The French Sugar Business in the Eighteenth Century

The French Sugar Business in the Eighteenth Century

Robert Louis Stein

Louisiana State University Press
Baton Rouge and London

Copyright © 1988 by Louisiana State University Press
All rights reserved
Manufactured in the United States of America

Designer: Albert Crochet
Typeface: Trump Mediaeval
Typesetter: The Composing Room of Michigan, Inc.
Printer: Thomson-Shore, Inc.
Binder: John H. Dekker & Sons, Inc.

96 95 94 93 92 91 90 89 88   5 4 3 2 1

LIBRARY OF CONGRESS CATALOGING-IN-PUBLICATION DATA
Stein, Robert Louis.
    The French sugar business in the eighteenth century/Robert Louis Stein.
        p. cm.
    Bibliography: p.
    Includes index.
    ISBN 0-8071-1434-0
    1. Sugar trade—France—History—18th century. 2. Sugar trade—West Indies, French—History—18th century. 3. Slave labor—West Indies, French—History—18th century.   I. Title
HD9115.F82S74 1988   87-26957
338.4'76641'0944-dc19   CIP

The paper in this book meets the guidelines for permanence and durability of the Committee on Production Guidelines for Book Longevity of the Council on Library Resources. ∞

Contents

Preface ix
Acknowledgments xiii
Abbreviations xv

Introduction: Sugar in the Old Regime 1

Part I: THE FRENCH WEST INDIES

1 The Slave Trade 17
2 The Plantations 40
3 Muscovado and Clayed Sugar 60
4 The French West Indian Sugar Business 74

Part II: THE SUGAR BUSINESS IN FRANCE

5 A National Perspective 93
6 Local Perspectives 106
7 Refining Sugar 120
8 The Local Refining Industries 135
9 To the Consumer 152
10 Conclusion 165

Selected Bibliography 175
Index 183

Maps

1 French Reexportation of Sugar in the 1770s 110
2 The French Refining Industry in the Seventeenth and Eighteenth Centuries 137

Preface

When crowds in Paris rioted in late January, 1792, they were not protesting against the rising price of bread, the usual reason for such actions during the French Revolution. Instead, they were reacting to the increased cost of sugar.[1] This was an unprecedented phenomenon that reflected the recent popular acceptance of sugar in Paris: for centuries confined to the wealthiest classes in French society and still almost unknown in the countryside, sugar was now considered a necessity by large numbers of the capital's residents. Coffee had entered the diet of Parisians, and this entailed a massive demand for sugar. What had long been an expensive luxury was becoming a cheap necessity—at least in Paris—and during the Revolution, the Parisian crowds treated what they believed to be unjustifiable price increases in sugar with almost the same gravity as they treated rises in the price of bread. They therefore took to the streets to demand that the government set a reasonable price for sugar.

The rapid expansion in the consumption of sugar forms the background, if not the *raison d'être*, of this book. The astonishing growth in the use of sugar in France and throughout Europe occasioned the development of one of the largest businesses in the Old Regime. By the time of the French Revolution, sugar was one of the most important commodities in French foreign trade, and raw French sugar from the French West Indies dominated the European market. In 1785, for example, sugar was responsible for some 60,000,000 livres' worth of French export sales to Europe out of a total of about 350,000,000 livres.[2] Small wonder, then, that sugar and the sugar business figured prominently in the thoughts of government officials and merchants

---

1. Albert Mathiez, *La vie chère et le mouvement social sous la terreur* (Paris, 1927), 29–49; George Rudé, *The Crowd in the French Revolution* (Oxford, 1959), 95–98. On parallel developments in the emerging mass market for sugar in England, see Sidney W. Mintz, *Sweetness and Power: The Place of Sugar in Modern History*, (New York, 1985), xxix, 5–6, 45, 161. Mintz claimed that "by no later than 1800, sugar had become a necessity . . . in the diet of every English person" (6).

2. Jean Tarrade, *Le commerce colonial de la France à la fin de l'ancien régime* (Paris, 1972), 752, 754; Théophile Malvezin, *Histoire du commerce de Bordeaux* (Bordeaux, 1892), III, 323; M. Avalle, *Tableau comparatif des productions des colonies françaises*

alike, although frequently in contradictory fashion. Indeed, the history of the eighteenth-century French sugar business is to a large degree the story of conflict between businessman and policy maker, with the latter struggling—usually in vain—to advance the national interest in the face of stiff opposition from various particular interests. Only the French Revolution could wipe the slate clean and allow the government to impose a more rational and uniform sugar policy on the country, ending the traditional practice of granting local privileges and guaranteeing local markets.

French sugar came from the French Antilles, and it was the extraordinary fertility of the French islands that enabled France to capture the European sugar market. The cornerstone of the French Empire was Saint Domingue, the colonial name for Haiti, supplier of up to 70 percent of all the sugar entering French ports.[3] So decisive was the contribution of Saint Domingue that the French sugar business never recovered from the Haitian Revolution; with the loss of Saint Domingue, France was relegated to a secondary role in the international sugar trade, at least as far as cane sugar was concerned. In addition to Saint Domingue, the colonies of Martinique and Guadeloupe produced significant amounts of sugar, while Saint Lucia, Tobago, and Guiana (French Guiana) made lesser contributions at different times during the eighteenth century. Together, the French colonies formed an empire that was the envy of France's rivals. It was a commercial empire whose value far outweighed its limited geographic size, a fact made obvious in 1762–1763, when France elected to part with the gigantic wastes of Canada rather than lose the lush fields of Guadeloupe.[4]

That the French Antilles should have been so highly valued in the eighteenth century was a most unexpected albeit welcome development. When the colonies were founded in the seventeenth century, few could have foreseen the eighteenth-century boom in sugar and the consequent prosperity of the Antilles. In fact, France had established the colonies primarily for military reasons, hoping that the islands' strategic location would balance the Spanish presence in the

---

aux Antilles avec celles des colonies anglaises, espagnoles, et hollandaises de l'année 1787 à 1788 (Paris, 1799?), table 1.

3. Avalle, *Tableau comparatif*, tables 2–5.
4. William L. Grant, "Canada Versus Guadeloupe: An Episode of the Seven Years' War," *American Historical Review*, XVII (1912), 735–43.

Caribbean area. When the colonies were formed, sugar was still a scarce, exotic commodity in Europe, reserved for the very rich.

The history of the eighteenth-century French sugar business is a part of the history of economic development both in the New World and Europe. Created in response to demand for sugar by European consumers and organized with a view toward profits, the sugar industries in the French West Indies and in France itself exhibited both traditional and modern features. Just as sugar consumption gradually filtered down through French society, so the sugar industry expanded beyond the traditional structures of French business. Part I of this study describes the French West Indian industry. Based on the use of slave labor on large plantations, it was responsible for growing sugar cane and producing raw sugar; in return, planters were given a monopoly over sales of sugar in France. Part II looks at the European end of the sugar business, analyzing France's role as a major distributor of raw and partly refined sugar to Europe and as a producer and consumer of relatively small amounts of fully refined sugar. In France the industry was divided into several local businesses, each enjoying special privileges. This was typical of the Old Regime, and only after the advent of a new regime was a truly national sugar industry able to develop. No longer could traditional social and political forces inhibit the changes demanded by the search for profit.

Acknowledgments

The history of sugar has been particularly gruesome in the Western world, for sugar was at the very center of a system that entailed the death or bondage of millions of people. Their suffering should not be forgotten.

In researching and writing this book, I received help from many people. Most were in France. The French government itself generously supported my research, while numerous archivists and librarians aided me in Paris and smaller French cities; I thank them for the warm welcome and the scholarly help they gave me. I would also like to thank the editors of *Business History* and the *Journal of European Economic History* for permission to reprint material from my articles that appeared in their journals: "The French Sugar Business in the Eighteenth Century: A Quantitative Study," *Business History*, XXII (1980), 3–17; and "The State of French Colonial Commerce on the Eve of the Revolution," *Journal of European Economic History*, XII (1983), 105–17 (published by Banco di Roma).

Above all, I would like to thank my wife, Mindy, who participated in every phase of the book's creation. She and our children, Robin Stephanie and Natalie Jill, have kept both this project and my interest in history alive during trying times. I gratefully dedicate this book to them.

Abbreviations

AC		Archives Communales
	B	Bordeaux
	N	Nantes
ACC		Archives de la Chambre de Commerce
	Dk	Dunkerque
	LR	La Rochelle
	M	Marseilles
AD		Archives Départementales
	BR	Bouches du Rhône
	CM	Charente Maritime
	G	Gironde
	IL	Indre et Loire
	L	Loiret
	LA	Loire Atlantique
	ML	Maine et Loire
	N	Nord
	S	Seine
	SM	Seine Maritime
AM		Archives Municipales
	R	Rouen
AN		Archives Nationales
	Col	Colonies
APL		Archives du Port de Lorient
BDM		Fonds Begouen Demeaux
BM		Bibliothèque Municipale
	N	Nantes
BN		Bibliothèque Nationale
	msfr	manuscrits français
	nafr	nouvelles acquisitions françaises

The French Sugar Business
in the Eighteenth Century

Introduction:
Sugar in the Old Regime

> Sugar is doubtles the finest gift given
> by Asia and America to Europe.
> —Jacques Savary des Bruslons

PRIOR TO 1664

It is impossible to date the introduction of sugar to France or Europe.[1] Originally from Asia, sugar cane took thousands of years to cross that continent to arrive in Europe. The Greeks and Romans probably did not know of sugar, and the Bible contains no mention of sugar either as a plant or a spice. Honey was the main sweetener at the time, and a "land flowing with milk and honey" reflected a biblical poet's conception of an earthly paradise. Sugar cane was, however, inexorably approaching the West, and by the year 1000, it was firmly implanted throughout the Middle East and particularly Egypt. Sugar itself, the processed product of the juices from cane, was sold by Moslems to Europeans, and in 996 it entered Venice, presumably for the first time. From there it spread throughout Europe, encouraged by the Crusades and by the revival of commerce. By the twelfth century an active trade in sugar appeared in the south of France, with duties imposed on it in Narbonne (1153) and Marseilles (1228). The troubador Chrétien de Troyes (ca. 1130–1195) mentioned it in his *Yvain ou le Chevalier au Lion* (ca. 1179).

> Et destanpre çucre de fiel
> Et mesle suie aveques miel.
>
> (He mingles sugar with gall
> And suet with honey.)[2]

---

1. On the early history of sugar, see Andrew M. Watson, *Agricultural Innovation in the Early Islamic World: The Diffusion of Crops and Farming Techniques, 700–1100* (Cambridge, England, 1983), 24–30. See also Paul Dorveaux, *Le sucre au moyen âge* (Paris, 1911); E. O. von Lippman, *Abrégé de l'histoire du sucre* (Paris, 1894); W. R. Aykroyd, *Sweet Malefactor* (London, 1967); Mintz, *Sweetness and Power*, 23–36.

2. Quoted in Dorveaux, *Le sucre au moyen âge*, 4–5; English translation by W. Wistar Comfort (London, 1914), 198.

2   The French Sugar Business in the Eighteenth Century

By the High Middle Ages, sugar was a relatively common delicacy among the richest classes throughout Europe. Imported from India or the Middle East, it came through Venice and Germany on its way to northern or western Europe. The best kitchens in France had several loaves of sugar on hand, purchased from grocers like Pierre Gilles, who had some ninety loaves in his store when he died in Paris in 1358.³ Kings in France and England were especially willing to indulge their sweet tooth, and the captive Jean II made sure that sugar was on his table in 1359.⁴ But the price of sugar was far too high to permit it to spread beyond a tiny group of the very rich; as long as sugar was imported in small quantities, it was doomed to be a trivial luxury item. Only the production and importation of appreciably larger amounts could drive prices down and encourage increased consumption, a fact that would in turn promote further increases in production, ever lower prices, and yet further demands. This cycle began in the fifteenth century and continued throughout the age of expansion.

During the fifteenth and sixteenth centuries the geography of sugar cane cultivation changed dramatically, mostly as a result of the European conquest of the New World. The first step in this new voyage westward occurred in the fifteenth century, when serious efforts were made to grow cane in Europe.⁵ Southern Spain and Sicily became important producers of cane at this time and went far toward replacing the Middle East, whose sugar was lost to Europe as a result of Turkish conquests. But Europe's rigorous climate restricted cane to the extreme south of the continent, in spite of numerous attempts to grow it elsewhere.

At least one of these attempts was made in France during the sixteenth century. According to a petition written by Sieur Gabriel le Sucrier in 1560, Francis I (1515–1547) had been interested in growing sugar cane in Provence.⁶ The king had gone so far as to get a sugar

3. J. C. Drummond and Anne Wilbraham, *The Englishman's Food* (London, 1957), 37–38; Dorveaux, *Le sucre au moyen âge*, 7. See also Alfred Franklin, *La vie privée d'autrefois* (Paris, 1888), III, 46. For fourteenth-century duties on sugar in Paris, see A. de Saint-Julien and G. Bienaymé, *Histoire des droits d'entrée et d'octroi à Paris* (Paris, 1887), 124–25.
4. Dorveaux, *Le sucre au moyen âge*, 8; Drummond and Wilbraham, *Englishman's Food*, 38.
5. Lippman, *Abrégé de l'histoire*, 13–16.
6. Francisque Michel, *Histoire du commerce et de la navigation à Bordeaux* (Bordeaux, 1866, 1871), II, 298–99; Louis Paris (ed.), *Négociations, lettres, et pièces diverses relatives au règne de François II* (Paris, 1841), 768–71.

expert—Sieur Gabriel himself—to come from Antwerp to supervise the project. Unfortunately, Francis I died and the idea was dropped. Gabriel, however, did not forget, and thirteen years later he requested royal aid in reconstructing the project. Gabriel wanted to grow the cane on the Hyères Islands, claiming that within three years he would be able to supply France with all the sugar it could use. In support of his petition, he also claimed that the project would create jobs in Hyères and would end French dependence on Portuguese cane. Gabriel asked the government for several commercial privileges, including the exclusive right to grow cane in France. Although all the details are not known, the project clearly did not succeed, and France, like the rest of Europe, had to look elsewhere for its sugar.

As Levantine and European sources proved inadequate, it became the practice to introduce cane into the newly discovered lands to the west and south. The Portuguese and Spanish were the early leaders in this field, and for nearly two centuries cane from their colonies dominated the European market. In the fifteenth century, cane was planted on Madeira and the Canaries with considerable success. Prices declined sharply in Europe and consumption increased. Throughout the sixteenth century the Canary Islands were major suppliers of raw sugar to Europe, and the earliest reference to sugar in Bordeaux was to Canary Islands' sugar.[7] Bordeaux merchants purchased their sugar in the Canaries and brought it to Bordeaux for redistribution in France.

The real breakthrough came when the Iberians brought sugar cane to the Americas. Early European settlement in the New World was centered on the tropical and subtropical zones, which were ideal for cultivating cane. Columbus himself introduced cane into the West Indies, and Cortez carried it to Mexico. Soon Spanish-American sugar began to compete on the European market. Heavy internal consumption prevented Spain from supplying all of Europe with sugar—indeed, in spite of its colonies, Spain was usually an importer of sugar during the Old Regime—thereby leaving the way open for Portugal to become the first great European sugar power. The heart of the Por-

---

7. Sydney M. Greenfield, "Madeira and the Beginnings of New World Sugar Cane Cultivation and Plantation Slavery: A Study in Institution Building," in Vera Rubin and Arthur Tuden (eds.), *Comparative Perspectives on Slavery in New World Plantation Societies,* Annals of the New York Academy of Sciences, CCXCII (New York, 1977), 536–52; Michel, *Histoire du commerce et de la navigation à Bordeaux,* 300. See also Drummond and Wilbraham, *Englishman's Food,* 38; and J. H. Parry, *The Establishment of the European Hegemony, 1415–1715* (New York, 1961), 45–46.

tuguese Empire was Brazil, which was first settled early in the sixteenth century. Although relatively insignificant throughout most of the century, Brazil finally emerged as an important factor in the developing "Atlantic economy" when it began to produce large quantities of sugar cane late in the century. According to J. H. Parry, the sugar industry in Portuguese America had several advantages over that in Spanish America.[8] Brazil had far more arable land than Hispanola or Mexico, and Portugal's superior shipping capacity together with its establishments in Africa meant a more reliable supply of the slaves so necessary to work the plantations. By the beginning of the seventeenth century, Portuguese sugar dominated the European market.

For most of the seventeenth century, France, like the rest of Europe, had to rely on Portuguese sugar for its growing needs, but by the end of the century, France was suddenly self-sufficient in sugar. This was the result of the rapid development of the French West Indian colonies, although it also reflected the still modest amounts of sugar being consumed. France had been in no hurry to colonize the Caribbean, waiting until the second quarter of the seventeenth century to establish permanent colonies in the area. Frenchmen had appeared in the Caribbean before then, of course, primarily as pirates or privateers preying on Spanish and Portuguese shipping and living in primitive settlements at strategic points in the West Indies. The most important of these colonies was formed in 1630 on the island of Tortuga, off the northwest coast of the Spanish island of Hispanola. Soon the French adventurers crossed over to Hispanola proper and began to occupy the western section of the island. Although the first settlers were few in number and created only a primitive economy on the island, they represented a French presence that did not go long unnoticed in Paris.[9] In 1664 Colbert ordered Bertrand d'Ogéron to impose royal authority over the French settlements on Hispanola, and by the time d'Ogéron died in 1674, the colony of "Saint Domingue"

8. Parry, *Establishment of European Hegemony*, 129–31. See also p. 72 on Spanish sugar.
9. G. T. Raynal, *Histoire philosophique et politique des établissements et du commerce des Européens dans les deux indes* (Geneva, 1775), II, 588, says there were only 400 whites in 1665. See also Robert Lacombe, *Histoire monétaire de Saint Domingue et de la République d'Haiti jusqu'en 1874* (Paris, 1958), 3. On the early days of Saint Domingue see Charles Frostin, *Histoire de l'autonomisme colon de la partie française de Saint Domingue aux XVIIe et XVIIIe siècles* (Paris, 1972).

was clearly French.[10] Some twenty-three years later, Spain reluctantly recognized French sovereignty over Saint Domingue in the Treaty of Ryswick. By this time, Saint Domingue was already sending small quantities of sugar to France.

Other French colonies were founded in more formal ways, although still with military considerations in mind. As the Spanish Empire was centered in the western Caribbean, France, like England, concentrated on the hitherto ignored eastern Caribbean, thereby gaining control over important sea-lanes. In 1627 the French settled on Saint Christophe (Saint Kitts), which they shared with the English until 1690.[11] Founded under the direction of Richelieu's Compagnie de Saint Christophe—soon called the Compagnie des Isles Occidentales and then the Compagnie des Isles de l'Amérique—Saint Christophe served as the "capital" and administrative center for the French West Indies for decades. The island also was used as the base for the French colonization of Guadeloupe and Martinique in the summer of 1635.[12] Both colonies were the property of the Compagnie des Isles de l'Amérique, but when they proved too expensive to maintain, the company sold them to individual proprietors. Finally, in 1664 Colbert reclaimed for the crown all the French islands in the Antilles and placed them under the control of the new Compagnie des Indes Occidentales. From then on, the commercial development of the colonies was paramount, and the subsequent history of the French West Indies formed a chapter of French economic history.

FROM 1664 TO 1717

As far as the colonies were concerned, Colbert's desire to stimulate French economic growth was well timed. French planters had recently mastered new techniques in sugar processing, and there was a

10. Frostin, *Histoire de l'autonomisme colon*, 115–16. See also d'Ogéron's correspondence in Michel Camus, "Correspondance de Bertrand Ogéron," *Revue de la Société Haitienne d'Histoire et de Géographie*, XLIII (1985), 3–188.

11. C. A. Banbuck, *Histoire politique, économique et sociale de la Martinique sous l'ancien régime (1635–1789)* (Paris, 1935), 24–25; Frostin, *Histoire de l'autonomisme colon*, 26.

12. Guy Lasserre, *La Guadeloupe, étude géographique* (Bordeaux, 1961), I, 263–382; R. P. du Tertre, *Histoire générale des Antilles* (1667–71; rpr. Fort-de-France, 1973), II, 9–20; Raynal, *Histoire philosophique et politique*, II, 571–84. See also F. d'Arcy, "L'industrie sucrière aux isles au XVIIe siècle," *Revue historique des Antilles*, II (1929), 3–16; and d'Arcy, "Aperçu de l'histoire du sucre sous l'ancien régime," *Revue historique des Antilles*, IV (1929), 11–32.

growing European demand for sugar. Until the mid-1650s, sugar cane had been eschewed on the French islands for two reasons: sugar processed in the French West Indies was inferior in quality to Brazilian sugar, and war in Europe kept demand for sugar modest.[13] With the end of the Thirty Years' War, a larger market for sugar existed in Europe. That French sugar was soon able to compete successfully in this market was largely due to the fortuitous arrival in the French colonies of a group of Dutch exiles from Brazil. Expelled by the Portuguese, the Dutch planters who settled in the French colonies taught their new neighbors better methods of processing cane. By the time Colbert came to power, the French West Indian sugar industry was firmly established and ready to expand rapidly. In fact, the colonies quickly became too productive, and there was a serious danger of overproduction. Soon the French controllers general were advising the intendants in the Antilles to encourage crop diversification on the islands.[14] Nobody wanted a repetition of the tobacco fiasco earlier in the century, when a glutted market had led to low prices and the ruin of colonists in both French and English colonies.

The impact of governmental policy on the economic development of the colonies is harder to measure. Although the government sought the growth and prosperity of the colonial economies, colonial interests were frequently sacrificed to metropolitan ones. In practice the government followed an inconsistent course between competing and often opposed groups, and the results were mixed. For the most part, the best that can be said is that the government did not actively hinder colonial growth. The problem was that the principles underlying French economic policy clearly placed the colonies in a subordinate position. These principles were enunciated primarily by Colbert, the minister responsible for formulating what has become known as the "colonial system." According to the colonial system, the colonies existed to increase the wealth of the mother country; in real terms this meant that the French West Indies became the colo-

13. Christian Schnakenbourg, "Notes sur les origines de l'industrie sucrière en Guadeloupe au XVIIe siècle (1640–1720)," *Revue française d'histoire d'outre-mer*, LV (1968), 267–92. See also Guy Josa, *Les industries du sucre et du rhum à la Martinique (1639–1931)* (Paris, 1931), 18–20, 33–34. For early documents, see BN, nafr 9323.

14. G. B. Depping (ed.), *Correspondance administrative sous le règne de Louis XIV* (Paris, 1850–55), III, 641–42. On the dangers of a single-crop economy, see Robert Carlyle Batie, "Why Sugar? Economic Cycles and the Changing of Staples on the English and French Antilles, 1624–54," *Journal of Caribbean History*, VIII–IX (1976), 1–41.

nies of the French merchants. Colonial planters could sell only to Frenchmen; colonial commodities had to travel aboard French ships; sales of French West Indian produce to foreigners had to take place in French ports; and colonists could purchase goods sold only by Frenchmen. As noted in numerous contemporary writings, "The colonies are made for the motherland."[15] Unfortunately for the colonists, the government did not believe that a thriving sugar industry in France necessarily implied a sound colonial economy.

The history of French sugar between 1664 and 1717 reflected the government's concern with maximizing the benefits accruing to France. Before Colbert, the colonies had been developing, but Holland was reaping the rewards. Dutch merchants purchased raw sugar in the French West Indies, shipped it to Holland for refining, and then sold it throughout Europe, including France. The loss to France in terms of shipping and jobs was obvious, and Colbert was determined to eliminate it. First, he created the Compagnie des Indes Occidentales, endowing it with a monopoly over trade with the colonies. This barred foreign merchants from the French Antilles, but it also hurt colonial and many French interests. The planters were upset because the chartered company was unable to supply the islands with all the European merchandise—including food—required; independent French merchants were unhappy because they were not allowed to participate in what promised to be a lucrative commerce. Faced with stiff opposition, Colbert and the company gradually relented: beginning in 1668, individual French merchants were permitted to trade with the islands, and in 1674 the company was dissolved. The French monopoly over the Antilles trade was retained, however, in the Ordinance of June 10, 1670, which prohibited "all foreign ships and vessels from docking in the ports of the American islands occupied by His Majesty's subjects." It also forbade "all the subjects residing in the said islands or doing business there from receiving any merchandise from foreign vessels."[16]

To appease the planters, Colbert tried to balance the French monopoly over trade with the Antilles by guaranteeing French West

15. See, for example, the series of mémoires in AN, Col F2B 8. As one eighteenth-century admirer of Colbert wrote, "The colonies were populated and were viewed not as conquered territories but as the acquisitions of commerce." Honoré Lacombe de Prezel, *Les progrès du commerce* (Paris, 1760), 49.
16. See ADLA, C735 for all of these laws. See also E. Boizard and H. Tardieu, *Histoire de la législation des sucres (1664–1891)* (Paris, 1891), 4–6.

Indian sugar a market in France. This he did through changes in the import duties collected in the metropolitan ports. As of September 15, 1655, raw sugar from foreign colonies was subject to steep import duties. Clayed sugar (high-quality raw sugar) from Brazil, for example, was taxed at 15 livres per hundredweight, and Brazilian muscovado (low-quality raw sugar) at 7.5 livres; all types of sugar from the French West Indies, however, were taxed at only 4 livres per hundredweight. These rates were confirmed by the Declaration of April 11, 1667, and three years later (on December 10, 1670), the duty on all French West Indian sugar was lowered to only 2 livres. These fiscal advantages assured the French West Indies of a competition-free market in France. This market, however, was as yet far too small to absorb all the sugar produced in the colonies, and the resolution of the problem caused by the surplus colonial sugar engendered a complicated conflict between merchants in France, merchants and planters in the West Indies, and refiners in both places.

Sugar refining had occurred in France at least since the mid-sixteenth century, although on a small scale.[17] With the establishment of a monopoly over trade with the Antilles, the number of refineries in France grew sharply. They were greatly helped by high duties placed on imports of foreign refined sugar. On September 18, 1665, for example, foreign refined sugar was subjected to a tax of 15 livres per hundredweight, raised to 22.5 livres the following year. According to F. d'Arcy, these measures led to the creation of some thirty-six new refineries in France, as well as to the demise of some thirty-three in Holland.[18] The French refineries were given yet further encouragement in 1671, when they were reimbursed the duties paid on the raw sugar that they refined and then reexported. Soon, however, the French refineries ran into unexpected competition from the colonies. To avoid a crisis brought on by overproduction, some colonial merchants and planters decided to refine their own sugar on the islands and thereby increase their profits. This was made all the more neces-

17. AMR, A19, June 30, 1572, mentions refining. See also Hector Valladier, "Histoire de la raffinerie de Nantes" (Typescript in ADLA), I, 11.
18. Schnakenbourg, "Notes sur les origines de l'industrie sucrière," 9. On the tariffs of 1664 and 1667, see S. Elzinga, "Le tarif de Colbert de 1664 et celui de 1667 et leur signification," *Economisch-Historisch Jaarboek*, XVI (1929), 221–73. On the confused conflict that ensued, see the conflicting accounts in Josa, *Les industries du sucre;* d'Arcy, "L'industrie sucrière" and "Aperçu de l'histoire du sucre"; and M. Forbonnais, *Recherches et considérations sur les finances de France* (Basel, 1758), I, 546–49.

sary in 1681, when the French refiners succeeded in obtaining a ban on the reexport of muscovado from France. Hitherto, only a small quantity of muscovado had been consumed in France, with the rest being sold in French ports to foreigners. The French refiners convinced the government that this raw sugar was being refined abroad and then used to undercut French refined sugar on the world market. The ban of exports, however, did not have the desired effects and served only to exacerbate the overproduction crisis in the Antilles and further encourage the West Indians to do their own refining. Faced with the new danger, the metropolitan refiners got the government on January 21, 1684, to prohibit further creation of refineries in the Antilles. This returned the colonies to a crisis situation, which lasted off and on until 1717.

Meanwhile, merchants in the French ports were furious, first over the restrictions on the reexport of muscovado and then over the increase in colonial refining, both of which hurt French shipping. Since it supposedly took some 225 pounds of muscovado to produce 100 pounds of refined sugar, French shippers lost more than half their cargoes. The merchants tried to persuade the government to return to the old system, and they achieved a partial success on September 28, 1684, when duties were raised on refined sugar from the colonies and French refiners were offered the reimbursement of all duties levied on muscovado refined for export. The planters retaliated by changing their production methods, and soon they were producing much more clayed sugar (*sucre terré*) than before. This was a more highly finished raw sugar that fetched better prices in France and even competed with French refined sugar. Although high duties were placed on it (15 livres per hundredweight as opposed to only 3 livres for muscovado, on June 20, 1698), clayed sugar replaced muscovado on most plantations in the Lesser Antilles.

In spite of these quarrels, the sugar industry in metropolitan France generally benefited from the protection offered by Colbert's measures and was on a firm footing from 1664 until 1717, the date of the next administrative reorganization. Growth, however, was restricted because of the warfare that plagued the last half of Louis XIV's reign. Although the wars of the late seventeenth century were fought primarily in Europe and for European reasons, French colonial trade experienced grave difficulties. Communications with the islands were difficult and occasionally impossible; slave trading was virtually nonexistent; commerce within Europe was precarious; and less money was available for luxuries like sugar. The sugar business needed peace to achieve real prosperity.

Peace came in 1713, and the sugar industry began to grow once again. It grew steadily and rapidly until the Revolution, slowing only during the three major wars of the century: the War of the Austrian Succession (1744–1748), the Seven Years' War (1756–1763), and the American Revolution (1778–1783). Annual colonial production of sugar went from under 50,000,000 pounds in 1713 to about 200,000,000 in 1789, or in terms of nominal value, from less than 15,000,000 livres to over 75,000,000. The vast majority of this sugar was reexported without further treatment, mostly to Holland and Germany but also to Scandinavia, Italy, Spain, and the eastern Mediterranean. The rest of the sugar was consumed in France, often after being refined in Orléans, Bordeaux, or any of several lesser centers. By the end of the Old Regime, France was importing nearly 60,000,000 pounds of sugar per year. This sugar was not distributed evenly throughout the realm, and in most rural areas and even many urban areas it was a rarity. In the biggest cities, however, sugar succeeded in creating a large market for itself, with all but the poorest segments of the population enjoying it at least occasionally. Parisians alone purchased a minimum of 6,500,000 pounds in 1789, or an average of at least 10 pounds per person. To the revolutionary Parisian crowds, it was indeed a necessity.

THE USES OF SUGAR

Sugar's great popularity was due to obvious factors: its taste and its extraordinary versatility in medicine and gastronomy. Sugar combined in one food the attributes of several, and when it became cheap enough for some of the less wealthy classes in society to enjoy, its attraction proved irresistible. In the eighteenth century virtually all sugar consumed by Europeans was cane sugar produced from West Indian sugar cane, a plant with large reserves of liquid sucrose.[19] Produced in the plant's leaves by photosynthesis, sucrose is a carbohydrate and a highly concentrated source of food energy that serves as a nutrient for the plant. When extracted from the cane and processed, sucrose forms sugar. The sweetness of sugar was highly valued in the

19. Aykroyd, *Sweet Malefactor*, 1–9.

Old Regime, and people who could afford it used it whenever possible. As one contemporary writer noted, "Today we put sugar into every sauce, to give food a more delicious taste."[20]

A pleasant taste also enhanced sugar's position in pharmaceutics, making it a medicine for the wealthy. Sugar was believed to have intrinsic medicinal powers, and it could be mixed safely with other, less palatable drugs. Most medical authorities stressed the beneficial effects of sugar on chest ailments. In 1683, for example, Constant de Rebecque wrote that "sugar is quite proper for hoarseness, cough, and other problems of the chest."[21] These sentiments were repeated throughout the Old Regime by authors of pharmaceutical handbooks. Said one: "Sugar in loaves and *cassonades* are good for chest ailments. They cut and reduce the phlegm; they excite the spittle." Another handbook maintained that "sugar is appropriate for colds. It sweetens the acidities of the chest." And according to P. Poncelet: "Sugar is excellent for chest and lung diseases because it attenuates and cuts the phlegms which commonly obstruct these organs."[22]

Besides being useful in combatting disorders of the chest, sugar was considered helpful in treating various other maladies. Philibert Guybert, for example, believed that sugar was good for the stomach and could serve as a laxative for breast-feeding infants. He also believed that a drink made from boiled water, sugar, and lemon juice was an effective remedy for persistent fevers.[23] One anonymous reporter went so far as to write in 1786 that "putrid and epidemic fevers are now less frequent in cities, an effect which M. Cullen attributes to the more general usage of sugar." Old people in particular were advised to consume sugar, both to strengthen their resistance to winter illnesses and to help prevent drying skin.[24] The usefulness of sugar in

20. Louis Lemery, *Traité des alimens* (3rd ed.; Paris, 1755), 523.
21. J. Constant de Rebecque, *L'apothicaire français charitable* (Lyon, 1786), 201–202. There is a debate on whether sugar was ever used primarily as a medicine. See Dorveaux, *Le sucre au moyen âge*, 36; and *Gazette de Santé*, no. 23 (1786), 89. On medicinal uses in England, see Mintz, *Sweetness and Power*, 96–108.
22. Nicolas Lemery, *Traité universel des drogues simples* (Paris, 1698), 668; Louis Lemery, *Traité des alimens*, 522; P. Poncelet, *Chimie du goût et de l'odorat* (Paris, 1755), 71.
23. Philibert Guybert, *Toutes les oeuvres du médecin charitable* (Paris, 1637), 17, 324. See also *Concise Observations on the Nature of Our Common Food So Far as It Tends to Promote or Injure Health* (London, 1787), 35.
24. *Gazette de Santé*, no. 23 (1786), 90; Louis Lemery, *Traité des alimens*, 522. But *Concise Observations*, 35, says too much sugar was "apt to occasion disorders of the skin."

medicine was recognized by the authorities when they decreed that only apothecaries and grocers should have the right to retail it.[25] Sugar was invaluable in making medicines, and it was so indispensable to the pharmacist's craft that a saying developed in the early seventeenth century—"apothécaire sans sucre" ("apothecary without sugar"), which meant "poverty-stricken." The druggist who had no sugar was a poor one indeed. The connection between pharmacist and sugar was recognized and made explicit in other ways; in Rouen, for example, the pharmacists' guild displayed two sugar loaves on its coat of arms.[26]

In spite of its medicinal benefits, sugar did have its disadvantages, and its supporters in the Old Regime thought it proper to warn of the possible dangers from overconsumption. There were two major charges against sugar: it discolored teeth, and it heated or excited the body. Even in the seventeenth century, Guybert advised his readers that sugar "blackens teeth and can, through frequent use, manifestly overheat [the body]."[27] This warning was reiterated throughout the Old Regime. In 1698 Nicolas Lemery claimed that sugar "slightly arouses the vapors and causes tooth decay," sentiments elaborated upon a half century later by Louis Lemery: "It excites the vapors a little; it easily turns into bile; it decays the teeth and blackens them; and it frequently causes overheating when used to excess." The tendency of sugar to overheat the body caused at least one author to caution extreme care when administering sugar, "particularly in cases of hysterical indisposition."[28]

Ignoring the possible negative consequences, people in the eighteenth century consumed sugar eagerly for nonmedical purposes. Although the pharmaceutical value of sugar was always respected, sugar owed its popularity mostly to its role as a sweetener and as a preservative. As a sweetener, sugar was especially appreciated in beverages. The eighteenth century witnessed great changes in the drink-

25. See, for example, René de Lespinasse, *Les métiers et corporations de la ville de Paris* (Paris, 1886), I, 500–11; M. Jèze, *Etat ou tableau de la ville de Paris* (Paris, 1760), 317; Franklin, *Vie privée*, III, 33.

26. Dorveaux, *Le sucre au moyen âge*, 37; E. Laruelle, *Les apothicaires rouennais* (Rouen, 1920), x.

27. Guybert, *Toutes les oeuvres*, 324. But M. Imbert de Lonnes, the "premier chirurgien de S.A.S. Monseigneur le Duc d'Orléans," writing in *Gazette de Santé*, no. 41 (1786), 162, claimed that sugar cleaned teeth and strengthened gums.

28. Nicolas Lemery, *Traité universel*, 668; Louis Lemery, *Traité des alimens*, 522; Poncelet, *Chimie du soût*, 71.

ing habits of Europeans, with tea and coffee challenging and even replacing beer and wine. As the new drinks spread, so did the use of sugar, since most people preferred their tea or coffee sweetened. Supplementing this sudden, spectacular increase in the demand for sugar as a beverage sweetener was a slower increase due to the more gradual acceptance of sugar as a necessity in the kitchen. Sugar was considered a preservative without equal, as an anonymous British observer wrote in 1787: "It preserves both animal and vegetable substance from putrefaction, and appears to possess this power in a higher degree than even salt."[29] It was particularly useful in preserving fruits. Large quantities were required to make jams; a typical seventeenth-century recipe called for three-quarters of a pound of sugar for each pound of fruit.[30] This helps explain why, as sugar became cheaper in the eighteenth century, the well-to-do and even those who were simply not poor needed ever increasing amounts of it. Richer people, of course, used sugar as an ingredient in more exotic recipes. Pierre de Lune's 1656 cookbook, for example, calls for sugar in a sauce for venison and in eggs Florentine, among other dishes, and a generation earlier, Lavarenne's cookbook offered a recipe for sugar-laden waffles. The rich clearly liked their sweetener, and they offered it as a gift to their friends or even to luckier residents of the poorhouse.[31]

29. Drummond and Wilbraham, *Englishman's Food*, 205; Michel Devèze, "Le commerce du sucre à la fin du XVIIIe siècle: La concurrence franco-anglaise," *93e Congrès des sociétés savantes, Tours, 1968: Section Histoire Moderne* (Paris, 1971), III, 37–39; *Concise Observations*, 35.
30. See for example, M. Lavarenne, *Le vray cuisinier françois* (Paris, 1628), 28, a recipe for apricot marmalade. M. Menon, *La cuisinière bourgeoise* (Paris, 1746), 337, called for the same proportions. Other writers suggested even more sugar. See, for example, Nicolas de Bonnefons, *Le jardinier français* (Paris, 1651), 273–314.
31. *Inventaire sommaire des archives hospitalières antérieures à 1790* (2 vols.; Paris, 1882), I, 354–55; Pierre Ponet, *Histoire générale des drogues* (Paris, 1694), 96.

PART I
The French West Indies

1

The Slave Trade

> There is no other commerce in the whole world which produces as many benefits as the slave trade.
> —Colbert

The cultivation of sugar cane first in the Iberian peninsula and then in the West Indies involved the creation of a new form of industrial organization: the plantation. In many respects, the plantation was a radically modern development. Organized with a capitalist's eye toward efficiency and profits, the plantation was more closely akin to the nineteenth-century factory than to the traditional, preindustrial workshop. The role of labor on the sugar plantations was particularly novel. Workers were dehumanized and conceived of in exclusively economic terms. The close personal ties that had characterized traditional economies were lost in the rush toward maximum production with minimum costs. As a consequence, slave laborers replaced small, free farmers.

The plantation economy was based on slave labor, and no discussion of the sugar business under the Old Regime could be complete without considering slavery and the slave trade. The entire sugar industry ultimately rested on the shoulders of the slaves, and although it may be argued that there was nothing inevitable about the success of slavery in the West Indies or that slave labor was not in fact the cheapest source available, plantation owners clearly believed that slavery was indispensable. They felt that slave labor offered the best and even the only means to make their plantations successful. Only the source of the slaves was open to question.

When the Europeans first arrived in the New World, they enslaved the natives and forced them to work in gold and silver mines. The Indians, however, could not long endure this treatment, and most of those who did not die fighting off the white invaders soon fell victim to newly introduced diseases. It then became necessary to import laborers, first for the mines and then for the plantations. In the eastern Caribbean and North America, the French and English tried to bring in their own citizens to work on plantations as indentured servants, or *engagés*.¹ On the French islands, *engagement* was virtually just slavery under another name, with one major, albeit frequently theoretical, difference: the engagés were free after three years of service. But many engagés never survived three years in the Antilles, and of those who did, most were in no position economically to establish themselves as freeholders and had to renew their contract or return to France. While under contract, the engagés were treated almost as slaves, having little control over their lives. Why, then, did they go? Many were all but shanghaied by unscrupulous captains, while others were lured by the thought of escaping the poverty of Old Regime France. The government actively encouraged the institution and required in the seventeenth century that all ships going to the West Indies carry up to six engagés. But by 1721 it had become clear that white engagés were never going to satisfy the labor requirements of the colonies, and the government allowed shippers to pay a modest fine instead of transporting engagés. The institution gradually declined. At no time since the introduction of sugar cane had the number of engagés alone been sufficient to work the plantations.

Given the failure of Amerindian and white indentured labor, the French, like the Spanish and Portuguese before them, turned to black slavery.² The importation of Africans as slaves offered several advantages. To begin with, it was cheap: several generations of labor might be purchased for a reasonable fee. Although this rarely occurred—disease and overwork killed most slaves within a few years of their arrival in the French West Indies—plantation owners were convinced that slavery provided the most economical source of manpower available.³ Next, and perhaps of even greater importance, was the seemingly endless supply of African slaves. Whereas France could supply perhaps 1,000 engagés in a year, Africa by the end of the eighteenth century was furnishing European buyers well over 100,000 slaves annually. The apparently inexhaustible human resources of Africa

---

1. On the engagés see Gabriel Debien, *Les engagés pour les Antilles* (Paris, 1952). On parallel developments in the British sphere, see David W. Galenson, *White Servitude in Colonial America* (Cambridge, Mass., 1981). On the decline of engagement see ADG, 6B85-115, and David W. Galenson, "The Rise and Fall of Indentured Servitude in the Americas: An Economic Analysis," *Journal of Economic History*, XLIV (1984), 1–26.

2. Arthur Percival Newton, *The European Nations in the West Indies, 1493–1688* (London, 1933), 47; Philip D. Curtin, *The Atlantic Slave Trade: A Census* (Madison, 1969), 17–21.

3. On the defense of slavery, see Léon Vignols, "Le travail manuel des blancs et des esclaves aux Antilles," *Revue historique*, CLXXV (1935), 308–15.

quickly made black slavery the basis of the West Indian economy and not just an exotic addition to it. Finally, the use of African slaves in particular helped overcome any moral qualms that the French may have had about the institution of slavery: being neither Christian nor white, the Africans could not claim the same natural rights as Europeans. As James Rawley put it: "Racism alone cannot explain the exploitation of blacks by the Atlantic slave trade. But racism, described as white belief in the inferiority of blacks, permeated the policy of the carrying nations."[4]

Black slaves arrived in the French West Indian colonies shortly after their foundation, but it took the successful introduction of sugar cane to encourage the development of a regular French slave trade. The first export crop on the French islands was tobacco, which was usually planted on small farms requiring few workers. When tobacco quickly proved unprofitable, it was replaced by sugar cane. The small farms were themselves replaced by large plantations, and the labor needs of the islands consequently soared. This required the creation of an organized French slave trade late in the seventeenth century. Hitherto, French West Indian demand for slaves had been low, and the occasional purchase from Dutch or English merchants had sufficed. Now, increased demand, coupled with Colbert's restriction on trade with foreigners, meant that French merchants were responsible for furnishing the planters with large numbers of slaves. Until the Treaty of Utrecht (1713), this was the assigned task of various chartered companies, for example, the Compagnie du Sénégal.[5] In return for monopoly privileges over the colonial slave market, the chartered companies agreed to supply the colonies with fixed amounts of slaves annually. Although fine in theory, the company monopolies never succeeded in practice. Planters found their slaves too few and expensive, and preferred to deal with smugglers either from France or other nations. For their part the companies invariably had financial difficulties stemming from a lack of working capital. This prevented them from operating on a large enough scale to turn a profit. The companies also had a high overhead, the consequence of maintaining a fleet of transatlantic vessels together with outposts in Africa. Further, the wars of the latter part of Louis XIV's reign frequently made French

4. James A. Rawley, *The Transatlantic Slave Trade: A History* (New York, 1981), 434.
5. Aboulaye Ly, *La Compagnie du Sénégal* (Paris, 1958).

slave shipping impossible; this caused drastic labor shortages on the islands and forced the planters to look elsewhere for their slaves.

By the time peace returned to Europe in 1713, it was obvious that major changes were necessary if the colonies were not to be forever short of slaves. These changes were incorporated into the Letters Patent of January, 1716, which served as the legal charter for the eighteenth-century French slave trade.[6] The trade was officially open to all Frenchmen who fitted out their ships in any of five major French ports: Rouen, Saint Malo, Nantes, La Rochelle, and Bordeaux. Gradually, merchants in other French ports were also permitted to engage in the slave trade, so that by 1741 the trade was open to almost all Frenchmen. Participating merchants did have to pay a modest tax for each slave imported into the colonies, but this money was to be used by the government to facilitate the trade through the construction and maintenance of outposts in Africa. The government also encouraged the slave trade by giving the traders important fiscal advantages. Exports to Africa were exempted from duties, while most imports from the colonies purchased from the sales of slaves were allowed to be reexported without tax or imported into France at half the normal duty rate. These exemptions were retained until 1784, when the government instituted a new system of subsidies based on slaving tonnage.

Given a growing demand for slaves, lengthy periods of peace, and a favorable legal foundation, the French slave trade boomed in the eighteenth century. The average number of French slaving expeditions went from 20 annually (1716–1721) to 110 (1783–1792). All told, French merchants organized over 3,000 slaving expeditions between the Treaty of Utrecht and the declaration of war between the French republic and Britain; these expeditions carried more than 1,000,000 Africans to the French West Indies, not counting some 150,000 to 200,000 who died on the way. These figures are all the more impressive when it is remembered that the French slave trade was only the third-largest in Europe during the eighteenth century. To appreciate the enormity of the Atlantic slave trade, the huge Portuguese and British trades must be taken into account, as must the lesser contributions of nations like Spain, Holland, and Denmark. Paul Lovejoy has estimated that more than 6,000,000 blacks were forcibly removed

6. The Letters Patent can be found in various places, including ADLA, C740.

from Africa during the eighteenth century alone, and more than 11,000,000 from the fifteenth through nineteenth centuries. Over 1,000,000 died before seeing the New World.[7]

The French slave trade grew in three stages during the eighteenth century.[8] The formative period was from 1713 to 1736, with an interruption between 1722 and 1725, when the Compagnie des Indes had a monopoly over French slaving operations. This first stage was a peaceful period that allowed France to develop its colonies as it wished. The colonies became successful producers of exotic commodities for the international marketplace, and the French slave trade reflected the prosperity. Instead of sending out only a half dozen or so slavers per year, as in the late seventeenth century, French merchants now organized an average of 23 slaving expeditions annually. The second stage lasted from 1737 until 1777, during which time the average number of expeditions rose by about 140 percent to 55 per year. This, however, considers only years of peace, and the period was broken by two disastrous wars, the War of the Austrian Succession and the Seven Years' War. The wars not only halted French slaving activity, but they also encouraged British incursions into the French West Indian slave market, which established new trading patterns that were detrimental to metropolitan French interests although highly welcomed by most planters. Thus, the French slave trade grew significantly but not as fast as colonial demand for slaves, and much of the colonial market was taken over by foreign smugglers. That the trade of both the French and the foreign smugglers could grow at the same time reflected the tremendous growth in colonial production, which in turn reflected the economic expansion in Europe. From the 1730s until the early nineteenth century, Europe experienced a cycle of economic growth. This growth encouraged the demand for colonial commodities, such as sugar and coffee.

The third stage in the development of the eighteenth-century French slave trade lasted from 1783 to 1792. This was another period of substantial growth, and it was preceded by the only war in the century that apparently had a positive effect on the trade, the Ameri-

7. Robert Stein, "Measuring the French Slave Trade," *Journal of African History,* XIX (1978), 519; Paul E. Lovejoy, "The Volume of the Atlantic Slave Trade: A Synthesis," *Journal of African History,* XXIII (1982), 483, 496.
8. Robert Stein, *The French Slave Trade in the Eighteenth Century: An Old Regime Business* (Madison, 1979), 13–42; Stein, "Measuring the French Slave Trade," 519–20.

can Revolution. French successes in the war helped regain the colonial slave market for French shippers, and in the decade following the war, French slaving departures increased by 100 percent to an average of 110 per year. For the first time in forty years French merchants were supplying the French colonies with almost all of their slaving needs. This was ironic, for only during this decade were imports of foreign slaves legal in the French West Indies: impressed by the colonists' constant complaints over the dearth of French slaving deliveries, the government finally allowed foreigners to sell slaves in the French Antilles under certain liberal conditions. In the event, the new policy was unnecessary. French merchants, encouraged by the ability of the French navy during the American war to keep communications open with the islands and keep out most smuggling, were determined to retain their advantage and supplied the colonies with nearly 40,000 slaves annually. But such massive deliveries had one negative result, at least over the short term: they led to a massive colonial debt. Planters were buying more slaves than they could afford, and French merchants had to accept what often proved to be poor credit risks.

This final period ended when war broke out between France and Britain in 1793. As during the other wars of the century, slaving operations were all but impossible. This time, however, the French gave legal status to the *fait accompli* and abolished slavery and the slave trade in 1794.[9] Until the eve of the Revolution, abolition had not been a significant political issue in France. Occasionally a writer like Montesquieu had condemned the slave system, but most had had little to say about it. In the 1780s, however, some French intellectuals, inspired by developments in Britain, began to call for the end of the trade and of slavery itself. The abolitionists formed an antislavery club, the Société des Amis des Noirs, and tried to arouse public opinion. They had been enjoying only limited success when the Revolution broke out, and more pressing problems quickly pushed abolition to the background. Merchant interests in France combined with colonial groups to form a powerful lobby in the National Assembly and protect slavery from the abolitionists' attacks. The Declaration of the Rights of Man and Citizen (1789) was not applied to the French West

9. On the illegal nineteenth-century trade see Serge Daget, *La France et l'abolition de la traite des noirs de 1814 à 1831* (Paris, 1969); on the eighteenth-century abolition see Robert Stein, "The Revolution of 1789 and the Abolition of Slavery," *Canadian Journal of History*, XVII (1982), 447–67.

Indian slaves, and it was not until May 15, 1791, that even some of the free men of color in the islands were given full civil liberty. As the Revolution became more radical, attacks on slavery and the slave trade became more frequent. Then, in 1793 Léger Félicité Sonthonax and Etienne Polverel, representatives of the French National Convention in Saint Domingue, unilaterally abolished slavery in that rebellious colony in a desperate attempt to regain control over it. Shortly afterward, the National Convention ended the system of premiums for slave-trading expeditions, and on February 4, 1794, it abolished slavery and the slave trade throughout the French Empire. France thereby became the first major power to abolish slavery in its tropical colonies, a moral victory lost only eight years later, when Napoleon reintroduced slavery and tried to reconquer Saint Domingue. Not until 1848 was slavery finally abolished in the French West Indies.

Supplying the sugar colonies with slaves gave rise to one of the most complex commercial networks in Old Regime France. Merchants in France, Africa, and the Caribbean participated directly in the slave trade, while others in Asia were involved indirectly through the sale of merchandise suitable for trading in Africa. Like the sugar trade it supported, the slave trade was a true international business representing at once the triumph and the shame of early modern commerce. The center of the slave trade was in the French ports, where merchants from Dunkerque to Marseilles organized and financed the expeditions. One port in particular was associated with the trade and came to be known as "the City of Slavers," Nantes.[10] Over 1,400 slave ships, or 45 percent of all French slaving expeditions in the eighteenth century, departed from Nantes. The early leader in commerce with the Antilles, Nantes began to concentrate on the slave trade when Bordeaux became the leading colonial port in the 1730s. By the end of the Old Regime, Nantes merchants were sending out an average of 39 slavers per year, almost twice as many as their nearest rival. The slave trade made the fortune of numerous individual businessmen in Nantes and was responsible for the tremendous wealth of the city as a whole. As Arthur Young remarked in 1788: "This town has that sign of prosperity of new building, which

10. On Nantes see especially Jean Meyer, *L'armement nantais dans la deuxième moitié du XVIIIe siècle* (Paris, 1969).

never deceives. The quarter of the *comédie* is magnificent, all the streets at right angles and of white stone. I am in doubt whether the *hôtel de Henri IV* is not the finest inn of Europe."[11] Compared with Nantes, the other major French slaving ports made modest contributions. Bordeaux was second, with over 450 eighteenth-century departures; then came La Rochelle and Le Havre, with about 400 each; and next were Saint Malo, Lorient, Honfleur, and Marseilles, with over 100 each. A half-dozen minor ports furnished the rest of the slavers.

Organizing a slaving expedition was an expensive, complex, and time-consuming project that demanded close attention from the *armateur*.[12] The armateur had two main tasks: he had to find adequate financing for the proposed expedition, and he had to prepare the expedition for departure. It was rarely easy to finance a slaving expedition, because of the great expense involved. For example, for expeditions originating in Nantes from 1783 to 1792, it cost an average of 275,000 livres to send a ship to Africa; a typical sugar refinery worker at this time earned well under 1,000 livres per year. Few merchants were willing or able to place that much money into a single venture, especially one as notoriously risky as the slave trade. It was therefore necessary to limit one's commitment and to diversify. Individual merchants formed long-term (at least in theory) partnerships as a first step toward minimizing risks. These partnerships were usually established between two or three relatives; if no suitable relatives were available, merchants joined with friends, coreligionists (in the case of Protestants or Jews), or colleagues from the local business community. Then the partners sought investors for the particular expedition under consideration; in effect, they formed temporary partnerships for each expedition. Typically, the armateur retained somewhat less than a 50 percent interest in his own expedition, selling the rest to businessmen locally and throughout France. Most of the ship interests sold were relatively small, so that each expedition had an average of eight to ten backers. Although most of the shares were sold to local merchants, including a high percentage to other slaving armateurs, many found their way to distant places and to people with few obvious connections with the trade; these men were encouraged

---

11. Arthur Young, *Travels in France*, ed. Jeffrey Kaplow (New York, 1965), 97.
12. "Outfitter" is the imprecise translation of the term. On financing see Robert Stein, "The Profitability of the Nantes Slave Trade, 1783–1792," *Journal of Economic History*, XXXV (1975), 786. On eighteenth-century wages see Chapter 8.

to participate by prospectuses published by the armateurs and suggesting fabulous profits. Examples of prospectuses can be found all over France and even outside of France, even though it was technically illegal for foreigners to invest in French slave shipping. Finally, many hard-pressed armateurs encouraged sales of slaving interests to the captain and crew; this was economical and convenient. It was also an excellent way to guarantee the crew's loyalty.

Most of the armateur's time was spent organizing the expedition. This involved several months of work and many decisions crucial to the success of the journey. The most critical decision was the choice of the captain, whose importance to the expedition rivaled that of the armateur himself.[13] The captain was in complete control from the moment the expedition set sail until it returned to France; he therefore had to be an excellent sailor and an astute businessman. Piloting a tiny vessel during the seven-thousand-mile voyage was no easy matter, and a man needed years of sailing experience before attaining the rank of captain. Besides knowing the sea, the captain had to be capable of dealing successfully with African and colonial merchants: the captain alone was responsible for the trade in Africa, and he had a large share of the responsibility for the sales in the islands. Such nautical and business talents were valuable assets, and successful captains who survived even two or three slaving expeditions could expect to amass modest fortunes. Indeed, the trade could be so profitable for captains that many left the sea to become armateurs.

The choices of crew, ship, and equipment were not nearly so important, and most armateurs paid little attention to them. A typical French slaving expedition had some thirty to forty crew members, divided almost equally between officers and sailors. Although the sailors were poorly paid—many owned only the ragged shirts on their backs—the officers had high salaries that considerably augmented the cost of the expedition. Since all were paid on a monthly basis, it was the great wish of the armateur to have as quick an expedition as possible; this would save considerable sums of money. Economic factors also affected the choice of a vessel. Slave traders wanted a ship that was cheap, that could carry the estimated number of slaves, and that could sail from France to Africa and the Caribbean. Most arma-

---

13. For the best description of a French slaving captain, see Dieudonné Rinchon, *Pierre Ignace Liévin van Alstein, capitaine négrier* (Dakar, 1964).

teurs preferred to use older vessels, and only a few ordered the construction of new ships for the trade. Slave ships were tiny by modern standards, displacing less than one hundred (modern) tons and providing less than ten cubic feet per slave.[14] Not surprisingly, the armateur did not want to spend much in equipping such a vessel: the pilot was given a few compasses and clocks to estimate the ship's position; the doctor had a small medicine chest that was hopelessly inadequate for combatting malaria or smallpox; the carpenter had a few tools to make the almost continual repairs to the ship that would be required. Only the captain's table was well stocked.

There was no compromise in the choice of a cargo.[15] The selection of trading goods regularly accounted for 50 to 70 percent of the outfitting costs and was frequently valued at over 200,000 livres. A poor cargo made a successful trade almost impossible, and the armateur was careful to keep abreast of current African tastes. There were four main types of goods appropriate to the slave trade: textiles, jewelry, arms, and alcoholic beverages. Most armateurs purchased some of each type, knowing that variety was much appreciated along the African coast. Merchandise for the trade was of diverse geographical origin: most of the cloths, for example, came from India, whereas beads were purchased in Amsterdam and rifles in England. Only the wines and liquors sent to Africa were invariably from France. Assembling an attractive cargo took a long time and often delayed the prompt departure of the ship. Sometimes a good cargo could not be put together in France for a reasonable price, and the expedition had to stop in Spain or Portugal in order to purchase the necessary merchandise.

The ship left for Africa as soon as the cargo was loaded. The voyage was usually uneventful but slow, taking from three to four months before arriving in sub-Saharan coastal waters. Once in Africa, the captain had to choose a trading site. Although the armateur usually specified a general area to trade in, the captain normally had complete discretion in picking the actual site, and he could ignore the armateur's orders if necessary. There were five main trading regions visited by French slavers: Senegal, Guinea, the Gold Coast, Angola,

14. J. M. Filiot, *La traite des esclaves vers les mascareignes au XVIIIe siècle* (Paris, 1970), 90.
15. Stein, *French Slave Trade*, 71–72.

and Mozambique. Of these, the Gold Coast and Angola were by far the most popular with individual merchants; Senegal was usually reserved for the chartered companies; Guinea (from the Gambia River to Cape Palmas) offered few slaves; and Mozambique was of trivial consequence until 1783.[16] The Gold Coast, particularly that section extending from present-day Ghana to Nigeria, was visited by about half of all French slavers during the eighteenth century. It boasted the only permanent French fortress south of the Sahara, Ouidah (Juda), which served as a good trading post and as an invaluable information center for French merchants in Africa.[17] The Angola coast was the most popular trading region in the second half of the eighteenth century. The southern portion of this coast was particularly appreciated by French slavers who had been forced away from the Gold Coast by aggressive foreigners. The Portuguese, who theoretically controlled commerce along the Angola coast, usually let Frenchmen trade there unhindered.[18]

Once at the chosen destination, the captain prepared to trade for slaves. Occasionally his job was made easy by contractual arrangements already established between the armateur and white merchants living in Africa. Slaves were more expensive this way, but many armateurs felt that the guarantee of a quick, large trade was worth the added cost. Captains could also try to make agreements with local white merchants, but there was always a strong chance that the merchant would simply vanish after receiving an advance payment. Usually the captain purchased his slaves from African merchants in a painfully slow manner.[19] Upon arriving at a trading site, the captain fired a salute to the local ruler and asked permission to trade there. This granted—with the aid of numerous gifts or bribes—the captain unloaded the ship's cargo and transferred it to a building that would serve as his office, trading post, and warehouse; it was either rented from the Africans or constructed by the ship's carpenter.

16. See Edward A. Alpers, *The East African Slave Trade* (Nairobi, 1967), and "The French Slave Trade in East Africa," *Cahier d'études africaines*, X (1970), 80–124.
17. On Ouidah see Simone Berbain, *Le comptoir français de Juda (Ouidah) au XVIIIe siècle* (Paris, 1942).
18. ADLA, C607, December 20, 1783.
19. Jean Mettas, "Honfleur et la traite des noirs au XVIIIe siècle," *Revue française d'histoire d'outre-mer*, LX (1973), 14–19; Rinchon, *Alstein*, 161; Stein, *French Slave Trade*, 83–85.

There the captain waited for African merchants to arrive with slaves to trade. This could be a slow procedure accelerated only by further gifts and bribes.

Eventually merchants would begin to offer slaves for sale. These slaves could come from both the coastal regions and the interior, depending on the trading site in question.[20] Large areas of Africa were thus affected by the Atlantic slave trade even though most whites never ventured inland. Africans themselves controlled the procurement, delivery, and sale of the captives, frequently adapting existing commercial networks to handle human merchandise. Nevertheless, the Atlantic slave trade implied major changes in many African societies; it did not, as its defenders claimed, merely involve the sale of surplus African slaves to Europeans. Before the Europeans arrived, chattel slavery of the "Western" type was virtually unknown in Africa. The slaves who did exist there were rarely denied their humanity; depending on the area, they could own property, attain positions of prominence, and develop bonds with their master's family. Only slaves with no such bonds—in other words, prisoners of war and criminals—were sold. With the advent of the Atlantic slave trade, demand for rootless slaves increased, and more warfare and lawlessness resulted. Africans far from the ports now enslaved people for the sole purpose of selling them ultimately to whites. African merchants served as middlemen in this process, acquiring slaves from their original owners and conducting them to the trading sites.

When a merchant arrived at a trading site with slaves for sale, he was approached by a broker who offered his services. The broker, often a member of the royal entourage, had the exclusive right to sell slaves to the captain, a right that earned for him large bribes and commissions. The trading process began when the broker entered the compound with one slave at a time. This slave was subjected to an extremely close inspection by the ship's doctor, who informed the captain of any faults in the captive. The French were meticulous in their choice of slaves and were proud to have what they considered to be the highest possible standards.[21] After the physical examination,

---

20. On the geographical origins of slaves see, among others, Philip D. Curtin, *Economic Change in Pre-Colonial Africa* (Madison, 1975), 59–91; and Kwame Yeboa Daaku, *Trade and Politics on the Gold Coast, 1600–1720* (Oxford, 1970), 23–24. On the effects of the trade on Africa, see J. E. Inikori (ed.), *Forced Migration: The Impact of the Export Slave Trade on African Societies* (New York, 1982).

21. ADLA, C738, October 21, 1762.

the doctor made his recommendation to the captain, who then bartered with the broker. There were two steps to this procedure. First, the abstract value of the captive had to be established with reference to a *pièce d'Inde*, or male slave in good condition. Then the captain and broker had to determine the amount of cargo that would be appropriate to pay for the quality of the slave in question. Since the African sense of values did not always coincide with the French one, it is difficult to figure out exactly how much slaves sold for in terms of French money. Depending on the time, place, and merchants involved in the transaction, captives sold for 100 to 600 livres' worth of merchandise, making meaningful generalizations difficult. Finally, once the broker and captain agreed on the terms of sale, the merchandise was handed to the broker, who examined it, accepted it, and left. This lengthy procedure ended in the purchase of one slave, who was branded on the shoulder or thigh and put aboard the ship.

Purchasing slaves in this piecemeal fashion made for lengthy stays along the coast. The average French slaver spent some five months in Africa, although some remained for more than two years. It was rare for a complete cargo of captives to be purchased at one site, and most ships had to visit several ports before leaving Africa. Some ships sailed up and down the coast for what appeared to be interminable periods of time, buying only a slave or two at each stop. Resorting to this practice was avoided if possible, for it not only raised expenses but also increased the dangers faced by the expedition. To begin with, the longer a ship stayed on the coast, the more likely the outbreak of a killing disease such as malaria or smallpox. Slaving crews and captives alike were frequent victims of contagious diseases. Slavers also had to fear people, both black and white. There were several instances of African antipathy toward the French traders, manifested in attacks on ships and attempts to free the captives. Although these attacks could be brutal, they were usually repulsed with ease by the whites, who did not hesitate to take advantage of superior firepower. Conflicts with other traders called for more circumspection from the French. Since the French were far weaker militarily along the African coast than the British, Dutch, or Portuguese, French slavers could not rely on force when confronted with hostile Europeans. Foreign traders frequently forced French merchants to leave hitherto "neutral" waters and trade elsewhere. Much more serious were the numerous instances of confiscation of French ships by foreign powers, usually just before, or at the very beginning of, a European war. The British were particularly aggressive in this respect, and French shipping suffered great losses before each of the century's major wars.[22]

For his own security the captain wanted to leave Africa as soon as his trade was completed, that is, when the ship was filled or when all the trading merchandise was gone. Before leaving African waters entirely, however, a stop was usually necessary on the Portuguese islands of Sao Tomé or Príncipe. Here the slaves were restored to good health and fortified for the middle passage. Also, the Portuguese islands supplied the French with food and fresh water, vital necessities for the approaching voyage. After some two to six weeks on the islands, the slaver finally set sail for the Antilles. The route followed was fairly direct, running west to near the Ascension Islands and then north toward the Antilles and, more specifically, Martinique. There were few nautical problems on the crossing; tropical storms during the Caribbean summer and a lack of winds near the equator presented the only such dangers. The other risk was that of Portuguese privateering off the Brazilian coast, but this danger could be minimized by maintaining a healthy distance from Brazil. Average crossing time was from two to three months, although it could take as little as four weeks or as much as a half year. These variations were significant because of the relationship between time at sea and death rates among the captives and crew: slow voyages tended to be deadly ones.

The slave trade took a heavy toll among both whites and blacks, with most of the deaths occurring during the middle passage. Sometimes there were spectacular death rates: half or even three-quarters of the captives might be stricken with fatal illnesses, or the entire crew might be wiped out in a bloody revolt. Most of the time, however, the slave trade was a more discreet killer, claiming from 5 to 15 percent of the captives and crew. Given the century's total of some 3,250 expeditions, each with an average of 300 slaves and 35 crew members, even a "low" death rate meant some 50,000 to 150,000 victims. This was quite acceptable to slaving merchants, and the Compagnie des Indes even granted bonuses to captains who lost "only" 20 percent of their cargo.[23] Although it is impossible to know exactly how many slaves died during the middle passage itself—most

---

22. Meyer, *L'armement nantais*, 227, 378–83.
23. APL, 1P256B.

documents mention the number of slaves traded and the number delivered alive to the Antilles, not distinguishing between deaths along the coast and deaths at sea—there are indications that most of the slaves who perished died at sea, while the crew members—about whom more exact information is available—tended to die along the African coast. A lengthy trade exposed the crew to more unfamiliar diseases, but survivors were strong enough to be relatively unaffected by the rigors of the middle passage. For the slaves, no such selection process had occurred, and a slow crossing gave birth to diseases that the weaker slaves could not withstand. All told, 13 percent of the slaves loaded aboard French ships in Africa during the eighteenth century never reached the Antilles.

Disease killed most of the slaves.[24] Scurvy and amebic dysentery were the biggest killers, and being slow to strike, they were most fatal on slow voyages. Thus, the only way to have a reasonable guarantee of a healthy expedition was to have a quick one: one in seventeen slaves died when the trade and crossing took less than seven months; one in five perished after more than nine months. No other factor had a significant impact on the death rate. Overcrowding, traditionally blamed for killing the slaves, had no real effect: there was no relation between the number of slaves per ton and the mortality rate. On the contrary, ships that had a large but quick trade suffered fewer deaths than ships that spent many months trading only a few slaves. Crew brutality had only the most marginal of effects on the captives' death rate. Mistreating the slaves was bad business, and although some slaves—particularly female ones—did suffer at the hands of whites, few died from such acts.

The crossing from Africa to the Caribbean was unpleasant for all concerned, with disease and revolt as ever present menaces. To create a more tolerable atmosphere, captains tried to establish daily routines.[25] The slaves were allowed on deck every morning to have their chains and their health checked. They then had a breakfast consisting primarily of beans and rice, a meal repeated late in the afternoon as dinner. During the day, some of the captives were ordered to clean the

---

24. Marie-Claire Chiche, *Hygiène et santé à bord les navires négriers au XVIIIe siècle* (Paris, 1957). See also Herbert S. Klein and Stanley L. Engerman, "Facteurs de mortalité dans le trafic français d'esclaves au XVIIe siècle," *Annales: Economies, Sociétés, Civilisations*, XXXI (1976), 1213–24.

25. Rinchon, *Alstein*, 184–87, 272–73.

ship, but most had nothing to do. Captains encouraged singing and dancing, and they occasionally offered little treats, such as beef or spirits, in order to give the slaves some hope. It was commonly believed that wise captains could avoid most problems simply by amusing their captives from time to time.

Enforced idleness, apprehension over their fate, and despondency over their captivity encouraged the slaves to revolt whenever possible.[26] There is no way of knowing how many slave revolts occurred aboard French slavers during the eighteenth century, but it seems probable that they were commonplace. Any act of negligence by a crew member could lead to a slave revolt, particularly if the mistake provided the captive with a source of arms. Suppressing possible revolts, therefore, was a preoccupation with the crew. Guards were posted wherever the slaves worked on the ship, and the captives were systematically denied access to any utensils that could serve as weapons. Guards were also posted at night, and as a final precaution the crew was trained in fighting off a revolt. Such training was necessary, and it made successful revolts almost unknown. It was virtually impossible for the slaves to gain control of a ship: their lack of a common language alone made them a poor match for the well-organized sailors. As soon as the initial surprise of a revolt wore off, the crew's superior discipline and weaponry invariably told. Most revolts ended quickly, with the death of the rebel leader and one or two of his followers. Economic interests dictated a certain restraint in dealing with the rebels, and wholesale executions were not allowed.

The middle passage finally ended when the ship arrived in the West Indies. French ships invariably landed first on Martinique in the southeastern Caribbean, either as a resting place or as a final destination. After two or three months at sea, the captives badly needed to be restored to the appearance of good health if their sale value was not to be compromised; thus, a few days on Martinique or on one of the tiny islands nearby was a good investment. Once the slaves looked better, ships not remaining at Martinique made for Saint Domingue. Although the occasional ship went to Guadeloupe, Guiana, or Louisiana, and although a handful went to Cuba or Puerto Rico, the overwhelming majority of French slavers either remained in Martinique

---

26. Stein, *French Slave Trade*, 102–106.

or went on to Saint Domingue. Martinique was the preferred destination early in the eighteenth century, whereas Saint Domingue became preeminent after 1730; by the end of the Old Regime, Saint Domingue received more than three-quarters of all French slavers.

Once in port, the captain completed certain formalities that, as in Africa, were accompanied by demands for bribes. He then prepared to sell the slaves. First, the captain contacted a colonial merchant or agent who would help with the sale. The colonial merchant was vital to the French trade: he knew the colonial market well, and he advised the captain in selling to the colonists. For his services the agent was well paid; taking a 1 to 5 percent commission on all transactions, he was the only man besides the captain certain to make a profit from the slave trade. The choice of a colonial agent was an important one that caused the armateur much concern. Finding an agent who would give priority to the armateur's interests instead of the planters' or other merchants' was no easy task, and the bigger French merchants usually had to operate their own businesses in the colonies. Whenever possible, brothers or sons of successful French slavers went to the Antilles to handle the family business there; if no relatives were available, wealthy French merchants had to deal with existing colonial merchant houses. In either case it was only by financially controlling the colonial merchant that the French armateur could be certain of having his personal interests protected, an important consideration in colonies notorious for not paying debts.

A few days after the ship arrived in port, the sale began. The agent printed announcements of the upcoming sale, posting them in town and mailing them to interested parties in the countryside.[27] The sale was usually held aboard the ship, although local authorities always tried to have it in a special marketplace in town; the captain preferred his ship because it made escape difficult and put the buyer at a disadvantage. Prospective buyers were ferried out to the ship and invited to inspect the slaves. As in Africa, the buyer examined the slaves as thoroughly as possible and then made an offer. Bargaining ensued between the buyer and the captain—the latter aided by the agent—until agreement was reached on a price and terms of payment. The slave was then led away. Again as in Africa, it was normal to purchase

27. ADG, 7B3041, March 27, 1785.

only one slave at a time, although some entrepreneurs or large planters might occasionally buy a dozen or more.[28] As there was usually considerable interest in a fresh cargo of slaves, the sale did not often take more than two or three weeks to conclude.

All but the poorest whites living on the islands bought slaves. Of course, plantation owners purchased most of them. Large plantations always seemed to need one or two more slaves and occasionally more; building new plantations or expanding old ones required many more. If a planter in need of slaves liked a particular cargo, he might purchase fifty or more at a time, much to the satisfaction of the captain and the armateur, both anxious to conclude a rapid sale. Not all slaves were destined for the countryside, however, and many found their way into towns, where they were employed primarily as domestics. Merchants, administrators, members of liberal professions, and even artisans owned slaves in the French West Indies; the whole of colonial society was characterized by slavery.[29]

With the sale of the slaves to the colonists, the histories of the slave and sugar trades converge and even tend to merge. Most of the slaves themselves went to work on the sugar plantations, which had made the entire slave trade "necessary." Not only was sugar the main product of slave labor; it was also used to finance further deliveries of slaves. The colonies had virtually no specie: it was illegal to carry any from France to the West Indies, and sales of French slaves to Spanish colonists produced only a minimal amount of currency. Hence, the colonists had to repay their debts by using their major commodities, sugar and to a lesser degree coffee. When the planter and the captain bargained over the price of the slave, they were also bargaining indirectly over the amounts of sugar to be delivered immediately and in the future. At issue was the size of the initial payment and the size and dates of subsequent ones. It was unusual for a planter to pay for all his purchases upon receipt, and captains considered themselves lucky to get a large down payment in the form of immediate deliveries of sugar and coffee. The typical down payment was about 25 percent, with the remainder promised within two years; planters, however, rarely honored these promises and unilaterally extended the period to five years and more.[30] Needless to say, the captain had long

28. Rinchon, *Alstein*, 314.
29. *Ibid.*
30. Stein, "Profitability of the Nantes Slave Trade," 790–91.

since returned to France, leaving the colonial agent with the difficult task of collection. Foreclosures were all but unknown in the French West Indies, so creditors had few weapons at their disposition.

Having completed the sale and taken delivery of the commodities in down payment, the captain looked for a cargo for the voyage back to France. Since the down payments filled only a third to a half of the ship, there was plenty of space available for carrying freight; this could be quite lucrative and was actually the major source of revenue for many ships sent to the colonies. With the agent's help again, the captain contacted planters or merchants with commodities to ship to France. The captain, however, had little time to spend on filling his ship: away from France for nearly two years, he was anxious to return to France and provide the armateur with the expedition's first returns. The armateur, for his part, encouraged the captain to do everything possible to return quickly; life in the colonies was expensive, particularly when a thirty-five-man slaving crew was still on salary. Hence, the captain took only what was immediately available for shipment to France and hastened to depart. The crew loaded the goods on the ship, the captain received official permission to sail, and the ship left, often only half full. After two generally uneventful months, the ship arrived in France, completing the slaving triangle.

Once the ship was back in France, the captain had to complete more formalities while the armateur disposed of the cargo and finally realized the first proceeds from the expedition. The captain had to file an official report on the expedition with the Admiralty; these reports, wherever preserved, form an invaluable source of information about the slave trade, giving details about the number of slaves traded and delivered, the dates and places of crew members' deaths, and any unusual occurrences. The captain also had to supply the Admiralty with an up-to-date copy of the crew list, which would insure that the armateur would pay all wages owed. This ended the captain's responsibilities, leaving the armateur in charge once again. The armateur arranged for the sale of the incoming merchandise and, finally, the distribution to the investors of the first, invariably modest cash proceeds. By this time, nearly two years had passed since the initial investments had been made, and it took an additional twelve to eighteen months before the expedition paid for itself and began to yield profits. More payments came in regularly for another two years and irregularly for up to twenty-five years. Occasionally, the original debtor and creditor died before all payments were made, and many debts were never repaid at all.

Was the wait worth it? Was slaving profitable? At first glance, the answer seems obvious; the very fact that armateurs financed more and more slaving expeditions throughout the eighteenth century apparently reflected their belief in the profitability of the trade. But the case is not that clear, for at the same time as they poured their money into the trade, French merchants complained bitterly that the trade was a losing and even a ruinous proposition. The ambivalence of the traders themselves has been reiterated, and even today a debate exists over the profitability of the French slave trade. Gaston Martin, the author of a general history of the French trade, pointed to the visible wealth of the great eighteenth-century traders and concluded that the idea of an unprofitable trade was preposterous. Subsequent historians have not been so sure and have tended to view the trade as a risky business venture that usually yielded only modest profits but that was almost unique in offering the possibility—albeit remote—of enormous riches.[31] Seen in the context of eighteenth-century business practice, the slave trade was a highly speculative affair that on the average rewarded investors with a slightly higher rate of return than more certain investments. At no time did participation in the trade guarantee a quick fortune, but again, it did offer the real possibility of huge profits.

Establishing the profitability of the trade is no easy matter. In addition to the normal problems that beset any study of eighteenth-century businesses, such as a lack of documentation, the slave trade is especially confusing because of its close ties to the general colonial trade. It is frequently impossible to distinguish between the two, and profits from one can easily be read as losses for the other. Some idea of slaving profits can be ascertained, however, by comparing an expedition's total costs with its net returns and ignoring such factors as commissions and government subsidies. The crucial elements were the costs of financing the expedition, the number of slaves traded and sold, the sale price of the slaves in the Antilles, and the amount of the colonial debt actually repaid. Financing a slaving expedition was expensive, with costs rising throughout the century; by the 1780s it

31. Gaston Martin, *Nantes au XVIIIe siècle: L'ère des négriers* (Paris, 1931), 425; Meyer, *L'armement nantais,* ch. 6; Stein, "Profitability of the Nantes Slave Trade," 779–93.

cost an average of 275,000 livres to send out a slaver from Nantes, although it could be done for as little as 22,000 livres or as much as 595,000 livres. What was crucial was the trade itself: the number of slaves purchased along the coast largely determined the ultimate result of the expedition. If a captain did not trade enough slaves, a loss was inescapable; similarly, a good trade all but guaranteed a profit as long as the middle passage was not disastrous.

When the slaves were sold in the Antilles, the paper profits of the expedition were established, and these were almost always substantial. Slaves who had cost 500 livres in Africa fetched 1,000 or more in the colonies, or even 1,500 "colonial livres," a money of account that the traders liked to use to make their gains—or losses—appear more impressive. Thus, the trade typically yielded paper profits of 100 percent and more in the Antilles, and further speculation in colonial commodities could double this amount. Unfortunately for the traders, the paper profits rarely became real profits, and even expeditions that were apparently huge successes in the West Indies sometimes ended up losing in France. The problem was getting the payments from the colonies to France. Some of the debts were simply ignored, and expenses and commissions ate away large shares of the rest. By the time the armateur counted out the net proceeds of an expedition, he was lucky to make more than a 10 percent profit, and that over a five- or six-year span. This is similar to the apparent profits in the British trade. Roger Anstey claimed that eighteenth-century profits in Britain averaged 9.5 percent.[32] David Richardson found that seventy-four expeditions from Liverpool gained about 8 percent between 1757 and 1784.[33] Although J. E. Inikori has questioned these figures by underlining the need to consider the limited amount of cash—as opposed to credit—actually risked, it seems clear that profits were relatively modest in the long run and that the speed and size of returns were critical.[34] Indeed, the slowness and the incompleteness of payments had an important effect on Franco-colonial economic rela-

32. Roger Anstey, "The Volume and Profitability of the British Slave Trade, 1761–1807," in Stanley L. Engerman and Eugene D. Genovese (eds.), *Race and Slavery in the Western Hemisphere: Quantitative Studies* (Princeton, 1975), 3–31.
33. David Richardson, "Profits in the Liverpool Slave Trade: The Accounts of William Davenport, 1757–1784," in Roger Anstey and P. E. H. Hair (eds.), *Liverpool, the African Slave Trade, and Abolition: Essays to Illustrate Current Knowledge and Research* (Liverpool[?], 1975), 60–90.
34. J. E. Inikori, "Market Structure and the Profits of the British Slave Trade in the Late Eighteenth Century," *Journal of Economic History*, XLI (1981), 745–76, esp. 775.

tions: they forced the French merchants to participate directly in the colonial economy. By the end of the Old Regime, Nantes merchants alone had holdings of nearly 80,000,000 livres in the colonies, most of which represented debts from slaving deliveries.[35] French merchants were becoming unwilling partners in colonial development and were no longer able simply to sell needed merchandise there at a profit. But the possibility of realizing enormous profits, reinforced by the fantastic size of the West Indian paper profits, lured more and more merchants into the slave trade until the very end of the Old Regime.

Thinking only of profits, the French merchants viewed the slave trade in a different light than did the planters. The merchants saw it as a business, while the colonists saw it as a service that provided the colonies with the manpower required to make the plantations productive. The conflict between independent business and necessary service was frequently a bitter one, with the government having to maintain a balance between the two. In the earliest days of colonial settlement, the French slave trade was a virtually unregulated business, primarily because it was so trivial. Soon Colbert realized that the colonies' economic future depended upon the development of a plantation economy, which in turn relied on slavery; so he treated the slave trade as an important service and tried to guarantee sufficient shipments of slaves through the creation of giant companies with monopolies. In the eighteenth century the trade was again deregulated, this time to encourage private merchants to succeed where the companies had failed. When the merchants became too greedy, that is, when they abandoned the Lesser Antilles in favor of the larger Saint Domingue market, the government stepped in again and opened Guadeloupe and Martinique to foreigners.

Each of these major changes and countless minor ones were accompanied by acrimonious debates between colonists and French merchants. By the end of the Old Regime the conflict had become so bitter that the colonists were screaming "exploitation" and the merchants "treason." Only when the entire slave system itself came under attack during the Revolution could these two groups work together, but by then it was too late. Neither could appreciate that both depended ultimately on the health of the economic relationship between France and the colonies, and that by pursuing one particular

---

35. ADLA, 6JJ30.

interest to the detriment of the other, the entire system suffered. Of course, a few traders succeeded in becoming very rich, and some plantation owners managed to amass and repatriate vast fortunes, but often there was only the appearance of wealth without the substance. When the French and Haitian revolutions ended the old colonial system, many merchants and planters were left in ruins.

2

The Plantations

> The wealth of Saint Domingue is not the gift of blind fortune; it is the fruit . . . of years of labor.
> —Hilliard d'Auberteuil

Many factors combined to encourage the French to establish plantation economies in their Caribbean colonies. A favorable climate, the natural fertility of the land, an abundant supply of cheap labor, a strong European demand for exotic commodities, and the influence of foreign precedents each contributed to the particular way in which the tropical French colonies grew. Nevertheless, it took several years for the plantation economies to develop in the French Antilles. Indeed, it was only after the "sugar revolution" of the mid-seventeenth century that large-scale plantation operations became the rule. Before the success of sugar cane, the colonies—in this case Guadeloupe and Martinique, the two major colonies whose settlement was organized by the government—were populated mostly by white freeholders whose chief export crop, tobacco, was conducive to small landholdings.[1] The first concern of the French government had been to settle the islands with sufficient numbers of French citizens to guarantee French possession. Accordingly, the early chartered companies were given the responsibility for attracting settlers to the islands, and the companies signed many contracts to that effect. For example, on February 14, 1635, the Compagnie des Isles de l'Amérique granted control over Martinique, Guadeloupe, and Dominica to Sieurs Olive and Duplessis in return for a promise to import 900 men within nine years; the Compagnie et les Marchands de Dieppe, associates of Olive and Duplessis, also agreed to send out a further 2,500 men within six years.[2] The first arrivals enjoyed a rough economic equality, claiming only enough land to farm at a subsistence level. As good land abounded, there were few problems, even when export crops of ginger, cotton, indigo, and especially tobacco were planted;

---

1. On the early days in Guadeloupe see Lasserre, *La Guadeloupe*, 263–326; on those in Martinique see Banbuck, *Histoire de la Martinique*, 21–62.
2. Lasserre, *La Guadeloupe*, 271; Banbuck, *Histoire de la Martinique*, 22.

small, self-sufficient farms were the rule until the late 1650s. Although slaves were present, they were not yet essential and formed a minority of the population: as late as 1656, Guadeloupe had 12,000 whites and only 3,000 slaves.

Sugar was of little importance to the early colonial economies. Although sugar cane had probably been present on Martinique and Guadeloupe since the arrival of the French, sugar was not commercially produced for several years. The first settlers concentrated on tobacco largely because of the favorable international market for it; they avoided sugar cane because the market was weaker and because of problems in processing it. But when tobacco prices began to fall in the late 1630s, the Compagnie des Isles de l'Amérique soon encouraged the cultivation of sugar cane. In 1638 the company promised exemptions from taxes to the colonists who sent the first sugar to France, and in the following year it commissioned Daniel Trézel to stimulate sugar production on Martinique.[3] Trézel received some 2,400 arpents of land on Martinique together with a six-year exclusive right to grow cane and manufacture sugar on the island; in return, he agreed to give the company 10 percent of all the sugar he produced. The plan soon failed, and the company shifted its attention to Guadeloupe. By offering various exemptions and by providing some capital, the company succeeded in establishing a rudimentary sugar industry on Guadeloupe in the early 1640s, but competition from the sophisticated Brazilian industry was too stiff. By 1648 the Compagnie des Isles de l'Amérique was virtually bankrupt and the French West Indian sugar industry moribund.

Within a few years, the sugar revolution altered the colonial economies and societies beyond recognition. The revolution began in 1654, when the Portuguese expelled the Dutch from northeastern Brazil.[4] Brazil was the chief producer of sugar in the Western world and owed its preeminence to certain technological advances. When the Dutch left, they took their knowledge with them, and the few who settled on the French islands taught the new processes to the French. In particular, the Dutch knew how to make the molds in which the hot sugar crystallized, and they knew how to whiten muscovado. With these

---

3. D'Arcy, "L'industrie sucrière," 3–8; Schnakenbourg, "Notes sur les origines de l'industrie sucrière," 275–83.
4. Schnakenbourg, "Notes sur les origines de l'industrie sucrière," 275–83; Batie, "Why Sugar?"

trade secrets, the French industry suddenly boomed, with sugar cane becoming the major crop on the islands; between 1644 and 1669 the number of sugar plantations on Guadeloupe increased from 1 to 113. By the end of the Old Regime, there were nearly 1,500 sugar plantations on the French West Indian islands. Saint Domingue had slightly more than half of them, with 314 in the West province, 288 in the North, and 198 in the South.[5]

The entire colonial socioeconomic system was reorganized to accommodate sugar cane. Unlike subsistence or even tobacco farming, sugar-cane farming was best done on large estates, but the creation of these estates or plantations implied the destruction of the small farms. Good land was not unlimited, and after most of it was given away in a few vast concessions, the new plantations had to take over the small holdings. Some dispossessed small farmers stayed to form a new class in colonial society, the poor whites. Most, however, simply left, and the white population declined sharply; on Guadeloupe, for example, the number of whites fell from 12,000 in 1656, to 5,009 in 1664, and 3,083 in 1671. Those who remained retreated to the foothills and other marginal areas to practice subsistence farming, often in nearly total isolation. In sharp contrast to the new class of poor whites was the new class of very rich planters. Characterized by one historian as forming a caste, the *grands blancs*—as opposed to the poor *petits blancs*—soon came to dominate colonial society and represented a unique interest throughout the Old Regime. But the most obvious social consequence of the sugar revolution was not the division of the whites into two often hostile classes, but rather the creation of a huge class of black slaves. With large sugar plantations requiring more than 100 workers each, the slave population grew tremendously until it far surpassed the free population. Abbé Raynal estimated in 1775 that there were 70,000 slaves and only 12,000 whites on Martinique and 73,000 slaves and 12,000 whites on Guadeloupe. The change was even more radical on Saint Domingue, where, on the eve of the French Revolution, Moreau de Saint-Méry calculated that there were 40,000 free whites but over 450,000

---

5. Lasserre, *La Guadeloupe*, 351–52; Raynal, *Histoire philosophique et politique*, II, 563; ACCM, H19; Médéric Louis Elie Moreau de Saint-Méry, *Description topographique, physique, civile, politique, et historique de la partie française de l'isle de Saint Domingue* (1797; rpr. Paris, 1958), 118, 723, 1165.

slaves.[6] The slaves did virtually all the manual labor on the islands and represented much of the planters' wealth.

The classic description of a French West Indian sugar plantation was given by Pére Labat.[7] According to him, the ideal plantation bordered a river for 3,000 yards and extended 1,000 yards deep; this made for a surface area of 300 hectares, or 750 acres. Along the front end, there was a 300-yard stretch of savannah, including some 50 yards of trees left to protect the plantation from winds. Then came an area for buildings, measuring 300 yards by 300 yards. In the center of this, preferably on a rise, was the master's house, surrounded by a garden with stores and offices. Then, a suitable distance behind the master's house, so as not to disturb the owner or manager with too much noise, came the mill and the various buildings in which the sugar cane was treated. Finally, there were the *cases*, or makeshift shacks for the slaves, arranged to form one or two streets with a small area at the end set aside for the plantation's animals. On each side of the building area was a field of sugar cane measuring 350 yards by 300 yards; a large cane field of some 40 hectares (100 acres) was directly behind the buildings. Next came the slaves' gardens, where they worked in their free time to grow food items that were frequently salable. Finally came the rest of the plantation, a large wooded area that could serve as arable land should the plantation grow; Labat suggested planting a cocoa crop on part of this spare land. A sugar plantation like this required 120 slaves, 4 oxcarts, 38 oxen, 20 cows with their calves, 12 horses, and flocks of sheep and goats.

Labat's ideal plantation was not too different from the typical sugar plantation in the Antilles, and his categories "land," "buildings," and "slaves and animals" were standard. All plantation inventories were divided into three such sections: for example, when Stanislas Foache bought the habitation Trou on Saint Domingue on January 14, 1777, the notary carefully described the amount of land involved (including 8 hectares, or 20 acres, claimed by Sieur Theil), then the buildings and their contents, and finally the slaves and animals.[8] The Trou planta-

---

6. Lasserre, *La Guadeloupe*, 275; Raynal, *Histoire philosophique et politique*, II, 563, 578; Moreau, *Description topographique*, 28.
7. Labat's description is summarized in Lasserre, *La Guadeloupe*, 354–55. For another description of an ideal plantation, see Avalle, *Tableau comparatif*, 3–4.
8. ADSM, BDM 1.49, January 14, 1777. See also AN, 107AP127; AN, 107AP108, dossier 4; AN, T256/2.

tion was on the Volrogue River and contained some 190 hectares (475 acres) of land, including 30 hectares (75 acres) of cane and 25 hectares (63 acres) of gardens for the slaves; the plantation had a house for the master, 2 buildings for processing sugar cane, 20 shacks for slaves, a store, and an infirmary; it counted 125 slaves, 18 mules, 7 oxen, and 8 cows. This plantation, although smaller than Labat's ideal, was probably more characteristic of reality. According to Christian Schnakenbourg, the average sugar plantation on late eighteenth-century Guadeloupe had 179 hectares (425 acres) of land, including 55 hectares (138 acres) of cane.[9] Plantations on Saint Domingue may have been somewhat larger, but they still devoted only a small fraction of their surface area to sugar cane. The grands blancs owned land that they had no intention of cultivating but refused to sell, fearing increased competition and loss of status. Only in some of the more remote areas of Saint Domingue were good lands available to small planters after the end of the seventeenth century.

All but the smallest sugar plantations needed a large number of slaves to function properly. Although the land on some plantations could occasionally be worth more than the slaves, it was still the number of slaves that usually determined the plantation's value. Unfortunately, it is difficult to establish the average number of slaves per plantation. Most figures from the French West Indies are unreliable, and only crude estimates can be made. At the end of the Old Regime, there were about 650,000 slaves in the French West Indies; from one-third to one-half of these probably belonged to sugar plantations, with most of the rest belonging to other plantations or to urban masters. On Guadeloupe, for example, there were 95,000 slaves in 1790, of whom some 42,000 lived on sugar plantations. The average sugar plantation on Guadeloupe had 112 slaves, including 85 adults able to work; but a large number of small plantations lowered the median figure to 86 slaves, with 63 adults able to work. The domination of the large plantations was also apparent on Martinique in 1770, when Raynal estimated that 100 large, rich, self-sufficient sugar plantations maintained 12,000 slaves, or 120 each, while the remaining 186 sugar plantations had only 11,000 slaves, or 60 each.[10] Much the same conditions undoubtedly obtained in Saint Domingue, where, if

9. Christian Schnakenbourg, *Les sucreries de la Guadeloupe dans la seconde moitié du XVIIIe siècle* (Paris, 1972), 53, 57.
10. *Ibid.*, 88–89; Raynal, *Histoire philosophique et politique*, II, 566.

anything, the large plantations probably had an even more telling impact.

The slaves represented a considerable capital investment, and replacing slaves was usually the largest operating expense encountered by a planter. The price of slaves increased throughout the eighteenth century, going from 600 livres in 1738 to nearly 1,500 in 1789. Official figures estimated that each of Saint Domingue's 455,000 slaves was worth 1,667 livres at the end of the Old Regime, for a total of over 750,000,000 livres—more than three times the estimated value of all lands and buildings in the colony.[11] An individual plantation owner might own hundreds of thousands of livres' worth of slaves: for example, the Belin family owned 205 slaves on Saint Domingue in 1790, worth nearly 300,000 livres, and Stanislas Foache's 125 slaves were worth 120,000 livres in 1777.[12] A truly great landowner had many more. In 1784, for example, the Marquis de Gallifet owned more than 950 slaves on 5 plantations; they were worth 1,400,000 livres. The value of individual slaves varied widely, depending on age, sex, and health. The Belins' 90 adult males were worth an average of almost 2,000 livres each, the 72 adult females only 1,350 livres each, the 18 boys and 25 girls 600 livres each. Old or handicapped slaves might have no value at all. Plantation owners tried to keep a rough balance between the numbers of males and females, a balance reflected in the 1789 Saint Domingue population figures, which showed an eight-to-seven male-to-female slave ratio.[13] Planters also liked children to account for one-quarter to one-third of the total number of slaves; a large number of healthy children meant fewer slave purchases in the future.

Having a naturally growing or even stable slave population was the goal of every planter, but few if any realized it. The death rate on the plantations exceeded the birth rate, and only a massive slave trade kept the captive population from decreasing. According to Philip Curtin, the slave population of Saint Domingue suffered an average natural decline of 2.6 percent annually from 1739 to 1774; yet the slave population actually grew by an average of 2.0 percent per year during the same period, the result of nearly 8,000 imports annually.

11. Stein, *French Slave Trade*, 141, 144; ACCM, H19.
12. ADCM, 4J2915; ADSM, BDM 1.49, January 14, 1777.
13. AN, 107AP128, dossier 4, May 12, 1784; Moreau, *Description topographique*, 118, 722, 1165.

The situation was even more dramatic on Guadeloupe: from 1730 to 1778, the average natural decrease was 5.4 percent, while the slave population grew by an average of 3.2 percent per year. Curtin's calculations have been criticized, not for exaggeration but for being too conservative: his most strident critic accused him of underestimating the death rate.[14]

Even if Curtin's "modest" figures are accepted, the view of an inhuman socioeconomic system vividly emerges. Disease and overwork killed slaves at a disastrous rate, and an abundant slave trade militated against improvement. In such a system the death of an individual slave was significant only for its economic consequences. Absentee plantation owners received, often without comment, annual reports of births and deaths among their slaves and animals. Only the death of an exceptionally productive slave was noted with any sense of loss, such as was felt by one manager in 1784: "We have just lost our Negro after five weeks of illness. It was first a cold, then a fever, then a trembling in the body, and then a sort of imbecility. In short, an almost unknown malady. I miss him because he was a good Negro and a good worker." Far more typical was the attitude of another manager who described the death of two slaves in 1792: "The first died of old age. This loss must be considered very modest, since the subject was no longer useful to you and had, on the contrary, occasioned expenses. As for the Negro named Jean Baptiste, a Congo and a mason, who died of illness, you should not regret his passing even if he was young. He was a bad subject who contributed much to the problems that took place."[15]

Even more typical were the deaths reported in passing on the annual accounts given owners by their managers. M. de Bongars, for example, learned of slave deaths on his Saint Domingue plantations at the end of each year when M. Chervain submitted his annual report. Of an average slave population of 210, there were 7 deaths in 1769, 8 in 1770, 12 in 1771, 14 in 1772, 10 in 1773, 9 in 1774, 2 in 1775, 14 in 1776, 8 in 1777, 7 in 1778, and 3 in 1779; 94 slaves out of a total of 302 had died. Things were no better on the Rochefoucault sugar plantation on Martinique. With an average slave population of

---

14. Curtin, *Atlantic Slave Trade*, 75–84; Lasserre, *La Guadeloupe*, 292–93; J. E. Inikori, "Measuring the Atlantic Slave Trade," *Journal of African History*, XVII (1976), 197–223.

15. ADSM, BDM 1.48, January 5, 1784; ADCM, 4J2915, August 31, 1792.

165, from 3 to 16 died each year from 1761 to 1766. Sometimes the death rate was so high that births and purchases could not keep pace; on the Marquis de Gallifet's five plantations, the net slave population declined from 1,000 in 1775 to only 915 in 1791, with as many as 16 dying in one three-month period.[16]

Some slaves did manage to survive, occasionally reaching old age. In 1762, for example, the Belin plantation on Saint Domingue had 113 adult slaves, including 22 in their forties, 33 in their fifties, and 26 above fifty-nine years. A few years later, the same plantation reputedly had a male aged ninety-one and a female aged ninety-six.[17] Resilient slaves such as these managed to reproduce and give birth to Creole, or French West Indian–born, slaves. There are indications that Creole slaves were fairly numerous; some lists of slaves have a high proportion of them. This meant, among other things, that the slave mortality rate was inflated by the large number of deaths of new arrivals from Africa and that slaves who did manage to adjust to the new diseases and the brutal work regime of the Antilles could survive, if not prosper.[18] Their offspring were much appreciated by some planters. As one absentee owner remarked to his foreman: "We believe that it is good to reward those women who raise their young with care. Humanity demands that we treat them favorably. It is also in the owner's interest, Creole slaves being much more valuable than African ones."[19] The preference for Creole slaves was not universal, although they were generally recognized to be without equal as domestics.

At any given moment, the majority of slaves on the French islands were from Africa. On the whole these slaves were not well liked by many planters, a sentiment that comes through clearly in the description of the African slaves given by Moreau de Saint Méry in his work on Saint Domingue. Moreau was from one of the oldest white families in the French West Indies and, if not particularly rich himself, was related to most of the major families on Martinique. He was

16. AN, T520/2; AN, T256/3; AN, 107AP127.
17. ADCM, E295, January 26, 1762; ADCM, 4J2914.
18. ADCM, 4J2915. See also Françoise Thésée and Gabriel Debien, *Un colon niortais à Saint Domingue, Jean Barrée de Saint Venant* (Niort, 1975), 79, 94; and Michel René Hilliard d'Auberteuil, *Considérations sur l'état présent de la colonie française de Saint Domingue* (Paris, 1776), I, 54.
19. ADCM, E310, April 8, 1774. See also Gabriel Debien, *Etudes antillaises* (Paris, 1956), 51.

most familiar with the planter mentality. According to Moreau, African slaves were naturally lazy and ignorant. He blamed much of this on the hot African climate, "which, in strictly limiting and easily satisfying all needs, relieves the African of all the worries and cares that man finds in the idea of the future." This was ironic, since one of the main defenses of the naturalness of slavery was that Africans were used to the torrid climate and could work in it without the problems encountered by whites. The planters obviously believed that they could force the African slaves to work in the Caribbean, although the whites never ceased complaining about the blacks' sloth. "In general," wrote Moreau, "the Africans living in Saint Domingue remain indolent and lazy, quarrelsome, overtalkative, lying, and given to larceny." They were also supposed to be profoundly superstitious and incapable of understanding refined French religious sentiments.[20]

This blanket criticism did not mean that the planters thought all Africans were alike and could be purchased indiscriminately. On the contrary much thoughtful care went into the selection of slaves for the French plantations, and colonial preferences in this area were almost as important as market conditions in Africa in deciding just which slaves a trader bought. Unfortunately, attempts to determine the exact ethnic origins of the slaves have met with scant success.[21] All that can be said with certainty is that the French West Indian slaves came from between Senegal and Angola, with a handful from Mozambique after the American Revolution. There is, however, nonstatistical evidence about the African slaves, particularly Moreau's lengthy description of the characteristics of the various black groups. Moreau recognized five major trading regions in Africa, which together sheltered a total of nearly forty slave-producing tribes. Only a few of these tribes consistently furnished good slaves, the rest of the tribes producing "unruly" or "lazy" captives.

Two areas in particular supplied Saint Domingue with slaves, the Gold Coast and the Congo–Angola coast. According to Moreau, slaves from the Gold Coast were barely acceptable for French West

20. Moreau, *Description topographique*, 47–55. The quotation is from Blanche Maurel's introduction to the book, vii–viii.
21. Even the most serious work on this subject is far from being comprehensive: Gabriel Debien, *Les esclaves aux Antilles françaises* (Basse-Terre, 1974), 39–68. See also David Geggus, "Les esclaves de la Plaine du Nord à la veille de la Révolution," *Revue de la Société Haitienne d'Histoire et de Géographie*, XLIII (1985), 16–51.

Indian plantations: "The Negroes of the Gold Coast are, in general, well made and intelligent; but they are criticized for commonly being deceitful, artificial, dissimulating, lazy, roguish, flattering, greedy, drunk, and lewd." Some Gold Coast tribes were supposed to have peculiar habits and had to be watched with care. For example, the Ibos were reputedly suicidal. Moreau wrote that "close surveillance of the Ibos is necessary because the least sorrow or discontent leads them to suicide, the idea of which, far from terrifying them, seems to have something seductive for them because they believe in the doctrine of the transmigration of souls. Only too frequently have all the Ibos of a plantation decided to hang themselves in order to return to their land."[22] In general, according to Moreau, most of the Gold Coast tribes tended to be bloodthirsty and difficult to enslave.

Most of Saint Domingue's slaves came from the Congo and Angola and were called "Congos." Some of the Congo and Angola tribes provided the French West Indies with the best slaves.

> The true Congos, or "Franc-Congos," to use the Saint Domingue terminology, come from the Congo and Angola kingdoms and are, like all those from this coast, of a much-sought-after mildness and cheerfulness. Loving songs, dances, and ornamentation, they make excellent domestics; and their intelligence, the ease with which they speak Creole, their playful and unmarked faces—particularly among the women, who have but two little marks near their temples . . . —make them preferred for home service. Congo women are much valued for tilling, as they are used to it in their native land; and in general, the Congos live on manioc and more so on bananas, which they like so much that they are described by the saying "Congo mangé banane" (Congo, eater of bananas). Besides being excellent mimics, always having a smile on their face, they are valuable in a workshop, where they bring cheer, which does not always convert work into neglect but which delays the ensuing fatigue.[23]

But even the Congo produced some unacceptable slaves, such as the Mousombés and Mondongues; members of these tribes reputedly resorted to cannibalism in Africa and even in Saint Domingue.

Most slave owners tried to have a large variety of language groups represented on their plantations in the belief that difficulties in communications discouraged revolt. Similarly, keeping the slaves content or at least not too miserable was a major concern of the planters, and individual planters frequently boasted that their slaves were sat-

22. Moreau, *Description topographique*, 51.
23. *Ibid.*, 53.

isfied and therefore not dangerous. Letters exchanged between absentee owners and their colonial representatives were full of reference to this matter; one plantation manager even considered applying the new techniques of Mesmer to those slaves "who have the greatest need for them." Usually, the more obvious prescriptions, such as adequate food and reasonable work load, were counseled, as one owner wrote to his manager: "We are strongly of your opinion of taking the greatest care with the Negroes, of feeding and clothing them well, of displaying attachment and friendship, and of not overburdening them with work."[24] Healthy, happy slaves presumably made for a more productive and profitable plantation.

Despite the surface tranquillity, however, the plantation was often filled with terror for both blacks and whites. The slaves feared their masters' arbitrary cruelty, and it was widely reported that the slaves expected to be eaten by their owners. The whites feared their slaves' revenge, to be taken not so much in night attacks but by poisoning. Tales of water or food poisoning circulated widely on the islands, and even an observer like Moreau was wary: "It is unfortunately all too certain that the old Africans profess in Saint Domingue the odious art of poisoning; I say profess, for there are some there who have a school where hatred and vengeance send more than one disciple."[25] The whites also feared wide-scale rebellion and escape. Slave revolts were not uncommon in the French West Indies and reached their peak in the great rebellion of August 22, 1791, when thousands of slaves fought to free the northern part of Saint Domingue from slavery. Marronnage was also common in the French Antilles, and local newspapers had regular accounts of runaway slaves. For example, one issue of the *Feuille du Cap Français* listed nine maroons in prison, including "Pierre, Mozambique, stamped on the right breast 'Sudre Cadet,' aged about eighteen years, four feet, ten inches tall, having facial markings from his land."[26] The goal of runaway slaves was to reach

---

24. ADLA, 1JJ5, August 25, 1788. On Mesmer's possible use, see ADSM, BDM 1.48, June 11, 1784.
25. Moreau, *Description topographique*, 56. On fears of being eaten, see Jehan Mousnier, *Journal de la traite des noirs* (Paris, 1957).
26. ACCM, H15, May 20, 1789. See also Leslie F. Manigat, "The Relationship Between Marronage and Slave Revolution in Saint Domingue–Haiti," in Rubin and Tuden (eds.), *Comparative Perspectives on Slavery*, 420–38; Debien, *Les esclaves*, 411–69; and Debien, *Etudes antillaises*, 173.

the mountains and live beyond the plantation system; penalties for failure were severe, ultimately including death.

Relations between master and slave were theoretically regulated by the *code noir*, a sixty-article edict promulgated in March, 1685, by Louis XIV and in effect with minor changes until the end of the Old Regime.[27] The code noir served as the legal charter for the French West Indian slave system, and it reflected official thinking about slavery. Since slavery was considered natural, no defense was required, as the preface made clear.

> As we owe our cares equally to all the peoples that Divine Providence has placed under our rule, we have had examined in our presence the essays that have been sent to us by our officials on our American islands, by which, having been informed of the need that they have of our authority and our justice in order to keep the discipline of the Catholic, apostolic, and Roman church there, and in order to regulate that which concerns the status and the quality of the slaves in the said islands; and desiring to make known to them that, although they inhabit climes infinitely distant from our usual seat, we are always present to them not only by the reach of our power but also by the promptitude of our application in supporting them in their necessities.

The code noir did not justify slavery; it merely organized it.

After a preliminary article reiterating the 1615 expulsion of the Jews from the French West Indies, the code noir successively dealt with the slaves' religious instruction, their civil status, their relationship to their master, and their enfranchisement. Perhaps reflecting the mature Louis XIV's preoccupation with religious orthodoxy—the Edict of Nantes was repealed only a few months after the promulgation of the code noir—the code began with a consideration of the slaves' religious welfare. All slaves in the French West Indies were to be baptized and instructed in the only lawful religion, Roman Catholicism (Articles 2 and 3); further, Sundays and Catholic holidays were to be observed as rest days for the slaves (Article 6). More mundane matters followed, as the code turned to the slaves' legal position. That the slaves were, in fact, slaves went without saying; what mattered here were the finer points, such as the status of a child born to a white and his concubine (Article 9) and the necessity of the

---

27. Reprinted in Lucien Peytraud, *L'esclavage aux Antilles françaises avant 1789* (Paris, 1897), 158–66.

master's consent for his slaves to marry (Article 10). The slaves also suffered from less obvious prohibitions designed to protect the master both physically and economically. All assemblies of slaves were banned, "even for marriages" (Article 16), and slaves could not under any circumstances own or sell sugar cane (Article 18).

The master's responsibility to, and powers over, his slaves formed the heart of the code noir. In an attempt to guarantee the slaves at least a minimal standard of living, the edict ordered the owner to feed and clothe them properly. Each slave more than nine years old was entitled to a weekly food ration of two pounds of salted beef or three pounds of fish, and six pounds of cassava bread or two and one-half *pots* of manioc flour; children received half of the adult ration (Article 22). Each slave was also to receive two outfits annually made from four aunes of cloth (Article 25). To insure that slaves would be adequately clothed and fed, the slaves could "notify our prosecutor [of inadequacies] and submit their petitions to him, on the basis of which and even on his own if the [same] opinions came from elsewhere, the masters will be prosecuted at his request and without cost; this is what we want observed for crimes and barbarous and inhuman treatment of the slaves by their masters" (Article 26). The master also had a special obligation to take care of old and sick slaves (Article 27), and he could not sell married slaves separately (Article 47).

The code noir demanded absolute obedience from the slave. Being themselves possessions, slaves could own no property; all belonged to the master (Article 28). Justice was equally uncompromising. Slaves who struck their master, their master's wife, or their master's child, either in the face or elsewhere, hard enough to draw blood, were liable to the death penalty (Article 33). Capital punishment was also prescribed for theft, as the case required (Article 35). On the other hand, the master was explicitly prohibited from torturing his slaves (Article 42), this a century before torture was abolished in France; masters could, however, chain their slaves and whip them (Article 42). The greatest power an owner had was the power to enfranchise his slaves. This power was unconditional: a master could liberate his slave without accounting to anyone (Article 55). Such enfranchisement could even follow an owner's death; if the master named a slave as principal heir, guarantor of the testament, or guardian over his children, the slave was automatically freed (Article 56). Although the liberated slaves were ordered to have great respect toward their former owners, they were considered the equal of all French citizens, sharing the same rights and obligations (Articles 57, 58, and 59).

Most plantation owners probably obeyed the letter and even the rather tepid humanitarian spirit of the code noir whenever convenient. For example, slaves were baptized, although scarcely instructed in the Catholic religion: Moreau mentioned newly arrived slaves anxious to be baptized "all too frequently without any preparation." Slave children were apparently baptized young, and one plantation manager thought it worthy of note that a baby of eight months had not yet been baptized.[28] Concern for profit and production, however, certainly outweighed interest in humanity or religion, and the high death rate attested to the cruel realities of plantation life. Slaves were mistreated and, contrary to the admittedly ambivalent wording of the code noir, had no legal recourse against oppressive masters. The code noir could not be enforced on the plantations, and only when it coincided with prevailing management techniques was it applied. Books about running plantations were of greater practical value than law codes.

The greatest discrepancy between legal theory and practice was in the treatment of enfranchised slaves or free men of color. Although promised full civil equality with white Frenchmen, the free men of color suffered discrimination in the most blatant fashion. As they complained in 1790, they formed "a class of men born French, but degraded by cruel and vile prejudices and laws."[29] Forbidden to enter France as of March 1, 1764, the free men of color were subject to significant restrictions in the colonies: they were denied all rights of assembly, banned from attaining noble status, kept out of most of the armed forces, and forbidden to hold positions of responsibility in the administration. In spite of their treatment, free men of color rendered the whites valuable services, particularly in controlling the slaves; free men of color were renowned for their ability to find runaway captives. The short-sighted bigotry of the white colonists, especially the Creoles, ultimately encouraged some of the free men of color to join forces with the slaves to end the French regime in Saint Domingue.

---

28. Moreau, *Description topographique*, 55; ADCM, 4J2915, October, 1778.
29. Michel Mina, *Adresse à l'Assemblée Nationale par les hommes de couleur libres de Saint Domingue* (N.p., n.d.), 1–2. On the free men of color see Auguste Lebeau, *De la condition des gens de couleur libres sous l'ancien régime* (Poitiers, 1903).

The issue of free colored or even slave "rights" was quite secondary for the planters, who were concerned almost exclusively with operating a successful plantation business. Central to the smooth functioning of the plantation was the work of the slaves, and making the slaves work was therefore a major concern for the planters. Owners and managers tried everything from brutal force to friendly persuasion to get their slaves to work, although none held out the prospect of automatic enfranchisement. In all cases, a firm discipline was recommended; the slave must never forget his station and must know that transgressions would be punished. So absolute was the distance between master and slave that a reform allowing slaves to testify in court against their masters was openly laughed at by the planters in 1785. The key to having the slaves work was to make the work bearable, as one owner wrote: "The slaves must work, but we must make their work as tolerable as possible, working them with humanity." "Humanity" usually meant giving the slaves some reason to continue living. The author of a manual on plantation life suggested, for example, giving all women four months' rest for pregnancies and completely ending forced labor for mothers with six or more children. The same author also recommended marriages between slaves to encourage personal stability in them, as well as interest in the plantation and in their own lives.[30]

But some owners rejected all notions of humanity and treated their slaves without pity. These planters defied even the possible negative economic consequences, pushing their slaves beyond the breaking point and earning their colleagues' animosity. One such slave driver was described by a plantation manager in a letter to the owner in France: "Lagrèze, whom you mentioned, was a very good farmer but not very humane. He dreamt more of sugar and of revenues than of food and Negroes. One year, he produced 450,000 livres' worth of sugar, but for that he pushed his Negroes. They held up as long as the food lasted, but this cruel man took a good field for cane and gave the Negroes a bad field for their gardens. They could not withstand this, and more than sixty of them fled at a time." Owners of similar persuasion were especially cruel to the elderly and infirm; early visitors to Guyane noted that some "work old and sick slaves to death rather

---

30. ADSM, BDM 1.50, April 14, 1785; ADCM, E301, April 1, 1770; Poyen Sainte-Marie, *De l'exploitation des sucreries* (Pointe-à-Pitre, 1803), 43, 49.

than let them sit around doing nothing but eat good food." Such attitudes, although not rare, were probably in the minority: most letters from owners to managers suggest a certain, albeit self-interested humanity, and at least one antislavery observer expressed surprise that old slaves were not destroyed like horses.[31] Most large plantations had an infirmary, and owners regularly reminded their managers to treat sick slaves with care. One pair of absentee owners congratulated their representatives for this: "We learn with pleasure . . . that you have had an infirmary built as needed to treat our poor Negroes with care and zeal." Sick slaves presented a difficult problem for the planters. Anxious as they were to nurse their slaves back to good health, the planters could never quite believe in the authenticity of the malady. Upon learning the latest news of illness on his plantation, one absentee owner sharply criticized his manager, saying, "Your infirmary is always full of malingerers."[32] Planters had to expect about one-tenth of their slaves to be sick at any given moment.

Slaves who were fit worked a full day.[33] They started at dawn, which was between 5:30 and 6:30 A.M. in the Caribbean. At eight o'clock there was a short break for breakfast, followed by more work until noon. Then they had a two- or, if unusually hot, three-hour break for lunch and working in their gardens. The slaves returned to work at two or three o'clock and continued until dusk, between 5:30 and 6:30 P.M. in the West Indies. In exceptional circumstances they might be required to work until far into the night. On Sundays and holidays they worked in their gardens, growing food for personal consumption or for sale. Particularly enterprising slaves could, with their master's permission, sell surplus crops in town for tobacco, rum, or clothing; these excess fruits and vegetables ultimately went to feed poor whites or domestics. In practice the slaves virtually owned their gardens and their proceeds, in obvious contravention of the code noir.

Just how much time the slaves had to devote to their gardens is

---

31. ADSM, BDM 1.48, June 6, 1784; Didier Guyvarc'h and Gabriel Debien, "Instructions des colons des Antilles à leurs gérants," *Anuario de estudios americanos*, XXIV (1958), 532–33; Justin Girod-Chantrans, *Voyage d'un suisse dans différentes colonies de l'Amérique* (Neuchatel, 1785), 176.

32. ADLA, 1JJ6, January 26, 1790; ADSM, BDM 1.50, January 25, 1785.

33. For the best description of the slaves' day see Debien, *Les esclaves*, 147–61. See also Avalle, *Tableau comparatif*, 18–21; and Gabriel Debien, "Les vivres sur une caféière de Saint Domingue," *Enquêtes et Documents*, I (1971), 144.

debatable. Some owners complained that slaves had up to ten days a month with no forced labor. M. Maillard of Cayenne, for example, claimed in 1768 that his slaves were free on no fewer than 108 days per year, including 52 Sundays, 30 holidays, and 26 Saturdays. If this was true, it was exceptional; evidence from other sources suggests that the holiday time in particular was exaggerated and that Saturdays were generally considered as normal workdays. On the Marquis de Gallifet's huge sugar plantation Grande Place on Saint Domingue, the 404 slaves rarely if ever had a free Saturday; they also had considerably fewer than 30 holidays, getting only about a dozen major Catholic festivals.[34] They did not, however, have to work on Sundays, at least in theory. Whether hard-driving foremen actually respected the prohibition is unknowable.

Slaves on sugar plantations did many types of work, depending on their abilities. One description of a late seventeenth-century sugar plantation on Martinique gave detailed information about the distribution of slave labor.[35] The plantation's two hundred slaves were divided into seven groups. Eleven slaves worked in the master's house; they included servants, cooks, guards, and other domestic workers. Forty were involved in the infirmary: one guard, twenty-five infants and children, two hospital workers, and twelve sick. Ten guarded or worked in the plantation's food-growing areas; nine dealt with the plantation's animals and grasslands; and five were artisans. Forty-one, including the aged and nursing mothers, performed moderately difficult manual labor, while the remaining eighty-four worked in the fields under the supervision of a slave driver. During the harvest season, more were undoubtedly assigned to various aspects of sugar-cane processing.

The elite of the plantations and of colonial society in general was made up exclusively of whites. Comprising less than 10 percent of the French West Indian population at the end of the Old Regime, the whites owned almost everything of value in the colonies; only the socially insecure free men of color shared the legal right to own property. Given the wealth of the islands and the quantity of slaves, the meager number of resident whites was astonishing: in 1789 a maximum of 55,000 lived in the French Antilles, with 30,000 on

34. AN, Col F3 91, fêtes, October 26, 1768; AN, 107AP130, dossier 1, travaux.
35. Josa, *Les industries du sucre*, 63–65. See also Thésée and Debien, *Colon niortais*, 81; and AN, 107AP130, May 22, 1775, which lists duties of Gallifet's slaves.

Saint Domingue alone—where there were more than 450,000 slaves. For purposes of comparison, South Carolina, the British North American colony with the lowest free-to-slave ratio, had 50,000 whites and 75,000 slaves in 1770. The white population in the French West Indies did not grow with anything approaching the speed of the black population; according to Charles Frostin, the whites increased from nearly 14,000 in 1700 to about 45,000 in 1775, while the slaves grew from about 27,000 to about 416,000. The overwhelming majority of the whites, like their slaves, lived in the rural areas. The largest town in the French West Indies was Cap Français, Saint Domingue; it boasted a population in 1790 of less than 20,000, most of whom were not white.[36] Most of the islands' whites were male, which was a prime factor in the growth of the mulatto population, whether free or slave; according to Article 13 of the code noir, all children of enslaved mothers were slaves, regardless of the father's status.

It was the whites' job to make the blacks work, and large sugar plantations had a relatively sophisticated administration. At the top was the owner, whether in the colonies or France. The question of absenteeism is an important one, and as Gabriel Debien has noted, it did not depend merely on the owner's place of residence but on his active interest in the plantation. There were large numbers of plantation owners living in France, and many others sought to leave the West Indies. According to one observer, most of the rich landlords from Cap Français and Port-au-Prince lived in France, and Moreau remarked that "the general mania is to speak of returning or traveling to France."[37] Owners of sugar plantations were the most likely to realize this dream. Having older and larger holdings than the lately arrived coffee planters, the sugar planters formed the backbone of the grand blanc community and were financially able to leave the colonies; this earned them the bitter enmity of the petits blancs, who tried to impose residency requirements at the end of the Old Regime.[38] Owners in France gave full powers of attorney to colonial

---

36. Charles Frostin, *Les révoltes blanches à Saint Domingue aux XVIIe et XVIIIe siècles* (Paris, 1975), 628–29; Moreau, *Description topographique*, 479.

37. Debien, *Les esclaves*, 105–107; Moreau, *Description topographique*, 34. See also AN, Col F3 84, June 2, 1787, "Lettre à l'auteur du mémoire intitulé 'Précis pour les grands propriétaires des colonies.'"

38. Gabriel Debien, *Les colons de Saint Domingue et la Révolution* (Paris, 1953), 40. On petits blancs see also his "La société coloniale au XVIIe et au XVIIIe siècles: petits blancs aux îles," *Annales des Antilles*, VII (1959), 1–37.

merchants or planters for running their plantations, and the correspondence between owner and proxy forms a major source of information about the islands. The absentee owners tried to play a political role while in France, and although they never exercised the same overt political power as their British counterparts, they did manage to influence government policy toward the colonies, especially during the early years of the French Revolution. Not all absentee owners were in France, however, and many planters residing in the Antilles were for all practical purposes "absent." This resulted from having a lack of interest in running the plantation, from owning more than one plantation, or, in the case of exceptionally large and well-organized plantations, from having the staff do most of the work independently. Planters frequently left the actual administration of their estates to specialists, theoretically employing one white for every twenty slaves.

When the planter did not run his plantation directly, a manager did.[39] Appointed either by the owner, his proxy, or his heirs when they did not wish to divide the legacy, the manager lived on the plantation and was responsible for all its daily operations. Often recently arrived in the Antilles without much money, the manager worked on contract and could earn a small fortune in a few years. Many therefore quit after a little while, although it was not at all uncommon for a manager to become attached to a particular plantation and spend the rest of his life on it; some even risked or lost their lives during the Haitian Revolution. The manager was interested primarily in increasing the revenues of the plantation; as Debien wrote, "His job was to force the agricultural and industrial machine by all means in order to increase the yield." Confronted daily with the realities of slave labor, the manager or owner-manager appeared far less humane than the absentee owner. Said Debien: "What was asked of the manager was not to be a philanthropist but to get the blacks to work in order to increase revenues."[40] Several other whites worked under the manager. Some kept track of the plantation's correspondence, others supervised the slaves, and still others performed specialized duties such as distilling rum or directing the processing of

39. Debien, *Les esclaves*, 105–17. For descriptions of the manager's duties, see AN, 107AP128, dossier 1.
40. Debien, *Les esclaves*, 108, 109. See also Françoise Thésée, *Les négociants bordelais et les colons de Saint Domingue* (Paris, 1972), 53.

sugar. These whites frequently were poorly paid and led lives only marginally better than those of the slaves. The colonies attracted far too many poor white fortune hunters than could be comfortably employed, and the resulting competition depressed wages and created major fissures in colonial society. The depth of these fissures became evident after 1789.

In spite of the legend, life for the whites on the plantations was usually far from luxurious. The lower ranks had *cases* similar to those that sheltered the slaves, and even the manager or owner-manager who occupied the large house in the middle of the plantation was scarcely comfortable. Only the oldest and wealthiest Creole families bothered to construct impressive residences on the islands; other planters were content with lower standards, wanting only to make their fortune and return to France. The whites also suffered from moral and intellectual shortcomings. Moreau, a planter himself, described white Creole children as little tyrants expecting to be served constantly by slaves. Once grown up, but still uneducated, the Creole, according to Moreau, "seemed to exist only for voluptuous pleasures"; he was not sociable and tended to be haughty.[41] He was, however, vitally concerned with producing large quantities of sugar.

41. Gabriel Debien, "Les grand'cases des plantations à Saint Domingue aux XVIIe et XVIIIe siècles," *Annales des Antilles*, XV (1970), 1–39; Moreau, *Description topographique*, 35, 37.

3

Muscovado and Clayed Sugar

> You see the Negroes coming out of their shacks, hoes on shoulders, baskets in hand. They perform different dances. The bell rings, the driver arrives, and they leave dancing to go to their place of work.
> —Tascher de la Pagerie

The *raison d'être* of the sugar plantation was the growing of sugar cane and, on all but the smallest plantations, the making of raw sugar.[1] These were labor-intensive operations that necessitated the entire slave system, at least in the eyes of contemporaries. The strongest slaves worked in the fields and were responsible for most of the duties involving the cane itself, such as planting and harvesting. Less fit slaves could also be compelled to work directly with cane, although in less demanding ways: they fertilized, weeded, and cared for the growing plants. Others worked in processing the cane. Under the supervision of a white specialist (the *maître sucrier*), these slaves performed the operations that transformed the cane into sugar. They fed the cane to a mill that crushed it and extracted the juice; this juice was cooked several times until it crystallized as muscovado, or *sucre brut*. On those plantations that did no further processing, the muscovado was then barreled and shipped to France. About half the sugar plantations in the French West Indies continued the processing and made clayed sugar, or *sucre terré*; this was a white sugar that earned higher prices and could be used by the consumer instead of refined sugar. In the eighteenth century, clayed sugar was generally the best quality of sugar produced in the French Antilles; only trivial amounts of refined sugar came from the islands, because high French duties favored metropolitan refining.

One of the most difficult tasks facing a plantation manager was minimizing periods of relative inactivity. The natural growth cycle of cane seemed to combine with the West Indian weather pattern to require lengthy work stoppages; up to half a year might theoretically be wasted waiting for the cane to ripen. First-growth cane took fifteen

---

1. For a general description of the entire process see Avalle, *Tableau comparatif*.

to eighteen months to mature and was best planted in the rainy season, that is, in the late spring or summer; *ratoons,* or second-growth cane, took twelve months to grow. Traditionally a five-year cycle imposed itself: plant in the rainy season of year one; harvest in the dry season of year three; harvest the ratoons one and two years later; and plant again in the rainy season of year five.[2] Such a calendar had obvious shortcomings because of the lengthy intervals between plantings and harvests.

Planters tried to avoid the problem by planting other fields at different times of the year in order to have some cane always ready for harvesting. At any given moment a planter might have up to six different cane crops growing. On the Bongars estate in 1778 there were eight fields with new cane, fifteen with first through fourth ratoons, and one fallow; the following year there were ten with new cane, twelve with first and second ratoons, and two fallow. Furthermore, each field was on its own schedule, providing steady work for the slaves. On the Bouzols plantation near Cap Français almost every month in 1775 saw some cane coming to maturity.[3] With twenty-four fields planted, the plantation was able to provide sugar almost continuously (see Table 1). This type of organization meant that the slaves nearly always had significant work to do, and their daily tasks were more evenly spread through the year.[4] Unfortunately, cane planted out of season could yield disappointing results. The problem was delicate and not easily resolved in spite of much effort.[5] Planters simply had to find other projects for their slaves during the quieter months, such as cleaning and repairing the factory.

According to Christian Schnakenbourg, there were several types of cane grown in the French Antilles. The best and most widely used was *creole cane,* a whitish plant originating in East Asia; other varieties included *otaiti,* from India, and the purple *Malabar* or *Batavia cane.* All were grown in the same way.[6] First, the slaves prepared the

2. Schnakenbourg, *Les sucreries de la Guadeloupe,* 62–63.
3. AN, T520/2, December 31, 1778; AN, T292/2, December 31, 1775.
4. AN, 107AP130, dossier 1, travaux, has lists of daily chores on Gallifet's plantations.
5. See, for example, the critique of traditional methods offered by M. Cazaud, *Account of a New Method of Cultivating the Sugar Cane* (London, 1779), 9–24.
6. Schnakenbourg, *Les sucreries de la Guadeloupe,* 60–61. For descriptions of planting cane see Duhamel du Monceau, *Art de rafiner le sucre* (Paris, 1764), 2–3; Sainte-Marie, *De l'exploitation des sucreries,* 52–55; F. R. Augier, *The Making of the West Indies* (London, 1960), 81; G. Tascher de la Pagerie, "Mes délassements à la

Table 1. Processing of Sugar Cane on the Bouzols Plantation, 1775

Month	Field Number	Type of Crop	Yield (in barrels)
January	21	new cane	37
January	1	new cane	24
January	18	third ratoon	19
February	17	ratoon	20
March	5	ratoon	19
March	14	first ratoon	21
April	20	first ratoon	27
May	2	new cane	24
May	15	first ratoon	19
July	3	new cane	26
August–September	23	new cane	44
September	4	first ratoon	20
October	6	second ratoon	18
November–December	19	first ratoon	16

land by burning or clearing away all grass and shrubs, and then they traced parallel lines from two to three feet apart across the entire field, the distance between the lines increasing with the quality of the soil. Along these lines, the slaves dug hundreds of trenches, each about fifteen inches long, four to five inches wide, and seven to eight inches deep; into each went two fifteen- to eighteen-inch lengths of mature cane stalk taken if possible from near the top of the plant. Earth was then lightly packed around the new plants and added as they grew; given favorable conditions, growth began within a week. There was little to do while the cane was growing besides protect it from weeds. Weeding was the perpetual task of slaves when nothing more important needed doing, and they weeded the entire field several times during the twelve- to eighteen-month growing period.

In spite of the care that the manager might have for his growing

---

Martinique en 1786 et 1787" (Ms in BMN), III, 4–20. See also ADSM, BDM, 1.48, June 3, 1784.

cane, a successful harvest depended in part on elements beyond human control. One danger was insects, and they were greatly feared. Between 1715 and 1720, insects destroyed the entire Martinique cocoa crop, and the fear of a similar disaster was vivid for the French sugar planters. Less spectacular losses were commonplace, as described by one manager to his absentee employer: "General Morin's canes are beginning to be hurt by caterpillars and plant-lice. These two bugs will do much damage if it does not rain to kill them."[7] Bad weather was another great menace to sugar cane, and too little or too much rain at an inopportune time could ruin the year's crop.[8] Managers complained incessantly about the weather, although perhaps to hide their own failings. In any event, droughts and hurricanes did occur with depressing regularity, particularly, it appears, in the western and southern areas of Saint Domingue. According to one manager on Saint Domingue, lack of rain held back planting, dried out the ratoons, and encouraged insects. Another manager blamed flooding for cane of inferior quality that fetched low prices. A third threat to the planter was earthquakes. They did not affect the cane directly but did cause general devastation, forcing the planter to concentrate on rebuilding rather than on farming.[9]

Assuming favorable conditions, most cane was ready for harvesting in the winter and spring, although, as we have seen, ambitious planters had at least small amounts maturing throughout the year.[10] At the height of the main harvest season, the plantation was working at its maximum, limited only by the number of slaves available. This was a difficult time for the slaves, often made worse by unseasonable rains and by the approach of planting season. Although the better fields did not have to be replanted after each harvest, they could not go for too long without new plants, as the practice of ratooning quickly exhausted all but the most fertile of soils. Poor fields, on the other hand, required regular replanting, which meant extra work. Delays in

7. ADSM, BDM 1.50, July 12, 1785.
8. For example, see ADSM, BDM 1.47, August 4, 1764. Paul Butel, *La croissance commerciale bordelaise dans la seconde moitié du XVIIIe siècle* (Paris, 1973), 221, mentions a drought in Saint Domingue in 1775–1776 and cyclones there in 1766, 1772, and 1777.
9. ADSM, BDM 1.47, August 4, 1764; ADSM, BDM 1.50, April 1, 1788. Butel, *La croissance commerciale bordelaise*, 221, mentions earthquakes on Saint Domingue in 1752 and 1770.
10. On planting and harvesting, see Hilliard d'Auberteuil, *Considérations*, I, 180, and Debien, *Les esclaves*, 96.

the harvest were obviously a manager's as well as the slaves' nightmare; the former worried about sacrificing future revenues, the latter about an intolerable work load. The harvest itself was quite straightforward although physically demanding: teams of slaves cut the mature cane with machetes and loaded it onto oxcarts for transporting to the mill. Both men and women performed these jobs.

Once the cane was cut, treatment of it had to begin within twenty-four hours, or it would start to lose its sweet juices. The processing involved a long series of operations that could take up to two months in the case of clayed sugar. Processing began at the mill, where the cane was crushed and its juices extracted. Relying at first on manpower or animals and then on water or wind, the mill was quite large and represented one of the biggest capital investments made by the planter; it demanded the services of four female slaves, two to bring and remove the cane, and two to feed the cane inside.[11] Three vertically mounted rollers made of wood and equipped with iron blades crushed the cane twice—besides frequently injuring the fingers, hands, or arms of the slave responsible for transferring the cane from between the first and second rollers to between the second and third. The juices thus released were collected in a trough underneath the rollers and channeled toward the boilers. The spent stalks were removed by the slaves and saved for fuel.

Transforming the juice into muscovado was the next major operation, and it was performed in the boiling house, or *sucrerie*—an open building averaging some forty to fifty feet in length and twenty-five feet in width. Of course, some were larger, like the one on the plantation purchased by Stanislas Foache in 1777. It was sixty feet long, twenty feet wide, and eleven feet high, and was "covered with brick tile"; another of Foache's sugar houses was seventy-two feet by thirty feet.[12] In the house was a series of red copper boilers, in each of which

---

11. On mills see Paul M. Bondois, "L'industrie sucrière française au XVIIIe siècle," *Revue d'histoire économique et sociale*, XIX (1931), 320. Suggestions for new mill designs were offered regularly. See, for example, AN, F12 1639A (1783). A new water mill on one of Gallifet's plantations cost 287,965 livres to build in 1779. AN, 107AP127.

12. Schnakenbourg, *Les sucreries de la Guadeloupe*, 70; ADSM, BDM 1.49, January 14, 1777. A sucrerie on one plantation was 84 feet by 28 feet by 13.5 feet. AN, T561, May 26, 1791. For the best descriptions of the process of making muscovado see Bondois, "L'industrie sucrière," 321–22; Duhamel, *Art de rafiner le sucre*, 4–5; and Tascher, "Mes délassements," III, 56–59.

the juice was cooked and purified until there remained only a thick syrup that crystallized into muscovado upon cooling. The freshly liberated juice was directed from the mill to the first of the boilers, called *la grande* because of its massive size: measuring four feet across and weighing three hundred pounds, the grande was the largest of the boilers, which successively diminished in size. Here the juice was slowly heated until a thick, black foam appeared on the surface; after this was skimmed off and put aside for the farm animals' consumption, the juice was boiled for an hour with a bit of ash and limewater for purification, then transferred to the second boiler, *la propre*. Over a slightly higher flame, the juice was now boiled more rapidly, again with limewater; this boiling also led to the formation of a foam that was removed. The actual production of sugar began in the third boiler, *la lessive*, where further detergents were added to the juice. These cleansed the juice, liberating various impurities that floated to the top and were again skimmed off. The fourth boiler was *le flambeau*, in which the juice began to clarify itself, again with the addition of detergents. The flambeau was suspended over a high flame that seemed to set the boiler itself on fire, hence the name *flambeau* ("torch"). The juice was then poured through a cloth filter into the fifth boiler, *le sirop*, where the juice became a thick syrup. Finally, after passing through a second cloth filter, the syrup entered the sixth and smallest boiler, known as *la batterie*. With the aid of more limewater and alum, the syrup was transformed into a liquid sugar and began to crystallize. By this time, only a third of the initial volume remained, the rest being lost as impurities or through concentration. Although six was the classic number of boilers, some plantations used as few as four (dropping the lessive and the flambeau) or as many as seven (adding a second flambeau).

After the final boiling, the thick, liquid sugar was poured into a tub to cool. If well-cooked and clarified, a crust of sugar formed within a half hour. This crust was stirred together with the liquid until it cooled to lukewarm; then the sugar was poured into different troughs for further cooling and stirring. Finally, when the sugar was cold, it was placed in uncovered pots. The pots had several holes in the bottom so that any liquid left in the sugar could easily drain; the pots were placed on a grill over a cistern in order to collect these wastes—known as molasses—for further processing. This settling process took place in the *purgerie,* or curing house, the largest building on the plantation, and it lasted three weeks. When all the liquid drained from the pots, only sucre brut, or muscovado, remained. This was the cheapest and poorest-quality sugar produced in the French West Indies and was good only for local consumption or for further processing either in the Antilles or in France. It was not particularly liked by Frenchmen, although its commercial value was uncontested. "*Sucre brut,*" wrote Dutrône la Couture in his treatise on cane, "is so named because from the moment it is produced, it enters into commerce without any preparation; it is still tainted with molasses, of which the more or less abundant proportion establishes the various qualities of muscovado distinguished in trade." A twentieth-century historian, Paul Bondois, was less charitable, characterizing muscovado as "raw, greasy, brown, and soft. It was still very impure in spite of being cooked and cleansed."[13]

With a little more work, planters could transform the liquid sugar into clayed sugar instead of muscovado. This was a common practice much liked by planters, since clayed sugar sold for 50 to 100 percent more than muscovado. The actual transformation procedure was simple, although it did demand a fair amount of time together with a certain expertise from the white supervisor. According to Dutrône la Couture, "clayed sugar differs from muscovado only insofar as it has been relieved of molasses by the claying operation."[14] The problem was to rid the liquid of its brownish color caused by the presence of impurities; this was achieved not by further cooking (as true refining required) but by cleansing it with water. After cooking in the batterie, sugar destined for claying was poured into a series of conical molds, "each made with a bunghole at the apex. The forms sit point down in pots into which the molasses is allowed to drain" for up to four days. Next a layer of wet clay was applied to the wide end of the mold. The water passed through the sugar and drained through the hole in the

13. Schnakenbourg, *Les sucreries de la Guadeloupe,* 70; ADSM, BDM 1.49, January 14, 1777. Jacques François Dutrône la Couture, *Précis sur la canne* (Paris, 1790), 264; Bondois, "L'industrie sucrière," 322.
14. Dutrône la Couture, *Précis sur la canne,* 264. On this process see Duhamel, *Art de rafiner le sucre,* 6; Tascher, "Mes délassements," III, 66–67; ADLA, C731, "Mémoire sur les différentes espèces de sucre," May, 1715; Bryan Edwards, *The History, Civil and Commercial, of the British West Indies* (1819; rpr. New York, 1966), II, 274–75; and Charles Coulston Gillispie (ed.), *A Diderot Pictorial Encyclopedia of Trades and Industry* (New York, 1959), I, plate 41.

narrow end; the movement of the water whitened the sugar by removing impurities. This took about nine or ten days, after which the entire process was repeated with a new layer of clay. After the second cleansing, the loaves of sugar were removed from the molds and placed on shelves in the *étuve*, or drying room. Once dried, they were taken out and broken into their constituent qualities. The narrow tops of the loaves tended to be less pure and were sold as *sucre têté* (from *tête*, or "head"; the name was derived from its position in the upright loaf); the rest formed various grades of clayed sugar.

Most planters considered the extra time and effort required to make clayed sugar well spent, and during most of the Old Regime production of clayed sugar in the French West Indies far exceeded that of muscovado. Since the late seventeenth century, clayed sugar's obvious advantages for the colonists had made it a favorite among planters and a source of anxiety for metropolitan refiners. Clayed sugar became popular in the 1680s, when the government discouraged refining on the islands.[15] Planters, particularly in the highly developed Lesser Antilles colonies, did not take long to realize that it was more lucrative to produce a clayed sugar that could compete in many areas with refined sugar, than a muscovado that required further treatment elsewhere; and by the end of the seventeenth century, muscovado was scarce on Martinique and Guadeloupe.

Only on Saint Domingue was muscovado more plentiful than clayed sugar. Developed after the seventeenth-century conflicts over refining, Saint Domingue was not fully and irretrievably converted to clayed sugar at that time, and the areas of Saint Domingue that were cultivated later—that is, the west and the south—preferred large muscovado plantations rather than the medium-sized clayed-sugar plantations such as were common in the north. In 1790 the west alone produced 70,000,000 pounds of muscovado on 203 plantations (in addition to 13,000,000 pounds of clayed sugar on 148 plantations), or 350,000 pounds per estate; the north produced 53,000,000 pounds of clayed sugar on 271 plantations (plus only 4,000,000 pounds of muscovado on 28 plantations), or 200,000 pounds on each. All told, however, clayed-sugar production in the French Antilles surpassed that of muscovado by 9,000,000 pounds in 1765 (71,000,000 to

15. D'Arcy, "Aperçu de l'histoire du sucre," 15; Josa, *Les industries du sucre*, 75–81.

62,000,000) and by 14,000,000 pounds in 1788 (110,000,000 to 96,000,000); muscovado, however, remained more popular on Saint Domingue itself (93,000,000 pounds to 70,000,000 in 1788).[16]

The triumph of clayed sugar in the French West Indies caused considerable irritation to French refiners. As we have seen, clayed sugar's development in the late 1680s was primarily the consequence of a conflict between planter and metropolitan refiner. When the government discovered that its policy of promoting the growth of both colonial and French refining discouraged the latter, it banned the former but permitted planters to produce clayed sugar; and as French refiners never tired of pointing out, this concession was unique in the West Indies. The second-largest set of sugar-producing colonies, the British, were restricted to making muscovado, but they were guaranteed high prices for it in Britain. French planters never had such security and were open to the vagaries of international competition; hence, they sought to manufacture the type of sugar that would be most profitable for them. Producing clayed sugar, however, provoked the enmity of the refiners, who feared that it was comparable in quality but not in price with their own product. Although exaggerated, these fears were not altogether groundless, and confusion between clayed and refined sugar was widespread. For example, on June 25, 1708, customs officers on the border between Brittany and France wrote: "We, the undersigned inspectors at the Ingrandes office, certify to all interested parties that all sugar passing through this office which is declared as 'white sugar from the islands' is much whiter than clayed sugar, which is always yellower and even has an odor of honey that is very easily identifiable. . . . Said sugar from the islands is nothing but sugar refined and broken up in Nantes."[17] Nonetheless, the so-called "white sugar from the islands" was in fact clayed, even if it took another generation and numerous tests to confirm it. In 1731 the Conseil royal de commerce finally decided that *sucre blanc*, which was of such high quality that Parisian grocers thought it refined, was actually clayed sugar and was therefore to be taxed at the lower rate. Interestingly, while first-quality clayed was taken for refined sugar, sucre tête was confused with muscovado, and terré and tête were

16. ACCM, H19; Tarrade, *Le commerce colonial*, 35. These are quantities exported to France, so they do not consider smuggling.
17. ADLA, C731.

mistaken for one another.[18] Obviously, the grading of sugar was as delicate as it was fiscally and even politically significant.

The French refiners waged a long and generally unsuccessful campaign against clayed sugar. The fight began late in the seventeenth century when the refiners realized that the planters had marketed a cheaper alternative to refined sugar; this turned the refiners' 1684 victory—won when the government all but eliminated colonial refining—into a Pyrrhic one. The refiners now wanted a ban on claying in the colonies, but this they never achieved. At most, the government was willing to discourage it mildly by imposing higher taxes and moderate controls. In 1694, for example, the government, complaining about the dearth of muscovado, decreed that a minimum of half of all colonial debt payments must be made in muscovado. Four years later the government raised the import duty on clayed sugar to 15 livres per hundredweight while keeping the duty on muscovado at 3 livres; the trivial amounts of colonial refined sugar were taxed at 22.5 livres. Finally, in the Letters Patent of 1717, which formed the legal cornerstone of eighteenth-century French colonial trade, the duties on clayed sugar and muscovado were set at 8 livres and 2.5 livres, respectively.[19] This represented more a loss for the refiners, who had to face more competition, than a gain for the planters, who still manufactured the vast majority of their clayed sugar for the reexport market.

Although the duty rates set in 1717 remained in effect until the French Revolution, the refiners kept up their fight against clayed sugar. In this they were occasionally aided by a most uncertain ally from the ports, the outfitters (armateurs). Concerned almost exclusively with the volume of trade between the French West Indies and France, the outfitter was usually opposed to the refiner; the shipper feared that the refiner would limit the sugar commerce to the small amounts required by French refineries and thereby ruin trade with the Antilles. For their own reasons, however, shippers occasionally fought a parallel fight against clayed sugar: they believed that clayed sugar was produced in smaller quantities than muscovado and

18. On problems with grading, see January 12, 1731, and ADLA, C731, mémoire (1748?); and ADLA, C730, August 27, 1763.
19. ADLA, C730, September 26, 1694, and June 20, 1698. See also ACCM, H13, April, 1717.

should therefore be discouraged. This argument was expressed from time to time throughout the eighteenth century, but never with great conviction; most outfitters preferred to transport a slightly smaller amount of clayed sugar than to risk losing most of the colonial trade altogether because of the narrow demands of French refiners.[20] These latter claimed that their industry could never stand the competition from clayed sugar and that a ban on claying would lead to higher tax revenues and higher employment in France. They also complained that claying was responsible for lowering the quality of sugar manufactured by French refiners: "A resident of Saint Domingue refines and whitens two-thirds of his muscovado; he keeps the other third, into which he mixes the molasses syrups produced in the refining process; and by the means of a little cooking, he gives body to these syrups mixed with the muscovado; and these are the materials that are sent to France to provision the refineries."[21] Unfortunately for the refiners, their arguments fell on deaf ears, and clayed sugar remained the primary sugar produced in the French West Indies until the Revolution.

Whether clayed or muscovado, once processed, the sugar was ready for packing and shipping to France. This occasioned yet another series of quarrels between planter and French merchant, with allegations of fraud commonly heard. The basic problem was simple: the merchant wanted to get all the sugar he paid for, but the planter either consciously or unconsciously engaged in practices that often cheated the merchant. The worst contentions occurred in the selection and weighing of the commodities, areas in which the planter could be particularly unscrupulous. So blatant were some abuses that the government had to intervene on several occasions. One 1744 decree "regulating the commerce of the French American colonies" cataloged the planters' crimes.[22] Planters were expressly forbidden to "deliver any barrel of clayed sugar or *tête* that is disguised or false, either by putting the fine sugar at the ends and the bad sugar in the middle, or by any other fashion." It was also illegal to "mix syrups or molasses with muscovado . . . or have less than three holes [for drainage] in the barrel." Barrels had to be of uniform thickness to prevent the intro-

20. ADLA, C730, February 9, 1706, and May 17, 1712.
21. ADLA, C730, "Mémoire pour les raffineurs d'Orléans, d'Angers, et de Saumur," March, 1732.
22. ADLA, C736, March 1, 1744.

duction of extra weight. The interminable disputes that occurred in French ports between merchants and tax collectors showed how little the official rules were followed; the tax men, following the colonial bills of lading, insisted on higher duties than the merchants, in possession of smaller and poorer-quality cargoes than expected, were prepared to pay.

Weighing the sugar presented special difficulties for the buyer. The barrels were weighed on the plantation by the manager or owner himself, but not until the sugar had been added; in other words, only a dubious gross weight was measured. Further, the scales were primitive, using stones to balance the barrels, and suspicious buyers were sure that all "error" systematically favored the seller.[23] In an effort to instill some order and confidence into the system, the government decreed in 1744 that all barrels of sugar had to weigh at least 1,000 pounds. To make it even more precise, the government ruled in 1787 that barrels of sugar had to weigh from 1,500 to 1,600 pounds; within ten months, however, the Lesser Antilles were exempted from this last order because of the difficulties in loading such barrels there.[24] In any event, the decrees still specified gross weight, forcing the purchaser to guess both the weight of the barrel and the size of future losses. The barrels themselves were significant also for their effect on the conservation of the sugar. Knowledgeable merchants insisted on wood from local trees and eschewed imports from Europe; the Farmers General gave larger exemptions for spoilage when sugar was carried in inferior barrels.[25] These exemptions were important and led to numerous disputes between the Farmers General and the merchants. Waste during the voyage to France, whether due to continued draining of molasses or water damage in the ship's hold, was generally calculated at 17 percent for muscovado and 5 to 6 percent for clayed sugar, but merchants always claimed that these figures were unrealistically low.

Besides muscovado and clayed sugar, many sugar plantations sold liquid by-products of sugar known in French as *tafia* and in English as

23. Schnakenbourg, *Les sucreries de la Guadeloupe*, 99. See also ACCM, H109, March 5, 1789.
24. ADLA, C736, March 1, 1744; ADLA, C730, February 11 and November 24, 1787.
25. On barrels see Jacques Savary des Bruslons, *Dictionnaire universel de commerce* (Copenhagen, 1762), IV, 823–24; ACCDk, deliberations of the Chamber of Commerce, October 14, 1761; and various tracts in ADLA, C734.

rum. According to some observers, sales of these beverages represented from 10 to 33 percent of a plantation's revenues.[26] Basically, rum was made by collecting the syrups or foams produced in the processing of cane and letting them ferment in vats for eight to ten days. The resulting liquid, known as *grappe*, was distilled and yielded both strong and weak rums, the latter appropriate for further distillation; this made a strong spirit able to withstand travel. Although rum was popular among French colonists, the British colonies in North America and the Caribbean formed the largest market, and most sales of French rum were to foreigners. Northern Europeans also appreciated rum, a fact that led indirectly to another controversy, this time between the French liqueur manufacturers on one hand and the planters and French merchants and refiners on the other. As early as 1680, French refiners had asked for permission to sell rum made, as in the West Indies, from wastes produced in the sugar-refining process, but pressure from the liqueur producers induced the government in 1713 to prohibit both the manufacture of rum in France and the reexport of French West Indian rum by way of the French ports. During the rest of the century, this prohibition was attacked with some success by merchants and refiners in France. In 1752 the government allowed French merchants to place West Indian rum in bonded warehouses in French ports for shipment to Africa, and in 1768 it authorized the reexport anywhere of rum coming from the Antilles in return for deliveries of dried cod. Finally, in 1777, all French West Indian rum could be shipped anywhere via the French ports without restriction.[27]

Each government decision was preceded by the appearance of several mémoires written by supporters and opponents of change.[28] The fundamental issue was clear: manufacturers of French eaux de vie were afraid of competition from cheap rum, although they pretended to have more noble sentiments. The liqueur makers, most of whom were from the La Rochelle area, stated their position most clearly in 1764.

26. ADLA, C730, mémoire, May 14, 1776; ADLA, C733, "Mémoire sur les guiliveries ou rumeries," 14. On making rum, see Tascher, "Mes délassements," III, 104; Schnakenbourg, *Les sucreries de la Guadeloupe*, 76.
27. ADLA, C733, letters of 1680, January 24, 1713, June 12, 1752, March 1768, and March 6, 1777.
28. These mémoires are gathered in ADLA, C733.

Self-interest, that passion which nature seems to have placed in man's heart only to degrade him, has inspired some residents of our colonies to make a branch of commerce out of the invention of types of eau de vie made from sugar that are as pernicious to health as they are unpleasant to taste. As this strong liqueur is cheap, the blacks use it, since their poverty will not allow them to numb themselves with a more satisfying brew. If there were no need to profit from the product of their labors and if human and divine laws did not order one to watch over their conservation, perhaps it would be an act of humanity to let them hasten the end of their days by its usage; but at least it is incontestable that one cannot excuse the effort to introduce this poison into our lands and climes, where the inhabitants, true men, enjoy the favors of humanity.[29]

The deleterious effects of rum were long considered severe enough to warrant its prohibition in France in spite of arguments of French merchants such as this one: "It is proven that this liqueur is good for the stomach and for injuries; that it has been used in the colonies . . . for almost two centuries without accident; and that doctors prescribe it for their patients with happy success."[30]

By the end of the Old Regime a substantial trade in both French West Indian and French rum had developed, much to the joy of colonial planters, metropolitan merchants and refiners, and Dutch and German consumers. According to Avalle, Saint Domingue alone produced some 66,000,000 pounds of sirop in 1787, of which 26,000,000 went to France and then to Northern Europe, and 40,000,000 to North America; the trade brought in 3,000,000 livres to the island's planters.[31] In the same year, Guadeloupe produced 12,500,000 pounds of it, Martinique 12,000,000, Saint Lucia 2,000,000, and Tobago 600,000. Although worth only a fraction of the value of even muscovado, rum could mean the difference between financial success and failure, particularly for smaller refineries and plantations.

29. *Ibid.*, June, 1764.
30. *Ibid.*, 14 mémoires, October 14, 1775.
31. Avalle, *Tableau comparatif*, tables 2, 3, 4, 5.

4

The French West Indian Sugar Business

> Political reason insists that the colonies always be dependent upon the mother country.
> —"Sur les retours des colonies" (anonymous mémoire)

Once the cane was grown and processed, it remained for the plantation director to sell the sugar, preferably at a profit. In selling his sugar, the planter entered into a complex relationship with French or colonial merchants that was often characterized by bitterness on both sides. The planters believed that the merchants were abusing their monopoly privileges over trade with the islands, while the merchants accused the planters of subverting the entire colonial system by illegally trading with foreigners. The debate became particularly acrimonious late in the eighteenth century, when colonial debts to French merchants reached unprecedented heights. It is against the background of increasing colonial indebtedness and growing French frustration that the West Indian aspects of the sugar business must be considered.

Any examination of the sugar trade in the colonies must begin with the quantities involved, both per plantation and per colony. In spite of limited and occasionally conflicting evidence, it appears that the average sugar plantation in the French West Indies produced anywhere from 100,000 to 250,000 pounds of sugar. The most reliable figures come from Christian Schnakenbourg's study of Guadeloupe: he estimated that in the late eighteenth century the average Guadeloupe sugar plantation of 181 carrés, of which 57.5 were planted in cane, produced some 900 quintaux (about 90,000 pounds) of sugar. This was clayed sugar, however, and must be converted into its equivalent in muscovado. Using Seymour Drescher's conversion factor of 1.42, the average Guadeloupe plantation produced from 1,250 to 1,300 quintaux of muscovado. This was considerably lower than contemporary estimates of good or even modest yields. Tascher de la Pagerie, for example, claimed in 1787 that an average 100-carré plantation should yield 3,500 quintaux of sugar, and a good one 4,000 quintaux. Even if Tascher was talking about muscovado and even if he meant 100 planted carrés, his figures would still be almost double Schnakenbourg's. D'Auberteuil was even more extravagant in 1776, believing that a 150-carré plantation should yield 12,000 quintaux of muscovado. Similar discrepancies existed in productivity-per-slave figures. Schnakenbourg has calculated that on Guadeloupe it took 112 slaves (of whom 85 were adult) to produce 900 quintaux of clayed sugar, each adult slave yielding some 1,500 pounds of muscovado. But contemporary estimates were again much higher. Tascher believed that 100 (adult?) slaves could produce 3,500 to 4,000 pounds of muscovado, a figure unequaled even by d'Auberteuil, who claimed 2,400 pounds each on a good plantation. D'Auberteuil admitted elsewhere that his figures were somewhat optimistic and that planters could hope to get 2,000 pounds per slave only on exceptionally fertile land.[1]

The contemporary estimates for Saint Domingue seem more reliable, although the data are incomplete. In 1791 Saint Domingue planters exported some 163,000,000 pounds of sugar to France, a figure that rises to 192,000,000 pounds when the 70,000,000 pounds of clayed sugar it includes are converted to their equivalent in muscovado.[2] This was produced on 800 sugar plantations for an average yield of nearly 240,000 pounds (2,400 quintaux) each; the 350 muscovado plantations produced 93,000,000 pounds, or 270,000 pounds (2,700 quintaux) each, while the 450 clayed-sugar plantations produced a bit more than 200,000 pounds (2,000 quintaux) each (muscovado equivalent). These figures are much higher than their Guadeloupe counterparts, reflecting the larger plantation sizes on Saint Domingue and, perhaps, their greater fertility. Some Saint Domingue plantations were immense, like Grande Place, owned by the Marquis de Gallifet.[3] With nearly 400 slaves, it produced up to 650,000 pounds of sugar (muscovado equivalent) in one year. This was nearly ten times the output of a small plantation on Martinique, such as the one at Anse à l'Ane owned by the Comtesse de la Rochefoucault and the Marquise de Cheylarfont. There some 150 slaves

1. Schnakenbourg, *Les sucreries de la Guadeloupe*, 88–89; Seymour Drescher, *Econocide* (Pittsburgh, 1977), 192; Tascher, "Mes délassements," III, 110–11; Hilliard d'Auberteuil, *Considérations*, I, 236.
2. ACCM, H19 (printed in Avalle, *Tableau comparatif*, table 11). The manuscript says 1794, but this is clearly impossible; internal evidence suggests 1791.
3. AN, 107AP127, May 22, 1775; AN, 107AP128, dossier 4, May 12, 1784. For production figures see AN, 107AP130, dossier 1 (1790–91).

produced about 70,000 pounds of sugar per year (muscovado equivalent) in the 1770s.⁴

Colonial production figures would be even higher if they were complete. Unfortunately, reliable statistics exist only for exports to France, and there is no sure way of ascertaining gross production figures. There are a few eighteenth-century estimates of colonial sugar production, but these are of limited value and usually ignore the problem of smuggling.⁵ In spite of numerous laws to the contrary, smuggling was a major business in the French West Indies, and it undoubtedly consumed a significant portion of the French colonial sugar crop. The most notorious smugglers were the Guadeloupeans, although they may well have been rivaled by residents of the south of Saint Domingue. Schnakenbourg has estimated that between 1667 and 1789, anywhere from 17 to 60 percent of the annual Guadeloupe sugar crop went to smugglers, with the overall average approaching 40 percent.⁶ This is probably higher than the rest of the French colonies, but there is no way of knowing for sure. It is dangerous enough to assume a constant rate of smuggling, let along attempt to identify that rate.⁷ All that can be said for certain is that Saint Domingue produced from two-thirds to three-quarters of all French West Indian sugar late in the Old Regime.

In selling his quarter of a million pounds, or 250 barrels, of sugar each year, the typical planter wanted both high prices and the security of a guaranteed market, a combination not always feasible. In practice, therefore, planters had to decide whether to use the services of a middleman based either in the colonies or in France. Al-

4. AN, T256/2.
5. See, for example, AN, F12 1639A, "Mémoire sur les sucres," by an anonymous author. This claims that the French West Indies produced 160,000,000 pounds of sugar annually, but it does not break this figure down by colony or by type of sugar. It also ignores smuggling.
6. Schnakenbourg, *Les sucreries de la Guadeloupe*, 118. See also Tarrade, *Le commerce colonial*, 111.
7. Drescher, *Econocide*, 46–47, 195–96, assumes a "steady rate of smuggling from 1770 to 1787" and sets this rate at 11.1 percent of total production. Unfortunately, evidence for these statements appears to be lacking. For a contemporary estimate of illegal sales to foreigners, see M. Weuves, *Réflexions historiques et politiques sur le commerce de France avec ses colonies de l'Amérique* (Geneva, 1780), 54. Weuves believed that one-quarter of the production of the Lesser Antilles and one-eighth of that of Saint Domingue went to smugglers. Avalle, *Tableau comparatif*, table 8, put the value of smuggled goods from the French islands at 5 percent of total production in 1787.

though most planters opted for these services, many did not and instead tried to market their own sugar. Basically, there were two ways of disposing of sugar without having recourse to merchant intermediaries.[8] Planters could sell directly to ship captains or to foreigners. Selling directly to captains was the time-honored means that had been so useful in the colonies' early days. It was essentially a barter system: the passing ship captain traded flour, wine, or manufactured goods from Europe to the planter for sugar either on hand or to be produced after harvest. Although such a system was apparently declining by the eighteenth century, it was still used until the Revolution, particularly by small shippers and out-of-the-way planters. Now, however, the shippers exchanged slaves for sugar, with both sides saving the commissions charged by merchants.

The second direct-sale system was illegal because it involved selling sugar to foreigners. Throughout most of the Old Regime, it was illegal for French West Indian planters either to sell sugar to foreigners or to purchase most commodities from them. However, in areas that proved to be unpopular with French merchants, such as the Lesser Antilles and the south of Saint Domingue, many planters came to depend upon the services of British, American, or even Dutch smugglers. Although present from the earliest days of colonial settlement, smuggling first became a major factor in the colonial economy during the War of the Austrian Succession (1744–1748). As the Conseil Superieur of Martinique noted in 1759: "That war, so glorious for the nation through its victories, became harmful for our colonies through the weakness of our navy. . . . The need to turn abroad forced the creation of a trading system."[9] This new system relied upon the sale of French colonial commodities to foreigners in return for flour, cod, manufactured goods, and especially slaves.

Illegal deals with foreigners took place in several ways.[10] One was quite traditional, with transfers of merchandise made in secluded inlets at night. Variations of this method were numerous and sophis-

---

8. On sales see Schnakenbourg, *Les sucreries de la Guadeloupe*, 100–26.
9. ADBR, C2561, March 7, 1759.
10. Schnakenbourg, *Les sucreries de la Guadeloupe*, 120–21. See also Frostin, *Histoire de l'autonomisme colon*, chs. 9–11; Tarrade, *Le commerce colonial*, 101–12; Frances Armytage, *The Free Port System in the British West Indies, 1766–1822* (London, 1953), ch. 3.

ticated, but all involved some nocturnal sleight of hand, such as this sugar-for-slaves trade described in 1730:

> To go to this island [the Dutch colony of Saint Eustatius] in total security to buy Negroes with the intent of reselling them, the French on Martinique make simulated declarations to the Bureau des Domaines claiming that they are shipping to Saint Domingue a certain number of local Negroes that [in reality] they have borrowed from their neighbors. The declaration made for form's sake, the Negroes return to their masters, and during the night the false claimants load their boats with sugar or other commodities and sail to Saint Eustatius, where they trade their cargo for the number of Negroes claimed on their declaration and proceed to sell them on Saint Domingue.[11]

Another means of smuggling was more innovative; it involved filling barrels labeled SYRUP with sugar and selling them openly to foreigners. After the Seven Years' War, the government allowed the colonists to sell the largely unwanted beverages to foreigners under well-defined—but scarcely obeyed—conditions. The planters viewed this as an open invitation to fraud and were encouraged to do so by the generally benign neglect of the colonial administration. As one observer put it: "Whole lots are sold in molds to be shipped to Havana and New England. How many other Americans are there who, while declaring 'syrups' and 'tafias,' are actually exporting [clayed sugar] . . . ?" So common were these and similar practices that the French consul in Boston wrote to his superior that "the illegal commerce is conducted openly between our islands and my department."[12]

Illicit transactions affected the colonial economy and aroused the ire of French merchants. According to the merchants, massive foreign purchases raised sugar prices in the islands, but low foreign shipping costs plus government subsidies prevented similar price increases in Europe.[13] Unaided by subsidies and faced with high shipping costs, the French merchants were hurt by high purchase prices and low sale prices. The French merchants also lost when foreigners illegally sold goods to the French West Indian planters. Although the

---

11. ADLA, C735, mémoire by the Chamber of Commerce of Guienne (Bordeaux), September 2, 1730.
12. ADSM, BDM 1.48, January 28, 1784; AN, Col F2B 8, July 21, 1784.
13. This was a common complaint. See, for example, ACB, HH49, April 22, 1786, and ADSM, BDM 1.48, January 28, 1784. On the problems caused by the smugglers, see Butel, *La croissance commerciale bordelaise,* 216–21.

French merchants had a theoretical monopoly over most kinds of sales to the islands, foreigners subverted that monopoly, particularly from 1744 to 1783, and introduced vast quantities of slaves, flour, cod, and manufactured goods. In 1765 one person observed, "The English are selling Negroes all over Saint Domingue." And the previous year he noted that "English flour continues to be introduced freely and with all kinds of abuses." The Dutch also participated in the illicit trade, although they specialized in selling manufactured goods to the planters. As Frances Armytage remarked: "The Dutch at St. Eustatius were rich and prosperous solely because they were the distributors of European manufactures to all the French islands in the vicinity. . . . The French had not been able to supply their own colonies with enough provisions and manufactures for some time, and St. Eustatius had become their chief source of supply." These purchases claimed a significant quantity of French West Indian commodities: "A paper . . . stated that the French West Indian produce loaded at St. Eustatius was enough to fill forty or fifty large ships in a year."[14]

Even so, most exports of sugar were legal and were facilitated by the services of one or two merchants. Basically, the planter had his sugar shipped to a French merchant, either with or without the intermediary of a local merchant, and then the sugar was usually sold to a Dutchman or a German. The contractual relationships, first, between the planter and the local and/or French merchant and, then, between the colonial and the metropolitan merchants varied according to the size and financial health of all concerned. Depending on the relative strength of the parties involved, the planter was either in control of the entire affair or very much at the mercy of the merchant(s).

Owners of small plantations had to limit their dealing to local merchants or, in the special case of Guadeloupe before the Seven Years' War, to merchants on Martinique.[15] The production of these small plantations was too small to necessitate direct dealings with the French ports, and local intermediaries were capable of handling it all. The colonial merchant, usually located in the larger towns, such as Cap Français, Port-au-Prince, or Saint Marc on Saint Domingue, Fort Royal on Martinique, and Pointe-à-Pitre or Basse Terre on

14. ADSM, BDM 1.47, January 14, 1764 [sic; it should read 1765], and September 19, 1764; Armytage, *Free Port System*, 35–36.
15. Schnakenbourg, *Les sucreries de la Guadeloupe*, 111.

Guadeloupe, could purchase the sugar from the planter for resale to French captains. More often, he could act as a commissioned agent, finding a buyer for the sugar and taking a substantial (usually 5 percent) commission on the transaction. In either case the merchant profited from the deal, and the small planter made a quick sale.

Larger planters required more sophisticated arrangements involving the active participation of merchants in France. The planter's sugar was shipped to France, where it was sold by a merchant who kept a commission on the sale and remitted the rest to the planter. Financially healthy planters had great freedom in choosing which French merchants to patronize and were under no obligation to be faithful to any one agent. Of course, sugar tended to follow family lines, with planters preferring to use the trustworthy services of relatives, but in the absence of convenient family connections good service was the only criterion to adopt. Not having a long-term contract with a French merchant house, the planter was free to ship his goods on the first available ship going to the preferred destination, and solvent planters could deal with merchants in several French ports.

Once planters were in financial difficulties, their range of options was limited, at least on paper. They had to accept long-term arrangements with French merchant firms even though such arrangements were often draconian.[16] In extreme cases, hard-pressed planters had to abandon real control over their plantations to the French merchants, who in turn took over the often substantial debts of the plantation. Some French merchant houses specialized in this type of transaction, and the Bordeaux firm of Henry Romberg, Bapst and Company had contracts with nearly sixty planters on Saint Domingue in the 1780s.[17] Romberg, Bapst and Company agreed to pay off plantation debts, guarantee the delivery of European merchandise and African slaves to the plantations, and run the estates efficiently; in return the company had exclusive rights to sell the products of one plantation and priority in shipping the commodities in its ships. Such arrangements had certain advantages for the planter. Relieved of his debts and usually guaranteed a reasonable pension by the merchant, the planter was put back on his feet while retaining ownership of,

---

16. Pierre Léon, *Marchands et speculateurs dauphinois dans le monde antillais au XVIIIe siècle* (Paris, 1963), 81.

17. This company is the subject of Thésée, *Les négociants bordelais,* upon which this section is largely based.

albeit not control over, his plantation. The merchant, on the other hand, was drawn into the quagmire of colonial debt and could be extricated only in the unlikely case of the plantation turning a profit. But to transform virtually bankrupt plantations into profitable enterprises took more time and more money than most companies could afford, and the new plantation owners—the French merchants— quickly became overextended.

As Françoise Thésée noted, indebted planters used the French merchants more as bankers than as commissioned agents. Planters in effect used their merchant associates to finance inefficient operations, and by the end of the Old Regime the colonies were in considerable debt to the port merchants. Most of this money represented slave purchases that the planters had made but could not afford. This was not necessarily a new phenomenon; even in 1765 Stanislas Foache of Le Havre remarked, "The old cargo debts are almost all for Negroes; there are very few for merchandise."[18] Since it was difficult to force colonial debtors to pay, especially with foreclosure almost unknown on the islands, the only way the merchants could get their money back was to lend or invest even more money, take over running the plantations, and once again hope to make a profit. The planter was well protected by local custom and had little reason to fear the loss of his estate. Local authorities were reluctant to force planters to pay their debts and all but refused to consider seizing real property. The problem originated in the early days of colonial settlement, when it appeared that a period of planter indebtedness was inevitable before profits could accrue. In order to protect the pioneering planters, laws were passed prohibiting the seizure of parts of the estate; in other words, slaves could not be seized by creditors. With the colonies developed, planters used their legal immunity to force loans from metropolitan merchants; they did this simply by contracting debts that they had no intention of repaying.[19]

Needless to say, merchant creditors did not acquiesce in this matter, but they had little chance of winning the battle. The legal administration on Saint Domingue sided with the planters, and exasperated merchants could only lament "the sad job of recovering debts on Saint Domingue." Actually, persistent efforts could reap some re-

18. ADSM, BDM 1.47, June 13, 1765.
19. Thésée, *Les négociants bordelais*, 261. See also ADSM, BDM 1.47, May 22, 1765; ADSM, BDM 1.48, February 7, 1784; and Article 48 of the code noir.

wards, but only at the expense of alienating the debtor and losing future business. Most merchants simply considered it impossible to get anywhere with the authorities. "Real seizures," wrote one merchant in 1749, "although permitted in America as in France, have not yet been concluded [successfully] on Saint Domingue. Some have tried this route more than once, but the infinite number of formalities, the lengths of time, and the dearth of legal procedures have disgusted all who have been involved with it."[20] Ship's captains seemed to have somewhat better luck in dealing with colonists, but even they had to give up when faced with the expenses involved. After a while it simply became too expensive to wait for all payments to be made.

The impossibility of foreclosing left the merchant with little leverage over the planter once the initial commitment was made. The merchant could refuse to make a commitment; he could simply serve as a commissioned agent with no banking role. This, however, was to run the risk of accepting a secondary position permanently. By not offering any exceptional services to the planter, the merchant could not hope to attract as much business. Of course, not all planters were in desperate straits, but it seems that enough were to affect the health of the entire system by the 1780s. On the eve of the French Revolution, economic difficulties put into sharper relief both the similarities and the differences between merchant and planter. On one hand the colonists had to rely heavily on the frequently willing merchant for money; on the other hand the colonists viewed this money as a long-term capital investment, while the merchant thought it was a short-term loan. The result was considerable misunderstanding and bitterness.

In the middle of the dispute were the major colonial merchants. Whereas the smaller colonial merchants were independent retailers purchasing European goods from arriving ships and speculating in small quantities of colonial commodities, larger merchants were usually associated with French commercial houses and acted primarily as representatives of French interests.[21] The major colonial

20. ADSM, BDM 1.48, February 7 and August 25, 1784; ACCM, BDM 1.48, June 4, 1749. According to Schnakenbourg, *Les sucreries de la Guadeloupe,* 235, there were but six foreclosures on Guadeloupe from 1778 to 1788, and this was a time of economic crisis.

21. For a description of the purchases made by merchants, see Weuves, *Réflexions historiques,* 29.

merchants served almost as frontline soldiers in the battle waged against the planters. As such, they had somehow to balance the unrelenting demands of the home office with the realities of colonial life. This was not always an easy task, a fact to which numerous impatient letters bear witness. As one colonial merchant complained to the head office, "We are between the hammer and the anvil, between your interests and those of our landowners."[22] The French merchant wanted all of his money immediately, the planter wanted to postpone repayment indefinitely, and the colonial merchant wanted to receive as much as possible from the former without forever losing the latter as a customer.

Most of the major colonial merchant houses were subsidiaries of French companies, although they did not necessarily begin that way. It was not at all unusual for small merchants in the French ports to go to Saint Domingue and make modest fortunes as commissioned agents; they then returned to France to establish major commercial houses using the services of the colonial companies they had created. But whether formed originally by a French merchant temporarily residing in the colonies or by one who had never left France, most significant colonial companies were accountable to parent companies in France. The French company always retained a controlling interest in the colonial one. For example, Stanislas Foache of Le Havre organized a company in Saint Domingue in 1777; Foache held a 50 percent interest, and two colonial merchants split the remaining 50 percent. Five years later, Foache reorganized the company as Stanislas Foache, Morange and Company, but again kept a 50 percent interest personally, in addition to advancing money to two of his three partners. This was quite typical, and similar arrangements existed for other colonial companies.[23] The French company supplied the capital and the colonial agent the labor; profits were split accordingly.

Large colonial merchant houses handled all the French merchant's affairs in the area. Among other things, this included running plantations either owned or managed by the merchant; acting as commissioned agents on purchases and sales of slaves, colonial commodities, and European goods; and collecting debts. One overworked colonial merchant complained of his burden in a letter to the main office: "I

22. ADSM, BDM 1.48, May 18, 1784.
23. ADSM, BDM 1.53, December 28, 1777, and May 15, 1782. For other companies, see Thésée, *Les négociants bordelais*, 29–30.

beg you to pay a moment's attention to our affairs and to their nature: five plantations in sugar that require constant surveillance: trials, credits . . . and all the costs of exploitation. Three coffee plantations that have the same needs to fill as the sugar plantations. In the office, books, letters, accounts, purchases, barreling, goods to sell, and finally recovering debts, this terrible thing in town and country"[24]

The colonial merchant also had to be a shrewd observer of the colonial scene: he frequently speculated in sugar or other commodities and had to know what, when, and at what price to buy and sell. Such a wide range of activities required a large staff, and the major colonial merchant houses employed several skilled workers. Preparing to return to France from Cap Français in 1777, Stanislas Foache described his staff in a lengthy letter to his brother in Le Havre.[25] Foache was particularly pleased with the abilities of his workers, whom he preferred above almost all others in the town. The chef de maison described no fewer than eight office workers, at least two of whom later became partners in the company. These two were Hellot, pictured as an honest, intelligent young man of twenty-two who already handled many of the legal affairs of the company and who was to assume responsibility for the company after Foache's departure, and Morange, the meticulous cashier from Saint Domingue who had never been outside Cap Français or seen a plantation. The other employees included the hard-working Pellier; Gerard, the bookkeeper from Martinique; Corneille, a local Creole who kept the books rather unsatisfactorily; La Croix, the director of the store or warehouse; and two traveling clerks.

Colonial agents were probably the only people in the colonies certain to make profits from colonial commerce. Taking a commission on all transactions, they were able to avoid the problems besetting the planters. Although it was commonly believed that sugar planters made vast sums of money, such was not the case. In spite of hypothetical calculations showing that a well-run estate should net profits of 25 percent per year, few planters ever realized such profits in practice, and plantation records show losses almost as frequently as gains.[26] Even large, well-organized, and presumably well-run plantations did not necessarily make money. This was the case with the five

24. ADSM, BDM 1.47, May 18, 1784.
25. ADSM, BDM 1.47, January 3, 1777.
26. For example, see Tascher, "Mes délassements," III, 110–11.

plantations owned by the Marquis de Gallifet.[27] Worth some 5,500,000 livres in 1784, Gallifet's three sugar plantations (worth 5,000,000 livres) and two coffee plantations (worth 500,000 livres) produced up to 300,000 livres' worth of goods per year. Unfortunately, expenses could be just as high, and in the thirty-two quarters from July 1, 1783, through June 30, 1791, the estate showed a profit in only sixteen. After eight years the five plantations actually had a net loss of 2,507 livres, even though revenues were nearly 3,000,000 livres. The more modest Bongars sugar plantation did little better in the 1770s.[28] With about 200 slaves, it produced 200,000 pounds of sugar per year, and from 1769 to 1779, total income was 1,114,000 livres. Expenses over the same period were 1,108,000 livres, leaving the plantation with a trivial surplus of 6,000 livres on what probably amounted to a capital investment of nearly 1,000,000 livres. Individual plantations were clearly not always prosperous.

The overall picture was similar, especially later in the Old Regime. Very rough estimates indicate that the French colonists sold a maximum of 300,000,000 livres' worth of goods annually before the Revolution. Jean Tarrade estimated that from 1784 to 1790 "imports from the colonies and from the Newfoundland fisheries" were worth some 200,000,000 livres per year, a figure that should be augmented by a maximum of 50 percent to account for smuggling and losses in transit. Colonial imports during the same period probably amounted to some 175,000,000 to 200,000,000 livres per year: close to 90,000,000 livres for goods shipped directly from France, some 80,000,000 livres for slaves, and the rest for goods purchased illegally from foreigners.[29] Thus, the colonists had an annual profit of from 100,000,000 to 125,000,000 livres. This, however, was based on a total capital investment of over 2,000,000,000 livres, for a profit of some 5 to 6 percent.[30]

27. AN, 107AP128, dossier 4, May 12, 1784, and dossier 1, July 1, 1783, to June 30, 1784 (brouillard).
28. AN, T520/2.
29. Tarrade, *Le commerce colonial*, 740, says that 70,000,000 livres' worth were exported, but the colonists paid far more than that once commissions, taxes, and profits—all paid by the colonists—were added.
30. On total investment, see ACCM, H19, which evaluates Saint Domingue plantations at 1,488,000,000 livres. Schnakenbourg, *Les sucreries de la Guadeloupe*, 88–89, estimates Guadeloupe's sugar plantations to have been worth 155,000,000 livres; other Guadeloupe plantations plus all of Martinique's plantations would easily amount to more than 357,000,000 livres. For a comparison of profits, see Richard B. Sheridan, *The Development of the Plantations* (Barbados, 1970), 102, which estimates a similar profit on investments in Jamaica at this time. J. R. Ward, "The Profitability of Sugar Planting

This figure must be lowered somewhat to ascertain the planters' net profit; commissions charged by middlemen, taxes, and the like prevented the planters from actually receiving all of their money. Indeed, the comité intermédiaire of Martinique estimated in 1787 that net profits for all plantations on the island were in the neighborhood of only 2 percent.[31]

It is commonly assumed that profit rates were higher earlier in the eighteenth century, but the data are not entirely convincing. Indeed, many historians seem to accept the notion of diminishing profits in order to explain the apparently unprecedented rancor that characterized merchant-planter relations following the American Revolution. Christian Schnakenbourg, for example, wrote of an economic crisis afflicting Guadeloupe, the other French West Indies, and perhaps even the entire Caribbean area from 1785 to 1790, an argument also advanced by Jean Tarrade for the French islands. Similar crises have been discerned in the French ports: Jean Meyer spoke of Nantes's declining profits, and François Crouzet implied much the same for Bordeaux.[32] The evidence for such statements, however, is often slight and usually rests on an unproven belief in an earlier golden age of high profits. Unfortunately, such a golden age, if it ever existed, was probably brief and of little significance. It is possible, as Schnakenbourg believes, that the first planters on Guadeloupe made annual profits of 25 percent or, as Meyer implies, that early slave traders made profits of over 100 percent, but such examples testify more to the high-risk nature of the early colonial and slave trades than to a subsequent crisis of declining profits. Once transatlantic commerce ceased being the preserve of a few adventurous souls and became another business run by calculating businessmen, it followed the normal laws of the marketplace, reflecting competition and supply and demand. In such conditions, astronomical profits were most unlikely and were due to some exceptional stroke of fortune, such as a sudden and unexpected dearth of ships in port. These quirks notwith-

---

in the British West Indies, 1650–1835," *Economic History Review*, XXXI, (1978), 208, says that profits averaged about 10 percent in the eighteenth century.

31. AN, Col F3 84, "Examen des observations du commerce de la Martinique sur le procès verbal colonial par le comité intermédiaire de cette assemblée," 1787.

32. Schnakenbourg, *Les sucreries de la Guadeloupe*, 127–239; Tarrade, *Le commerce colonial*, 776, 783; Meyer, *L'armement nantais*, 248, 250; François Crouzet in François Pariset (ed.), *Histoire de Bordeaux* (Bordeaux, 1968), V, 316–17.

standing, colonial commerce normally provided a 5 percent annual profit, about the same as good investments in France. Colonial trade did involve greater risks, but it also held out the possibility of greater profits and perhaps the prospect of greater or at least more rapid growth based on loans. In other words, credit was much looser in the colonies than in France.

What was unique about the last decade of the Old Regime was the very size of the entire operation, the increasing needs for capital to keep it functioning smoothly, and the sources of that capital. After the American war, the volume of trade between France and the colonies doubled, and debts increased accordingly. Instead of a recession, as in France, there was a tremendous boom in the 1780s for colonial commerce, and this boom was ultimately financed by credits provided—often voluntarily—by French port merchants on the verge of overextension. The central problem was with the slave trade, and for French slavers the American war was a critical turning point. Before the war, English slavers provided the French West Indies with a large proportion of its slaves, perhaps up to 50 percent.[33] These slaves were notoriously cheap and provided the French planters with an economical source of labor. After the war the English were effectively excluded from the French West Indian slave market just when that market was expanding appreciably. Now the French merchants were supplying the colonies with virtually all the required slaves, and the French slave trade nearly doubled relative to prewar levels, going from an average of less than 60 expeditions per year to 110 per year. This meant that more than twice as much of the merchants' capital was being tied up for lengthy periods of time in slaving, and colonists' delays in repaying debts provoked an exceptionally strident response from the merchants.[34] Also, it should be noted that during the last decade of the Old Regime more medium-sized merchants were involved in slaving than ever before; these men had far smaller reserves than the large merchants who had dominated slaving in earlier periods, and they were affected more directly by the delays in payment.

Things looked no better from the planters' point of view. Expansion forced them to purchase more slaves than ever before, and the slave

33. Curtin, *Atlantic Slave Trade*, 211, 216, as corrected by Stein, "Measuring the French Slave Trade," 519–20.
34. Stein, "Profitability of the Nantes Slave Trade," 791.

population of Saint Domingue alone went from an estimated 260,000 in 1775 to 465,000 in 1789.[35] The new slaves were supplied almost exclusively by French traders and were much more expensive than prewar English (or even French) slaves. In short, planters' expenses were rising rapidly, but revenues were temporarily lagging behind. It would be two or three years before the larger labor force affected harvest sizes and plantation income, and it was the question of who was to finance the waiting period that sharply divided merchants from planters during the 1780s. Thus, the impressive growth of colonial trade created short-term problems of considerable proportion. Had there been sufficient time available, these problems probably would have been resolved to the satisfaction of both planter and merchant, but the French and Haitian revolutions brought the postwar period to an early end and made any such readjustments impossible.

The problems of the 1780s were "growing pains," aggravated by the intense dislike of the merchants by the planters and the deep suspicions of the planters by the merchants. Tied together in a colonial economy and dependent upon that economy for their prosperity, the merchant and planter nonetheless pursued conflicting short-term policies and had opposing views of their respective roles in the system. The planter believed that the health of the colonial economy was the first priority, as one planter said in 1791 or 1792: "There are two classes of men on Saint Domingue: the planter and the merchant. The first is the true colonist; he belongs to the land, either through possession or his work. Behold the citizen. The merchant . . . sacrifices all to his cupidity. He lives in Saint Domingue as a gambler lives by a gaming table. Behold the troublemaker."[36] The French merchant, on the other hand, believed in the subordination of colonial interests to French commercial ones. The colonies should consume French goods and produce exotic commodities that French merchants could sell throughout Europe. Typical were the sentiments of the deputies of commerce: The colonies, they declared, "consume the excess of the production of our soil and our manufactures. . . . They deliver in return luxury commodities that we lack and that habit has made necessary. . . . It is through sales of colonial com-

35. Frostin, *Les révoltes blanches*, 28.
36. *Discours historique sur la cause des désastres de la partie française de Saint Domingue* (Paris, [1792?]), 56–57.

modities—after our own consumption—that we obtain a tribute of 70,000,000 livres from foreign lands."[37]

Thus, on the eve of the Revolution, there was a split between merchant and planter, but this must not overshadow the close ties between the two throughout the Old Regime. Although neither was completely satisfied with the colonial system and although both tried to gain advantages during the early days of the French Revolution, they realized that their fates were closely linked and that they both relied on the continuation of the slave trade and the slave system for their livelihood. The eighteenth-century French colonial economy depended on the use of slave labor, and slaves bore the burden of the entire operation. In determining just who profited and who lost from the system, it appeared that all were winners save the slaves. Planters, colonial merchants, French merchants, and African merchants made profits from the sales of either slaves or sugar or both, while the use of slave labor helped keep sugar prices relatively low in eighteenth-century Europe.[38] By keeping prices down, merchants helped create a demand for sugar and coffee, which alone seemed to justify the entire operation.

37. AN, Col F2B 8, "Avis des deputés du commerce," 1785.
38. Robert Paul Thomas and Richard Nelson Bean, "The Fishers of Men: The Profits of the Slave Trade," *Journal of Economic History*, XXXIV (1974), 885–914.

PART II

The Sugar Business in France

5

A National Perspective

> The French islands and colonies form the
> kingdom's most important branch of commerce.
> —Arrêt, July 29, 1767

From the vantage point of a sugar planter in the colonies, there appeared to be one great French sugar business, a monolith solid in its opposition to the planters. French merchants encouraged this perception by appealing to national interests in defending themselves against colonial attacks. Merchants in France warned against sacrificing the national commerce to the narrow interests of the planters; they also questioned the loyalty of the planters. "One must not count on the patriotism [of the colonists]," wrote some concerned merchants from Nantes. "They are cosmopolitan in commerce."[1] Upon closer inspection, however, a different view emerges, and the French sugar business becomes a series of local businesses, each centered in a port and each in conflict with the others. Indeed, even the merchants' occasional outbursts of "nationalism" were merely reflections of a more exalted form of particularism; their conception of empire implied the supremacy of metropolitan interests over colonial ones. Only the government held a truly national outlook, but even that was subject to change when necessary. The Old Regime was one of privilege and legal difference, features that often conflicted with a national perspective. Each port had its own interests consecrated by long years of usage, and few merchants would sacrifice traditional local privileges for a new national organization based on legal or fiscal equality.

It is therefore difficult to speak of a French sugar business except insofar as it related to other national units. Only in relation to the colonies or to the rest of Europe did France have some sort of a national sugar trade, meaning little more than the sum of several local trades. The French government tended to view the sugar business in the context of international commerce and tried to elaborate

---

1. ADLA, C608, September 8, 1789.

some sort of national sugar policy to insure the supremacy of French sugar in Europe. The government sought to encourage French West Indian sugar production and French reexports of sugar to Europe in order to improve the national balance of trade. This national policy worked, and in the eighteenth century France served as a giant redistribution center. It received sugar from the Antilles and forwarded it throughout Europe; relatively small amounts remained in the country. The particulars of the national policy, however, were typical of the Old Regime, with most ports placed under special laws designed to guarantee them certain markets both within the country and abroad. In the next chapter the local sugar businesses will be considered; this chapter analyzes the structure of the national business.

Sugar from the Antilles arrived in French ports aboard French ships. The voyage to France took from six to nine weeks, but this represented a small fraction of the ships' time away from France. Some had been away for more than two years; these were the slavers, carriers of about a fifth of the incoming cargoes of sugar and coffee. With the exception of a few expeditions that before 1759 went both to Canada and the West Indies, the remaining ships had all sailed directly from France to the Antilles. This direct trade was known as *commerce en droiture*, and by the end of the Old Regime, more than six hundred ships per year were participating in it.[2] Even in 1687 an estimated seventy-three ships had made the voyage from Nantes alone, most of them delivering a variety of European goods, including food, and using the proceeds to purchase cargoes of sugar, coffee, indigo, cotton, and cocoa.[3] Some ships, especially those leaving Nantes after 1750, carried little merchandise to the Antilles and served as freighters on the return voyage. Sugar was by far the most common commodity to be shipped like this; according to Jean Tarrade, the French received 183,000,000 pounds of sugar in 1789, but less than 105,000,000 pounds of all the other colonial products combined.[4]

The voyage to France was simple but nonetheless significant for

2. Tarrade, *Le commerce colonial*, 730–35.
3. Meyer, *L'armement nantais*, 66. At this time Nantes was the major trading partner of the French West Indies.
4. Tarrade, *Le commerce colonial*, 34, 747–49. After the American Revolution, the value of arrivals of coffee in French ports exceeded that of sugar. Tarrade, *Le commerce colonial*, 747, 754, 772.

the sugar merchant because of losses in transit. As noted, during the voyage up to 20 percent of the sugar might be lost through seepage alone. The poorly processed sugar had been loaded in the French West Indies before completely settling, and it continued to dry in the ship's hold. Although such losses were expected, they could lead to disputes between French merchants and colonial planters. Further, losses in transit could also cause trouble between merchants and tax collectors. In 1747 the latter suddenly attempted to collect taxes on the gross weight loaded in the Antilles rather than on the net weight arriving in France.[5] Merchant response to this initiative was predictably strong, and the tax collectors soon retreated.

With the arrival of the ship in port, a long series of formalities began, most involving the collection of taxes or duties.[6] The hogsheads of sugar had to be removed from the ship, taken to shore, weighed, and then either placed in bonded warehouses if to be reexported or delivered to the merchant's own warehouse if to be kept in France. In the eighteenth century, all arriving sugar was subject to a tax payable to the Domaine d'Occident; this was left over from the days of chartered company monopoly.[7] In 1664 the crown had given the newly created Compagnie d'Occident exclusive trading rights with the French West Indies. Soon, however, it became clear that the company was incapable of effectively using this privilege, and it began to allow private merchants to trade in the Antilles in return for 5 percent of the exports. In 1671 the crown lowered this amount to 3 percent and in 1681 redirected it to the Domaine d'Occident; this latter—ultimately assimilated into the General Farm—received the tax until the Revolution, by which time the rate had increased to 4.5 percent. The tax was thus the fee charged by the crown for permission to trade in the colonies. Originally, it had been paid in kind in the West Indies, but by the eighteenth century, merchants paid it in specie in the metropolitan ports. It was payable on 80 percent of the value of the incoming produce, 20 percent being deducted for various expenses.

5. For this debate see the various mémoires from 1747–48 in ADLA, C734.
6. See BN, nafr 20539, fol. 238–42, for a list of the twenty-seven types of registers that the General Farm kept in each port to deal with arrivals of foreign goods. There were some modifications for Breton ports.
7. See "Dissertation sur les droits du Domaine d'Occident," a "mémoire sur les droits du Domaine d'Occident," the mémoire of September 27, 1728, and a 1745 mémoire, all in ADLA, C734.

How much sugar arrived in French ports during the eighteenth century? This is one question that can be answered with a reasonable degree of accuracy. Port officials, tax collectors, and chambers of commerce kept relatively reliable records of arrivals of sugar in ports from Dunkerque to Marseilles; they either itemized the cargo of each ship from the Antilles or estimated the quantity of commodities arriving in port each year.[8] Needless to say, the statistics were not uncontested: merchants and tax collectors disputed everything from the capacity of a single hogshead to the size of an entire shipment. Still, it appears that statistics within each port were gathered in a consistent fashion, although it is possible that different ports may have used slightly different recording techniques, which would have yielded consistently low or high figures for each port.

Assuming the basic reliability of the manuscript data, a clear picture of growth in sugar arrivals emerges. From 1730, when the data become fairly comprehensive, until 1790, arrivals of sugar in French ports increased from an annual total of nearly 60,000,000 pounds to over 180,000,000 pounds. Fragmentary figures for earlier times suggest that this growth had been occurring at a similar rate since the seventeenth century. Christian Schnakenbourg has estimated the French West Indian sugar production at 26,000,000 pounds in 1670; allowing for spoilage, this would imply an arrival figure of some 21,000,000 to 22,000,000 pounds.[9] Thus, arrivals of French colonial sugar tripled every sixty years from 1670 to 1790.

Growth was uneven, coming in clearly marked stages lasting several years rather than at regular annual increments (see Table 2). With the exception of the period 1736–1743, each new period was preceded by a major colonial war, and these wars gave the French trade its distinctive growth pattern. War had two main effects on the trade, one immediate, the other delayed. First, war sharply depressed the sugar commerce, and the more arduous the war at sea, the more

8. Major published documents include Malvezin, *Histoire du commerce de Bordeaux*, III, 302–309; Noel Deerr, *The History of Sugar* (London, 1949–50), I, 235, 236, 240; Pierre Dardel, *Navires et marchandises dans les ports de Rouen et du Havre au XVIIIe siècle* (Paris, 1963), 523–741; Paul Jeulin, *L'évolution du port de Nantes* (Paris, 1929), tables. Archival materials include ADLA, C715–17, and ACCM, I29. For further statistical information about imports and reexports see Robert Stein, "The French Sugar Business in the Eighteenth Century: A Quantitative Study," *Business History*, XXII (1980), 3–17.

9. Schnakenbourg, "Notes sur les origines de l'industrie sucrière," 285.

Table 2. SUGAR ARRIVING IN FRANCE, 1730–1790 (in millions of pounds)

Dates	Average	Maximum	Minimum	Increase over Previous Period
1730–35	59	64	53	
1736–43	86	100	71	+46%
1749–55	114	135	90	+33%
1764–76	138	164	111	+21%
1784–90	178	200	149	+29%

SOURCES: See footnote 8.

severe the decline in trade. The War of the Austrian Succession reduced French colonial commerce by more than 50 percent, whereas the Seven Years' War cut it by more than 90 percent. Even the relatively benign American Revolution entailed a decline of at least 33 percent. Then, following each of the three wars, the sugar business registered record volumes, as merchants rushed to satisfy the demands of sugar-starved markets in France and Europe. Finally, the French Revolutionary Wars and the English blockade reduced the French sugar business to a nullity after 1792.

War also affected the English sugar trade, but not in the same manner as the French. While the War of the Austrian Succession sharply reduced the quantity of sugar arriving in French ports and reexported from France to Europe, it encouraged the English to attempt to satisfy continental demands for sugar; and although amounts of sugar arriving in English ports remained at their prewar levels, reexports of the expensive English sugar more than tripled. The Seven Years' War encouraged the growth of all branches of the English sugar business, as the occupation and exploitation of Guadeloupe and Martinique enabled arrivals and reexports to reach record levels. Only the American war hurt the English sugar business, with arrivals in England falling by a quarter; but these English losses were more than overcome when the French Revolutionary Wars allowed the English sugar trade to reach unprecedented heights. The behavior of both the French and English sugar trades during the century's major wars underscores once again the commercial significance of eighteenth-century colonial warfare.

In keeping with colonial preferences, French merchants received somewhat more clayed sugar than muscovado.[10] The claying of sugar was peculiar to the French West Indies, and the availability of this relatively high-quality product may have helped France assume a leading position in the reexport trade. Until late in the century most of the clayed sugar originated in the Lesser Antilles, but by 1789 Saint Domingue was the leading supplier. Throughout the century Saint Domingue also led in supplying muscovado, which Guadeloupe and Martinique planters had all but abandoned in favor of clayed sugar or coffee. Although French shippers may have complained about the colonial practice of claying, they never refused to buy clayed sugar and at times clearly preferred it.

The vast majority of the sugar arriving in the French ports was quickly reexported in the eighteenth century, and the *raison d'être* of the entire colonial system was the sale of tropical produce, especially sugar, to Europe. From the time of Colbert, the government organized its empire to encourage commercial growth with a maximum of benefits accruing to French merchants. As we have seen, Colbert successfully reestablished French control over the colonies' trade and encouraged colonial production, French shipping, and, above all, French processing of sugar. Indeed, Colbert and his successors under Louis XIV placed so much emphasis on the necessity for French refining that they discouraged and even prohibited the reexport of muscovado. This threw the whole French sugar business into a chaotic state, which ended only in 1717. The ban on muscovado, accompanied by restrictions on colonial refining, served only to encourage the claying of sugar in the French West Indies. By the beginning of the eighteenth century the Lesser Antilles had turned decisively to the production of clayed sugar.

The Letters Patent of April, 1717, returned the colonial system to an orderly state that lasted until the Revolution.[11] They also served as the charter for the eighteenth-century French sugar business, and together with the Letters Patent of October, 1727, they provided the clearest statement of the government's conception of a national sugar business. The main goals of the letters were, by that time, traditional: to reserve the French West Indian trade for French merchants, to

---

10. For statistics on 1765 and 1788 see Tarrade, *Le commerce colonial*, 34.
11. The Letters Patent can be found in many places, including AN, F12 1639A.

reserve the tropical commodities market in France for French West Indian goods, and to encourage the reexport of colonial commodities. Instead of a chartered company, merchants in thirteen ports—ultimately expanded to include virtually all French ports of any consequence—received the exclusive privilege to trade in the French colonies. Foreigners were prohibited in 1717 from trading in the French West Indies; in 1727 the prohibition was reiterated in greater detail.[12] The government clearly wanted to guarantee that France would receive as much of the profit generated by colonial trade as possible. To insure the planters of a competition-free market for their goods in France, the Letters Patent of 1717 imposed favorable duty rates on French West Indian produce entering France: 2.5 livres per hundredweight for French muscovado and 8 livres for French clayed, as opposed to 7.5 livres and 15 livres, respectively, for their foreign counterparts. More important, the Letters Patent encouraged the reexport trade by eliminating all duties on all French West Indian sugar to be reexported; only the 3 percent tax due the Domaine d'Occident remained. Although modified in certain particulars, the 1717 rules remained in force throughout the century and provided the national sugar business with its legal and fiscal foundation. They reflected the government's belief that the sugar trade was most significant for commercial reasons, to augment French exports rather than help the French refining industry. France was to be a vast entrepôt, linking the New World plantations to Dutch and German refineries.

The national policy was a success, and French West Indian sugar dominated the European market during times of peace in the eighteenth century. France's nearest competitor was England, but the distance between the two countries grew steadily throughout the century. In 1730, for example, France reexported some 30,000,000 to 35,000,000 pounds of sugar, and England 20,000,000; in 1790, the two reexported 125,000,000 and 36,000,000 pounds, respectively.[13] During the same period, arrivals of sugar in French ports increased from between 55,000,000 and 60,000,000 pounds to 187,000,000, and in English ports from 116,000,000 pounds to 192,000,000. Obviously,

12. See, for example, ADBR, C2561.
13. See footnote 8 for sources of French statistics; for English statistics see Elizabeth Schumpeter, *English Overseas Trade Statistics, 1697–1808* (Oxford, 1960), tables 8, 9, 18. This considers a pound of refined sugar to be the equivalent of two pounds of muscovado.

the French reexported a much higher proportion of their sugar, regularly sending out from 60 to 70 percent of it. The English, on the other hand, usually reexported less than 20 percent of theirs; only during the Seven Years' War did reexports exceed 40 percent.

Although the French sold their sugar throughout Europe, sales to Holland and Germany accounted for nearly two-thirds of French reexports. These were the refining capitals of Europe, and they relied heavily on France for the raw sugar. At the very end of the Old Regime it was estimated that four-fifths of Hamburg's sugar came from France.[14] This commerce came to a quick end when France declared war on England in 1793; by 1795 the English were supplying nearly all of Hamburg's sugar. In peacetime, German and Dutch merchants, often residing in France, purchased huge quantities of both muscovado and clayed sugar, shipping them aboard foreign vessels to the great ports of the North: Amsterdam, Rotterdam, Hamburg, Bremen, and Stettin. Other significant, albeit secondary, destinations for French sugar included Italy, Spain, and the Levant.

With most of its sugar going abroad, France imported relatively small amounts, particularly in view of its large population. The French consumed on average some 30 to 40 percent of its arriving sugar. This was in striking contrast to the English, who regularly kept about 75 percent of theirs. England consumed from two to three times more sugar than France in the eighteenth century, and average per capita consumption favored the English by eight or even ten to one. Although French economists may have been pleased by the huge reexport trade and the restricted national market, English observers thought otherwise. John Campbell noted in 1763 that, "notwithstanding France in times of peace exports such great quantities of sugar, yet as this visibly arises from the smallness of her home consumption, it must be considered as an incontestable evidence, she has not as a nation drawn the same advantages from her trade as we have."[15] Campbell believed that England could afford to consume so much sugar because it sold so many manufactured goods to the colonies; France, however, was content with merely being an intermediary between northern Europe and the French West Indies. Thus, for

---

14. ADSM, BDM 1.52, "Specifications du sucre . . . ."
15. John Campbell, *Candid and Impartial Observations on the Nature of the Sugar Trade* (London, 1763), 33. For speculation on why England consumed more sugar than France, see Mintz, *Sweetness and Power*, 189–90.

Campbell, the colonial trade helped England to develop industrially but had no such impact on France. Even French shipping did not fully benefit from the reexport trade, as almost all French reexports were carried on foreign ships.[16]

Total French sugar consumption did grow during the eighteenth century, but not as rapidly as French reexports of sugar. Growth in consumption was quite regular from 1730 until 1770, going from 25,000,000 pounds per year to 84,000,000. After 1770 there was a sudden and sharp drop, as consumption fell from 84,000,000 pounds to 44,000,000 in one year and remained at that level until the American Revolution. Even after the end of the war, the recovery was incomplete, and consumption averaged some 57,000,000 pounds annually until the French Revolution. The obvious cause for the post-1770 decline was the general economic crisis that beset France. Unlike the reexport trade, which reflected economic conditions in Amsterdam or Hamburg, the internal market for sugar was dependent to a large degree on the state of the French economy, and the crisis beginning in the early 1770s discouraged sugar purchases in France. Interestingly, consumption of refined sugar continued to grow in the 1780s. Purchased only by the rich, its market did not shrink at all. It was the less wealthy purchaser of clayed sugar who was affected by the recession.

Both muscovado and clayed sugar were imported into France during the eighteenth century. Muscovado was not suitable for immediate consumption but was appropriate for refining. During the eighteenth century a modest refining industry developed in France to serve the home market; exports of French refined sugar were rare. Clayed sugar, on the other hand, was moderately priced and accessible to a wider population. High-quality clayed sugar provided refined sugar with stiff competition, and refiners never ceased in their efforts to have it banned from France.

The nominal value of the sugar handled by French businessmen grew more quickly than the quantity because the price of sugar rose throughout the century. Given the French sugar trade's reliance on the reexport market, this rise in price was a significant factor in the success of the French sugar merchant. Acting basically as a commis-

---

16. Paul Butel, *Les négociants bordelais, l'Europe, et les Iles au XVIIIe siècle* (Paris, 1974), 22, 50, 57.

sioned middleman, the merchant in the port gained both from the increase in quantity and the rise in price, and commissions on sugar transactions ultimately proved more lucrative than the occasional windfall profit gained by speculating on sugar. Similarly, armateurs of ships for the islands gained more from selling European merchandise in the Antilles or from carrying freight back to France than from sugar speculation.[17] There was a close similarity between sugar prices in the French West Indies and the French ports; competition was simply too keen to allow for large price differences between the colonies and France.[18] Although over the very short term there could be significant differences in price due, for example, to a sudden dearth or excess of shipping activity, these differences did not necessarily operate in the French merchant's favor. Losses on shipments of colonial commodities were almost as common as gains, and reexport prices were generally considered to be only 10 percent greater than arrival prices.[19] This scarcely covered various costs such as warehousing, transport, and local taxes.

Wholesale prices in the French ports showed a steady increase from 1730 until the French Revolution (see Table 3.) From the 1730s to the 1770s, nominal sugar prices increased by 42 percent. Since this was somewhat less than other French price increases, it meant that real prices were down; this reflected the quickly growing supply. After the American Revolution, sugar prices acted quite exceptionally relative to most French prices: instead of declining markedly, sugar prices continued to rise, carried along by a strong reexport market. Tied to the international Atlantic economy and not to the largely agri-

17. See, for example, the accounts of the Chaurand brothers of Nantes in ADLA, 1JJ26–28.
18. Tarrade, *Le commerce colonial*, table between 138 and 139, 647; Thésée, *Les négociants bordelais*, 220. There are still those who insist that speculators made great profits; for example, Michel Morineau, "Quelques recherches relatives à la balance du commerce exterieur français au XVIIIe siècle," in Colloque National de l'Assemblée française des historiens économistes, Paris, 1973, *Aires et structures du commerce français au XVIIIe siècle* (Paris, 1975), 3: "It was thanks to the differences in price between the metropole and the colony . . . that Bordeaux, Marseilles, Nantes, and Rouen became rich." Even seasonal differences were regular and expected. ADSM, BDM 1.47, January 26, 1765.
19. See, for example, ADLA, C864, 1749–54, which shows average prices of clayed sugar in Nantes to be 35 livres per hundredweight upon arrival and 39 livres upon departure. See also ADCM, I19 and I29, which evaluate clayed sugar at Marseilles during the 1760s at 40 livres per hundredweight upon arrival and at 45 livres upon departure.

Table 3. WHOLESALE PRICES OF SUGAR IN THE FRENCH PORTS, 1730–1790 (in livres per hundred pounds)

Years	Muscovado	Clayed Sugar	All Sugar
1730–39	17	31	24
1740–43	22	33	28
1749–54	19	33	26
1763–77	26	42	34
1783–90	32	51	42

Sources: ADLA, C706; ACCMx, I29; Tarrade, Le commerce colonial, 771–72.

cultural French national economy, the sugar business grew in spite of a general recession in France.[20]

Given the steady rise in sugar prices and the increasing volume of sugar sold, the nominal value of the sugar trade soared during the eighteenth century. The total value of sugar arrivals went from 15,000,000 livres in 1730 to 75,000,000 in 1790 (see Table 4), for an annual growth rate of over 4 percent for the forty-one years of peace. This was far in excess of the growth rate for the economy as a whole and, when accompanied by an even more spectacular boom in coffee, helps explain why the ports were so much richer than the rest of France. Arthur Young, for example, was shocked by the sight of a wealthy Nantes in the midst of an impoverished Brittany: "'Mon Dieu!' Cried I to myself, do all the wastes, the deserts, the heath, ling, furze, broom, and bog that I have passed for 300 miles lead to this spectacle? What a miracle, that all this splendor and wealth of the cities in France should be so unconnected with the country! There are no gentle transitions from ease to comfort, from comfort to wealth; you pass at once from begging to profusion—from misery in mud cabins to Mademoiselle St. Huberti, in splendid spectacles at 500 livres a night (£21 16s 6d)."[21]

The obvious wealth of the French ports seemed to vindicate the government's sugar policy in particular and its colonial policy in general. Early in the century the government had realized its goal of

20. Ernest Labrousse, La crise de l'économie française à la fin de l'ancien régime et au début de la Révolution (Paris, 1944).
21. Young, Travels in France, 115.

Table 4. VALUE OF SUGAR ARRIVING IN FRENCH PORTS, 1730–1790

Year	Value
1730	15,000,000 livres
1750	30,000,000 livres
1770	45,000,000 livres
1790	75,000,000 livres

Sources: See Tables 2 and 3.

establishing French domination over the European sugar market, and by 1730 cheap French sugar forced British sugar out of Europe and back to the protected market in Britain.[22] For the rest of the century, the government sought to maintain its hegemony over what was one of Europe's largest trades. This implied action on two fronts. First, France had to protect its Caribbean colonies, even at the price of abandoning its North American and Indian ones. Second, France had to provide continued encouragement to merchants involved in the reexport business.[23] The results of government policy were positive, although it is clear that legislation did little more than help provide favorable conditions for business growth and that the international demand for sugar was the key factor involved.

There were, however, problems. In spite of impressive growth in both volume and value, the colonial trade in general was in a delicate position in the 1780s, as merchants and planters had to contend with the consequences of rising costs and increased competition. The rapid expansion of the trade in sugar and coffee—and it is impossible to distinguish between the two—in the 1780s was made possible only by the importation of vast quantities of slaves into the French islands. These were supplied in unprecedented numbers by merchants in all the major French ports. Unfortunately, slave imports outpaced colonial production, thereby committing the planter to a cycle of indebtedness that proved impossible to break in the short term.[24] Greater

---

22. Drescher, *Econocide*, 51–53.
23. For encouragements given—even to refined sugar—see Boizard and Tardieu, *Histoire de la législation*, 6.
24. Annual slave imports into the islands doubled from the 1760s and 1770s to the 1780s (see Stein, "Measuring the French Slave Trade," 519–20), while colonial production increased by only a third (if smuggling did not vary). This is still true even in the

capital investment led only to increased competition and low profit margins, while overfarming exhausted the land, limited productivity, and necessitated yet further investment in slaves, in more distant and less attractive land, or in a combination of the two.

Thus, a century of growth appeared to lead to an impasse, and complaints were common in both the Antilles and France. Had the colonial economy been allowed to develop without outside interference, a way out may well have been found. A lengthy period of peace both in Europe and the Caribbean could have brought stability and solidity to the sugar business; in time the larger labor force would have yielded larger harvests. Peace, however, was not forthcoming in the 1790s, and war brought a quick end to the entire French colonial system in 1793. The British navy put an end to almost all commerce between France and the colonies and quite coincidentally justified the exaggerated air of crisis of the prewar period.[25]

---

unlikely event that smuggling went from the lowest estimated level to the highest from 1763 to 1789. Slave prices increased much as sugar prices did. See Robert Stein, "The State of French Colonial Commerce on the Eve of the Revolution," *Journal of European Economic History*, XII (1983), 105–17.

25. For a typical "crisis interpretation," see Meyer, *L'armement nantais*, 249–54; and Schnakenbourg, *Les sucreries de la Guadeloupe*, passim.

6

Local Perspectives

> The refineries of Orléans were established at great expense and maintained by the ability of our entrepreneurs. . . . Those at Rouen, because of limited knowledge, are forced to use foreigners.
> —"Mémoire pour les raffineurs d'Orléans"

Impressive and cohesive as it appeared in official statistics, "the French sugar business" was in reality a series of local sugar businesses, each operating semiautonomously in a major French port. In most respects, France in the Old Regime was a confused and often contradictory patchwork of jurisdictions and customs, with regional interests conflicting both with one another and with the national one. The sugar business was therefore quite typical in its divisions: interested merchants in Nantes, Bordeaux, and Marseilles fought one another frequently and even bitterly in order to gain the most concessions for their home port and united only when confronted with a common and particularly dangerous threat. It was the duty of the national government to calm these local rivalries by granting each town its particular rights and privileges. Throughout the eighteenth century the sugar business in each of the major ports operated under special laws peculiar to that port. This allowed a balance to be achieved, as each port became in some sense a specialist concentrating on reexporting or importing sugar to certain areas or on refining sugar.

The geography of the reexport and import trades tended to follow natural boundaries. With respect to reexports, the great division was between the Atlantic and the Mediterranean: ports on the Atlantic coast concentrated on trade with northern Europe, while Marseilles—the only significant commercial port on the Mediterranean coast—had a virtual monopoly over trade with Italy and the Levant. Competition was stiff in the west, as Nantes, Bordeaux, Le Havre, and La Rochelle vied for supremacy in the lucrative Dutch and German trades. The import trade was more rigorously controlled and less open to competition. Special tariffs, for example, gave Nantes a virtual monopoly over Brittany's sugar business but effectively prevented Marseilles from selling sugar on the internal French market. Bordeaux filled the gap and supplied most of southern France. Paris was served by Nantes, Le Havre, and La Rochelle, whereas Dunkerque tried to dominate the market in French Flanders. The extreme particularism of the import trades reflected the traditional outlook of both the government and the merchant communities: local interests had to be protected at almost any cost. Although this outlook prevented the creation of a unified, national French sugar business, it did guarantee the survival of several small, local industries.

There were three great sugar ports for most of the eighteenth century: Nantes, Bordeaux, and Marseilles; and together they handled more than three-quarters of all sugar entering France. Nantes was the early leader in the sugar business and was not decisively displaced by Bordeaux until after the Seven Years' War. Perhaps because of its privileged position near Lorient and the favors shown the port by the Compagnie des Indes Occidentales, Nantes was deeply involved with colonial trade by the late seventeenth century. In 1730, when reliable figures became available, Nantes received some 23,000,000 pounds of sugar, a figure that rose steadily until the end of the War of the Austrian Succession, when 39,000,000 pounds arrived annually in port.[1] Following the Austrian war, sugar arrivals continued to grow, averaging 40,000,000 pounds until 1755. Increased competition from Bordeaux put an end to Nantes's growth after the Seven Years' War, and arrivals remained fairly constant until the American Revolution. In the years preceding the French Revolution, however, Nantes succeeded in sharing in the boom in colonial trade and increased its average annual sugar arrivals to some 55,000,000 to 60,000,000 pounds.

The pattern of growth of the Nantes sugar trade closely resembled that of the Nantes slave trade: regular growth until the 1740s, stability from then until the 1770s, and rapid growth in the 1780s.[2] At Nantes the sugar business was to a large degree dependent upon the slave trade, particularly after the development of a major Bordeaux sugar commerce. Unable to compete with the Bordelais in furnishing the colonies with European merchandise, the Nantais turned in-

1. For the Nantes import and export figures, see ADLA, C706, 716, and 717.
2. See Stein, *French Slave Trade*, 207–209.

creasingly to the slave trade. Only by selling slaves to the colonists could local merchants retain their status in the colonial market and guarantee shipments of colonial produce to Nantes. By the end of the Old Regime, more than one-third of all sugar arriving in Nantes was in payment for slaves sold by Nantes merchants, and most of the remaining sugar was simply sent to Nantes on consignment. Slaves provided the real motivation for Nantes's economy; sugar merely followed the paths charted by the slavers.

Most of the sugar arriving in Nantes came from Saint Domingue. From the early days of official French settlement on Saint Domingue, Nantes merchants had concentrated on commerce with the colony, and this concentration remained high throughout the eighteenth century. Again, this phenomenon was related to the slave trade, as Nantes slavers dealt almost exclusively with Saint Domingue in the second half of the eighteenth century. Specializing in the Saint Domingue trade meant that Nantes received more muscovado than clayed sugar. As we have seen, the Lesser Antilles produced clayed sugar almost exclusively after 1700, but the more recently developed colony of Saint Domingue always produced much more muscovado than clayed. Nantes sugar arrivals reflected this preference, and for most of the eighteenth century, some 60 to 70 percent of all sugar arriving in Nantes was muscovado.

The predominance of muscovado at Nantes matched the wishes of at least one group of purchasers of Nantes sugar: the refiners.[3] Situated near the mouth of the Loire River, Nantes was in an ideal position to supply the refiners of Angers, Saumur, Tours, and especially Orléans with raw sugar, and a higher percentage of the sugar arriving at Nantes remained in France than that arriving at Bordeaux or Marseilles.[4] Most refiners preferred cheap muscovado to expensive clayed sugar. Besides selling sugar to refiners inside the Five Great Farms—the customs union in France—Nantes merchants also sold it to retailers in Brittany. The Letters Patent of April, 1717, gave the Nantais a virtual monopoly over the Breton sugar market.[5] Located outside

---

3. Paul Bois *et al.*, *Histoire de Nantes* (Toulouse, 1977), 139. See also figures on the amounts of muscovado and clayed going from Nantes up the Loire, between 1699 and 1727, in ADLA, C855.
4. ADL, 11J239, cahier 2, "L'art et le commerce du raffineur."
5. AN, F12 1639A.

the Five Great Farms, Brittany could receive sugar from Breton ports duty free; this represented a savings of 2.5 livres per hundredweight for muscovado and 8 livres per hundredweight for clayed sugar. The Breton market, however, was small.

In spite of sales to France and Brittany, from 55 to 60 percent of the sugar arriving at Nantes was destined for reexportation (see Map 1). From 10 to 20 percent of this went to southern Europe. Early in the century, Spain took about 1,000,000 pounds per year, and Italy took similar quantities later in the century. Portugal was a modest and occasional buyer throughout the century. Significantly, all three purchased clayed sugar almost exclusively; this was probably retained without further processing. The rest of Nantes's sugar reexports went to northern Europe, with the bulk going to Holland and Germany. As early as the 1730s, the Dutch purchased over 8,000,000 pounds of sugar per year at Nantes; this increased to an average of some 10,000,000 pounds after the Seven Years' War, with a record of 16,000,000 pounds coming in 1774. Most reexports to Holland were of muscovado. A close second to the Dutch as purchasers of Nantes sugar were merchants from northern German cities, such as Hamburg, Bremen, and Stettin. They bought roughly equal amounts of muscovado and clayed sugar, although there was somewhat of a preference for the former until the Seven Years' War and for the latter afterward. The third major northern destination for Nantes sugar was Belgium or Austrian Flanders, which after the Seven Years' War took up to 5,000,000 pounds per year. Minor purchasers of Nantes sugar included the Danes, the Swedes, the Russians, and even the English.

If Nantes dominated colonial trade early in the eighteenth century, Bordeaux was the leader later on. Bordeaux's sugar arrivals nearly matched Nantes's as early as the 1730s, and after the Seven Years' War pulled far ahead.[6] From 1767 to 1776, for example, an average of 63,000,000 pounds of sugar arrived in Bordeaux, compared with only 42,000,000 in Nantes. Bordeaux's preeminence in the sugar trade was due to the port's domination of the trade in European goods shipped to the French West Indies. By the end of the Old Regime, nearly 40 percent of the ships sailing from France to the Antilles were from

---

6. For the Bordeaux import and export figures see ADG, C4269; Malvezin, *Histoire du commerce de Bordeaux*, III, 302–309; Butel, *Les négociants bordelais*, 24–82.

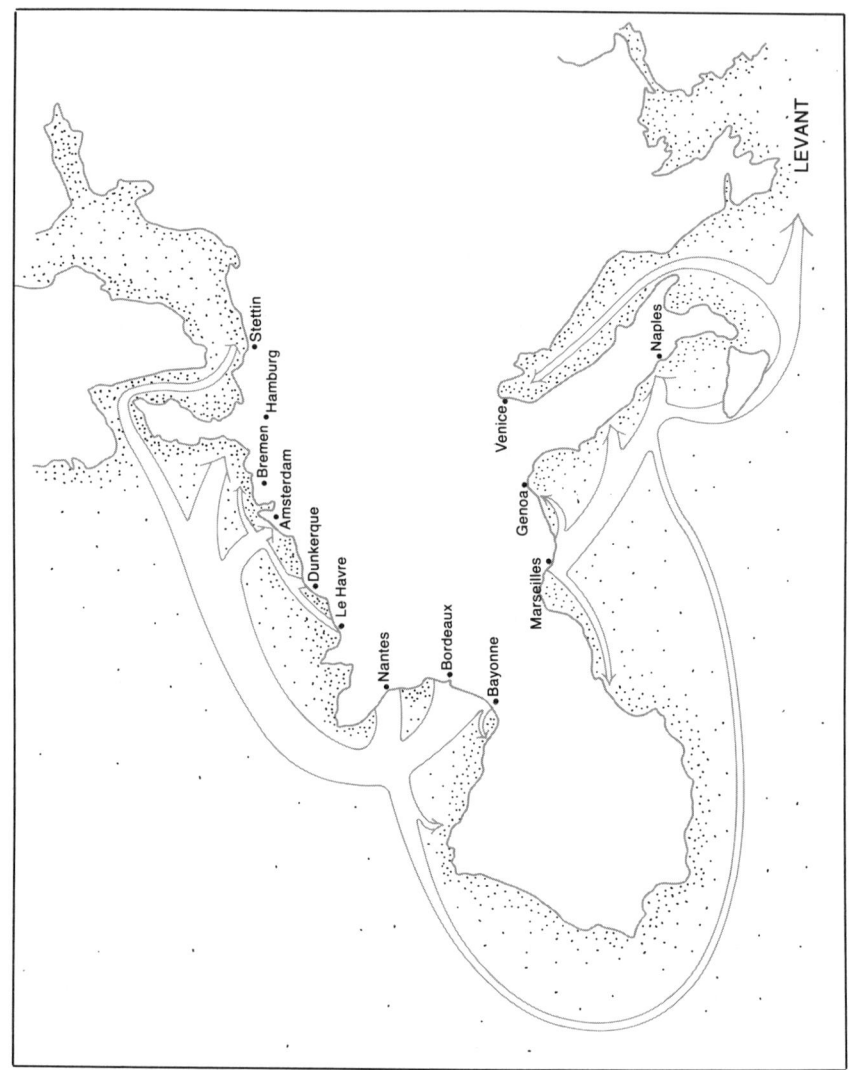

Map 1: French Reexportation of Sugar in the 1770s

Bordeaux; they supplied Saint Domingue with 72 percent of its salted beef, 88 percent of its flour, and 93 percent of its wine.[7] The traditional products, particularly foodstuffs, of Aquitaine were much sought after in the islands because of their exceptional quality. Indeed, the only important food commodity that the Bordelais did not supply was oil, which was furnished mostly by the Marseillais. By controlling the flow of European goods to the French West Indies, Bordeaux assured for itself the lion's share of colonial commodities.

The breakthrough in Bordeaux's sugar trade came when its merchants shifted their focus from Martinique to Saint Domingue. Until the middle of the century, Bordeaux merchants specialized in trade with Martinique, and even in the 1750s they sent out more than 50 percent of all French ships going there.[8] In return the Bordelais received virtually all of their coffee and clayed sugar from Martinique; Saint Domingue supplied the majority of muscovado only. Later in the century the Saint Domingue market grew at the expense of Martinique, and by the end of the Old Regime, Bordeaux shippers were concentrating on Saint Domingue, although not as exclusively as their counterparts in Nantes. There was one major difference: whereas the Nantais had always purchased a majority of muscovado and continued to do so until the Revolution, the Bordelais dealt primarily in clayed sugar. At first they got it from Martinique, but when they switched to Saint Domingue, they insisted on purchasing clayed sugar there. Thus, even in the 1780s Bordeaux still received much more clayed sugar than muscovado in spite of the fact that most of its sugar originated in Saint Domingue.[9]

Bordeaux's sugar found a ready market abroad, and higher percentages of it were reexported than Nantes's sugar. This may have been related to the preeminence of clayed sugar in Bordeaux, although it seems that foreign merchants were prepared to buy virtually any unrefined sugar available in the city. In any event, some 70 to 80 percent of sugar arriving in Bordeaux was regularly reexported, with the vast majority going to Holland and northern Germany. According to Paul Butel, the Dutch and Germans together purchased an average

7. Butel, *Les négociants bordelais*, 33–34; Tarrade, *Le commerce colonial*, 734.
8. "Martinique" represents Martinique and Guadeloupe, since before the Seven Years' War virtually all trade between Guadeloupe and France passed through Martinique.
9. Tarrade, *Le commerce colonial*, table between 730 and 731; D'Arcy, "Aperçu de l'histoire du sucre," 30–31.

of 32,000,000 pounds of sugar from 1751 to 1753 and an average of 61,000,000 from 1774 to 1776; Théophile Malvezin reported total Bordeaux reexports to have averaged 32,000,000 and 65,000,000 pounds, respectively.[10] Although comparisons between Butel's and Malvezin's figures are of dubious precision, they do give a reasonable idea of the extent to which the Dutch and Germans dominated the Bordeaux reexport trade. Little sugar could have been left for sale elsewhere, and what was available went primarily to Sweden and Denmark.[11]

As with Nantes's sugar, reexports of Bordeaux's sugar were usually handled by Dutchmen or Germans residing in the French ports. This was because French merchants had little interest in the carrying trade with other European ports. By the end of the Old Regime, French shippers were sending out nearly eight hundred expeditions annually to the Antilles, either directly or via Africa; this represented an investment of at least 50,000,000 livres. Transatlantic shipping on such a vast scale apparently drained the resources of French armateurs, and they fitted out few if any ships for Holland or Germany.[12] Sugar was invariably sold in bulk to foreign purchasers in the French ports. This was done for two additional reasons. One was speed: slave traders and merchants selling European goods in the West Indies were anxious to sell their sugar and finally realize some cash returns on investments that had been made several months or even years earlier, while merchants selling sugar on consignment from the Antilles needed quick sales to get their commissions. The other was cost: Dutch shipping was far too cheap and efficient to suffer from competition from the French. Hence, the sugar was sold almost immediately after its arrival in port and was shipped abroad in foreign vessels.

The sugar that was not reexported from Bordeaux was imported into France. Upon payment of appropriate duties—2.5 livres per hundredweight for muscovado, 8 livres per hundredweight for clayed—sugar arriving at Bordeaux could be sold anywhere in the Five Great Farms. Bordeaux was one of the few important ports not having special duty status, and it had no legally reserved areas for marketing its

10. Butel, *Les négociants bordelais*, 308–309; Malvezin, *Histoire du commerce de Bordeaux*, III, 302–309.
11. Butel, *Les négociants bordelais*, 72. Butel does not mention sales of sugar to Spain or Italy. See, however, his map 13, which indicates some such sales.
12. Tarrade, *Le commerce colonial*, table between 730 and 731; Butel, *Les négociants bordelais*, 61–64.

sugar. In practice, however, Bordeaux dominated the sugar business in the south of France, primarily because of a lack of competition. The only other major commercial port in the Midi was Marseilles, but it was effectively prohibited by its status as a free port from importing sugar into France. Indeed, so great an advantage was held by Bordeaux sugar that much of it was refined and then sold at the Beaucaire Fair, practically on Marseilles' doorstep.[13] Bordeaux refined sugar was about 10 to 15 percent cheaper than Marseilles', and it regularly outsold its rival at Beaucaire by nearly two to one. Marseilles refiners complained bitterly about this, charging that Bordeaux sugar was inferior, but they never succeeded in having it banned from the fair.[14]

The Marseilles sugar business was much smaller than that of either Nantes or Bordeaux, but still clearly larger than those of the secondary ports of Le Havre, La Rochelle, Dunkerque, and Bayonne. Unlike Nantes or Bordeaux, however, the Marseilles economy did not rely heavily on the sugar business in particular or on colonial trade in general. Whereas the overwhelming majority of Nantes's or Bordeaux's trade involved the colonies, Marseilles had traditional trading relationships with Mediterranean lands that remained more significant than the transatlantic trade. Thus, although Marseilles was generally the most active of the eighteenth-century French ports and handled the largest percentage of total French foreign trade, it ranked behind Bordeaux and Nantes in trade with the Antilles.[15] For the Marseillais, the sugar trade was a lucrative windfall, not a vital necessity.

Arrivals of French West Indian sugar at Marseilles grew steadily throughout the century.[16] In the early 1730s an average of 6,000,000 pounds arrived per year; this increased to 15,000,000 pounds before the War of the Austrian Succession and 17,000,000 before the Seven Years' War. In the years preceding the American Revolution, the port received over 19,000,000 pounds of sugar annually, and there are indications that this rose to some 25,000,000 before the French Revolution. Until the very end of the Old Regime most of this apparently came from the Lesser Antilles. As late as 1773, for example, Mar-

13. See AN, F12 1229 and 1230, for sugar sales at Beaucaire.
14. See ADG, C4269, mémoire on Beaucaire, 1732. See also Bondois, "L'industrie sucrière," 339; Gaston Rambert, *Histoire du commerce de Marseille* (Marseilles, 1951–66), VII, 119; ACCM, H110; AN, F12 1501.
15. Dardel, *Navires et marchandises*, 736.
16. Marseilles sugar statistics are in ACCM, I19, 20, 24, 25, 29, and 30.

seilles merchants sent out forty-three expeditions to Martinique and Guadeloupe, but only thirty-six to Saint Domingue. The picture changed in the 1780s, however: in 1788 eighty-nine ships went to Saint Domingue, and forty-nine to the Lesser Antilles.[17] Saint Domingue's sugar production was simply too large to ignore, particularly when the colony began to produce vast quantities of the clayed sugar so much demanded by the Marseillais. Throughout the century, more than 90 percent of all sugar arriving in Marseilles was clayed.

The concentration on clayed sugar reflected the wishes of foreign purchasers. The Marseilles sugar business was devoted almost totally to the reexport trade, with 80 to 90 percent of all sugar regularly going abroad. Virtually all of this sugar went to Mediterranean destinations, where it was probably retailed without further processing; as noted, Nantes's exports to Italy and Spain had also been almost exclusively clayed. Italians purchased more than half of Marseilles' sugar reexports. In 1769, for example, Marseilles reexported some 17,000,000 pounds of sugar, 16,000,000 of which was clayed. "Italy" took 6,000,000 pounds, Naples and Sicily 3,000,000, Venice 2,000,000, Genoa 1,000,000, and Savoy and Piedmont 1,000,000; Spain and the various Levantine ports took most of the rest. The major buyers in the eastern Mediterranean were Constantinople, Smyrna, Aleppo, Acre and Syrian Tripoli, and Salonika; occasional buyers included Tunis, Algiers, Cyprus, and Egypt. The success of French sugar in the Levant reversed ancient trading patterns and put the final nail into the coffin of the eastern Mediterranean sugar industry. By the 1770s the Marseillais were virtually the only sellers of sugar in the area, leading an anonymous writer to comment, "The only competitor French West Indian sugar has in the Levant is Egyptian, whose quality is so low and whose quantity so minimal that it scarcely warrants attention."[18]

Marseilles sugar merchants specialized in reexports for two reasons. To begin with, there was an obvious foreign demand that could easily be satisfied by the port. Second, Marseilles' unique legal position encouraged reexports and discouraged imports of sugar. In 1669 Marseilles was proclaimed a free port. Although it is possible that

17. D'Arcy, "Aperçu de l'histoire du sucre," 30–31. Tarrade, *Le commerce colonial*, table between 730 and 731. See also Charles Carrière, *Négociants marseillais au XVIIIe siècle* (Paris, 1973), 1052–53.
18. ACCM, I19, 20, 24, 25, 29, and 30; BN, nafr 6530, fol. 147.

Marseilles' special privileges may not have positively encouraged reexports of sugar, and although it is certainly true that, after the Letters Patent of April, 1717, all French ports were almost free ports as far as the reexport of sugar was concerned, a combination of high duties and low quotas kept Marseilles from selling sugar to France.[19] These restrictions were established to prevent Marseilles merchants from fraudulently introducing foreign sugar into France: since Marseilles was officially a free port, foreign sugar could legally be present there, and the government feared that unscrupulous merchants would try to pass it off as French. Thus, only relatively small amounts of sugar were allowed to enter France from Marseilles. At most, some 2,000,000 to 3,000,000 pounds per year were imported, all of it going to the neighboring provinces of Provence, Dauphiné, Languedoc, and Roussillon.[20]

The other French ports had more modest sugar trades and tended to specialize in certain areas according to specific market demands. Beside Nantes, Bordeaux, and Marseilles, only Le Havre, La Rochelle, Dunkerque, and Bayonne made significant contributions to the French sugar business. Le Havre was guaranteed a foothold in the colonial market because the port had a wide range of items wanted by the colonists, especially salted beef and textiles. Le Havre's sugar trade experienced the same pattern of regular growth apparent in Bordeaux and Marseilles.[21] Amounts of sugar arriving rose from an average of 1,000,000 pounds per year in the early 1730s to 7,000,000 in the 1740s, 10,000,000 in the 1750s, 13,000,000 in the 1760s and 1770s, and probably higher in the 1780s. Most of this was clayed sugar, and most was reexported to Holland and northern Germany. The rest of Le Havre's sugar was shipped along the Seine River either to Paris or to the gates of Paris, where it was unloaded and taken by land to Orléans for refining.[22]

Unique among the French ports trading with the French West Indies, La Rochelle experienced stagnation and decline both relative

19. BN, nafr 6530, fol. 147. See also ACCM, H110, "Réponse aux Fermiers Généraux," December, 1742.
20. For an estimate of French imports from Marseilles see Jules Julliany, *Essai sur le commerce de Marseille* (Marseilles, 1842), III, 214. See also Rambert, *Histoire du commerce de Marseille*, VII, 66–68.
21. Le Havre import and export statistics are in Dardel, *Navires et marchandises*, 55, 222–23, 566. See also D'Arcy, "Aperçu de l'histoire du sucre," 30–31.
22. Dardel, *Navires et marchandises*, 483 and 483 n. 2.

and absolute during most of the eighteenth century. Like Nantes, La Rochelle turned to the slave trade to remain a force in the colonial market, but this policy met with only limited success. In spite of sending many ships to Africa, La Rochelle's colonial trade was trivial by the end of the eighteenth century: only six ships left the port bound directly for the Antilles in 1788.[23] This was a sad ending to what had begun most auspiciously. In the early 1730s an average of 8,000,000 pounds of sugar arrived annually in La Rochelle, placing the port ahead of Marseilles.[24] But the average fell to 7,000,000 in the next decade, returned to 9,000,000 in the 1750s, and then dropped to only 5,000,000 in the 1760s and 1770s. In the 1780s it fell even further to a mere 4,000,000 pounds per year. As in Nantes, merchants in La Rochelle took a majority of muscovado, but the Rochellais refined much of it locally.

Dunkerque and Bayonne, minor ports near the borders, relied on special concessions from the government to bolster their sugar trades. Both were free ports and—like Marseilles—both relied on reexports of sugar. Dunkerque specialized on sales to French Flanders, which for customs purposes was foreign to France (a *province reputée étrangère*). This market was small and, in spite of sales to Belgium and Holland, Dunkerque's sugar arrivals never exceeded 10,000,000 pounds per year and rarely went over 5,000,000. One reason for the limited scale of Dunkerque's sugar business was local merchants' fear that a large French West Indian trade might conflict with the port's traditional franchise. The general feeling was that nothing should be allowed to endanger Dunkerque's status as a free port, and only the local sugar refiner, Sieur Langheté, seemed prepared to sacrifice this privilege.[25]

Bayonne's sugar industry was centered on reexports to Spain. Smaller than Dunkerque's industry, Bayonne's probably never ac-

---

23. On the La Rochelle trade see Henri Robert, *Trafics coloniaux du port de la Rochelle au XVIIIe siècle* (Paris, 1960).
24. Tarrade, *Le commerce colonial*, table between 730 and 731.
25. See the deliberations of the Dunkerque chamber of commerce, January 21, 1718, February 24, 1718, March 28, 1718, May 25, 1718, in ACCDk. See also Paul M. Bondois, "L'exportation du sucre au XVIIIe siècle: La question de la Flandre française," *Annales du Nord*, IX (1923), 123–28. See also Carrière, *Négociants marseillais*, which claims that Marseilles' status as a free port hindered rather than helped its trade with the colonies.

counted for more than 1,000,000 or 2,000,000 pounds per year.²⁶ Although Bayonne was admirably situated to supply Spain with sugar, competition from the major ports was simply too great, and the capital necessary to establish a major trade was lacking. Spanish demand was clearly strong enough, as an eighteenth-century essay noted: "The widespread use of chocolate leads to a consumption of cocoa and sugar that can scarcely be imagined. It is the principal expense of rich and poor." Bayonne merchants tried to satisfy this demand, but in spite of a local refiner's claim that "the city of Bayonne has become the city of supply for Spain," it never managed to develop into more than a minor provincial port.²⁷

The structure of the French sugar business—its division into a series of semiautonomous units—along with traditional assumptions about the need to protect and encourage local industry, provoked the outbreak of numerous conflicts among the ports. A look at these conflicts sheds light not only on how business was actually conducted in eighteenth-century France but also on how merchants believed business should have been conducted. The power of the marketplace was never allowed to become absolute, and government controls were considered both natural and necessary by businessmen. At the same time, the exact impact of such regulation is difficult to establish and can be easily overestimated: in the long run, economic factors determined the success or failure of the local businesses. What was significant about the government's role was the attitudes toward business it reflected. Businessmen appealed to the government, and the government acted in support of certain views of commerce.

Quite naturally, disputes about what was fair stood at the heart of each conflict. "Fairness," however, was measured not so much by abstract principles as by traditional practice and economic necessity. Like most people in the Old Regime, businessmen were profoundly conservative in that they believed that anything sanctioned by time should probably continue to exist. Frequently, of course, this served

26. Statistical information is limited. See D'Arcy, "Aperçu de l'histoire du sucre," 30–31; Tarrade, *Le commerce colonial*, table between 730 and 731.
27. BN, nafr 20540, "Mémoire concernant le commerce du royaume d'Arragon," fol. 43; request by Sieur La Salle (1784 or 1785), AN, F12 1502.

to mask economic self-interest: old rules that helped one port or hindered a competitor would be fervently praised by local businessmen claiming only to support the ancient customs of the kingdom. Still, tradition did play a powerful role in determining government policy and was probably responsible for retaining many privileges that went against the national interest. The integrity of local business had to be supported. It might, for example, have been more rational to abolish the special status of some ports, but such was almost inconceivable.[28]

In the disputes between ports, economic self-interest was usually evident. Merchants seemed to believe in a type of domestic mercantilism which held that one port's advance was related to a competitor's decline and vice versa. Proposals to enlarge colonial trade by allowing other ports to participate in it were therefore roundly condemned by all those already enjoying such a right; even when the new port was clearly too small to affect established trading patterns, merchants reacted strongly.[29] Similarly, proposals to improve the status of any town already dealing in sugar were bitterly contested by merchants in other towns. For example, in 1637 or 1638, Rouen sugar refiners elected to pay a special tax of 2.5 livres per hundredweight on raw sugar entering their city rather than pay a direct tax on their wealth.[30] At the time, there was little competition from other cities, and an increase in the price of Rouen sugar did not hurt sales. A century later the situation had altered: there was stiff competition, especially from Orléans, and the more expensive Rouen sugar was in danger of disappearing. Further, Rouen merchants claimed that the Le Havre sugar trade, which supplied Rouen with raw sugar, was also in danger of vanishing. The refiners asked for the special tax to be suppressed, but their competitors outside Rouen were opposed to any change. Only in 1786 was the tax eliminated.

Other internal disputes pitted Bordeaux against Marseilles, Nantes against La Rochelle, and the ports of Normandy against the free ports of Marseilles, Bayonne, and Dunkerque. These were paralleled by a series of international disputes between French and English

---

28. John F. Bosher, *The Single Duty Project* (London, 1964).
29. ADG, C4382.
30. AMR, A25, March 20, 1637, February 17, 1638, February 19, 1638, November 19, 1638; AMR, A26, December 9, 1653, June 5, 1655; AMR, A27, January 5, 1656; ADLA, C733, September 21, 1733, August 26, 1733.

or Dutch sugar merchants. At issue here were the nominally French markets in French Flanders and eastern France, regions with special customs status.[31] The French merchants complained that foreigners were monopolizing the sugar trade in the outlying provinces and that the government should either ban all sales of foreign sugar or subsidize French shipments there. The French merchants, however, were not concerned with the views of the residents of the disputed areas, who were quite content to buy their sugar cheaply from the Dutch or English. Refiners in Lille, for example, complained bitterly in 1789 when their province lost its special status and was forced to purchase French sugar. Like merchants elsewhere in France, the Lillois demanded exemptions or subsidies or special laws. Particularism was a powerful force in eighteenth-century French business, and few merchants had any conception of a national market.

31. See, for example, AN, F12 1639A, "Avantages et facilités des anglais et des hollandais dans la fabrication des sucres" and "Compte rendu . . . sur l'affaire des sucres . . ."; BN, nafr 20541, "Réflexions sur le renouvellement d'un traité du commerce . . ."; ADLA, C730, mémoire, March 4, 1786, and "Déclaration de M. Jan Jacobi Elzerier, rafineur à Rotterdam," January 21, 1786; AN, C1269, December 30, 1789; and AN, F12 1502, mémoire by the chamber of commerce at Lille, January 14, 1790.

7

Refining Sugar

> The best sugar is solid, light, extremely white and sweet, brilliant as snow, hard, not spongy, and dissolves quickly in water.
> —Jacques Savary des Bruslons

At the gastronomic heart of the French sugar business was the refining industry. Although only a small fraction of French West Indian sugar was refined in France, refiners took great pride in their work and went about it with dedication and even enthusiasm, transforming raw sugar into a highly polished product worthy of gracing the best tables in the land. They also produced some more modest varieties of refined sugar that somewhat less wealthy customers could afford. Still, if sugar was generally reserved for the better-off classes of society, refined sugar was the preserve of the rich: it was a true luxury item and the glory of the French sugar business. This chapter describes the refining process and the economics of refining. The next chapter discusses the history of French refining, on both the national and the local levels.

What is refined sugar? Quite simply, it is pure sugar marketed in a crystalline form. Today, refined sugar is 99.9 percent pure sucrose. In the Old Regime the degree of purity may have been somewhat lower, but the refiner's goal was the same: to produce a sugar as free from impurities as possible. Although high-quality clayed sugar from the islands could replace refined sugar in more modest homes and although the highest-quality clayed could appear to the biased observer to be refined, French refineries produced a refined sugar that exceeded any nonrefined import in purity.[1] In practical terms this meant that it was whiter, having lost all trace of brown residue. It had less of a distinctive taste and was more of a neutral sweetener than a characteristic spice; this was considered an advantage.

The basic idea behind the refining process was a simple one, al-

---

1. Tax collectors frequently tried to tax incoming clayed sugar at the higher rate for refined sugar. For example, see January 12, 1731, and ADLA, C731, mémoire by the Farmers General(?), 1748(?).

though it took an experienced refiner to realize it properly. Still, a primitive form of refining had existed for centuries and was practiced in private kitchens; sixteenth-century cookbooks even offered a recipe for "clarifying" sugar, which was similar to the fundamentals of seventeenth- and eighteenth-century refining. According to Michel de Nostredamus, *cassonade* or *sucre noir* could be clarified by a relatively easy process.[2] First the sugar was dissolved in warm water and then brought to a boil. Egg whites and white vinegar were added, and the mixture was stirred. This produced a foam that had to be skimmed off before the liquid was strained through a white cloth and left to sit for two days. The cooking process was then repeated, and after six more days of sitting, the clarified sugar was ready. This was indeed a refined sugar, and although relatively impure, it was satisfactory for all but the most discriminating of households.

Refining on a large scale followed the same basic steps of cooking, straining, draining, and drying.[3] The process began when the refiner received the hogsheads of raw sugar at his establishment. After verifying the weight of the shipment, the careful refiner put the barrels into a dry cellar, where the sugar finished draining; weeks at sea had not permitted all the syrup to drain from the imperfectly processed sugar. Once dry, the barrels were carefully opened and the contents removed and sorted according to quality, usually into three categories corresponding to sucre terré, têté, and brut. As one barrel might contain more than one quality of raw sugar, the selection process was as long and tedious as it was important. The worst raw sugar had to be treated before it could be refined; in other words, muscovado had to be elevated to near the level of clayed.

With the sugar divided and the muscovado prepared, the actual refining could begin. Workers filled large, clean, copper boilers two-thirds full with limewater, which would cleanse the sugar, and one-third full with raw sugar; being more dense, the sugar weighed the same as the limewater. The type or types of raw sugar added depended on the quality of refined sugar to be produced; one expert suggested

2. Michel de Nostredamus, *Excellent et moult utile opuscule à tous necessaire qui désirent avoir connaissance de plusieurs exquises receptes* (Lyon, 1552), 151–54.
3. The following description of the refining process relies heavily on Duhamel, *Art de rafiner le sucre*, and "L'art et le commerce du raffineur" (1772), part of a manuscript, perhaps by the refiner Ravôt of Orléans, ADL, 11J239. The account of the refining process given by Bondois, "L'industrie sucrière," 323–27, is singularly confusing. See also Deerr, *History of Sugar*, II, 464–66.

that 3,600 pounds of limewater might be used to purify a combination of 600 pounds of clayed sugar, 1,440 pounds of muscovado, 840 pounds of intermediate-quality sugar, and 720 pounds of syrup or the dregs from a previous refining operation.[4] Similarly, the exact proportion of limewater to sugar could vary according to the quality and cleanliness of the latter; high-quality clayed needed much less than common muscovado. The boiler loaded, a fire was lighted underneath and the mixture began to cook. In many refineries the fire was fueled by coal, which had to be imported from England. Throughout the century, refiners begged the government for permission to import English coal without paying high duties. As refiners in Bordeaux wrote in 1729: "Commerce with America depends principally on the number of sugar refineries established in the kingdom. These refineries can work only at a certain price." The government reacted favorably to such requests, and refiners were usually allowed to import cheap English coal.[5]

The use of fire, both in boiling and later in drying, made refining a dangerous enterprise, and several refineries burned down in the Old Regime. Fire claimed at least three in Orléans and two in Nantes.[6] The danger of fire made refineries unwelcome in residential neighborhoods, and there were concerted drives in many towns to have them relocated beyond the city walls. These enjoyed only limited success: even when laws were passed prohibiting it, some refineries were still constructed in the city.[7] Although most were built in the suburbs, stubborn merchants preferred to build in the city even if it meant a legal battle against the neighbors.[8] Guillaume Lefebvre, for example, insisted on constructing a refinery in a heavily populated section of Tours.[9] Outraged residents complained of the fire hazard as well as the air pollution that would result from the smoke, but their efforts were in vain. Lefebvre's assurances that the surrounding

    4. ADL, 11J239, "L'art et le commerce du raffineur," cahier 2, 4ᵉ partie.
    5. ADG, C4269, mémoire, May 4, 1729; ACCDk, deliberations, October 11, 1724; ADG, C4264, letter from the chamber of commerce to Trudaine, December 20, 1763; BN, nafr 2721, June 20, 1769.
    6. ADL, 2J354, August 23, 1775; ACN, AA81, June 18, 1786; ACN, CC187, January 21, 1694.
    7. For example, in Nantes: ACN, DD331, September 12, 1761; also Orléans: AN, F12 1501, August 12, 1775.
    8. For example, in Nantes: Valladier, "Histoire de la raffinerie," I, 13, 19, 20; and in Bordeaux: ADG, C1642, letter from Lassabathies to the intendant, n.d.
    9. ADIL, C142 (1755).

houses were not threatened, and his claim that all industry would have to cease if the effects of burning coal were to be eliminated, won the day, and the refinery was built as planned.

Another problem arose in the cooking process, when at some stage—some authors said near the beginning, others just before the mix reached a boil—from one to twenty pounds of ox blood were added. This was a controversial step added early in the eighteenth century, perhaps by a Swedish immigrant to Bordeaux named Dohrmann.[10] It soon became popular among refiners, particularly in La Rochelle, who justified its use by a shortage of eggs (the earlier cleansing agent) and by a reduced refining time. In spite of complaints for hygienic reasons by people living near refineries and in spite of the prohibition put on its use by the Conseil de Commerce, ox blood became a standard cleanser in sugar refining. Indeed, in Hamburg more ox blood was reputedly used than limewater in producing most kinds of refined sugar.[11]

With or without ox blood, the mixture was heated over a high flame while being constantly stirred with a giant wooden spatula. This was known as *moving*, and it served to melt the raw sugar. After an hour or so, the liquid reached the boiling point, the stirring ceased, and the fire was greatly reduced. Now the simmering sugar began to "rise." On the surface there appeared a thick, black foam that was distinct from the liquid underneath (unless the flame remained too high, in which case the sugar and the foam mixed). When this scum was thick enough, the fire was extinguished altogether, and the mixture left to cool a bit. After fifteen minutes, the scum dried and hardened a bit, and a worker skimmed it off with the help of a large copper skimmer. Even if done properly, only part of the impurities were removed in a single boiling, and the whole procedure had to be repeated one or two more times. By the third boil the scum was white, and after it was removed, the sugar was kept simmering until it became quite clear. It was then poured through a *blanchet*—a large white cloth that filtered the mixture—and cooked again in a different boiler.

The second cooking clarified the sugar. Here the master refiner had

10. So he claimed. AN, F12 1501, January 14, 1704. See also AN, F12 1501, complaint by Sieur Gresseau, 1708.
11. ADLA, C730, "Théorie du raffinage des sucres bruts mise en pratique par M. Jean Othon Dédé de Hamburg, dirigeant la rafinerie de la Compagnie à Trieste," September 20, 1780.

to use all of his skill to produce the finest possible sugar. The liquid was quickly brought to a boil over a high flame and allowed to cook for nearly an hour with further additions of ox blood. When the sugar was almost cooked, it became thicker, and it was up to the refiner to determine exactly when the proper consistency had been reached. If removed from the fire much too early, it remained watery; if taken off just a bit too soon, it formed huge crystals; if left on too long, it began to ferment. But if done correctly, the "separation of the grain occurs quickly; all of a sudden it forms a large number of tiny crystals."[12] By feeling a sample of the liquid with his fingers, the refiner decided when it was properly cooked, and he removed it immediately from the boiler. The critical phase was over.

It remained to drain and dry the sugar. Although relatively simple operations, they took a long time and could last up to a month. The hot sugar was poured into a cooling vat, from which it was poured into conically shaped molds made of terra cotta. Proper clay for the molds apparently was difficult to obtain, and refining towns with local supplies were loath to sell to out-of-town refiners.[13] The molds came in several sizes that were more or less standardized throughout the nation; in general, the smaller molds contained the highest-quality sugar. The smallest in most refineries was the *petit deux:* 11 inches tall, 5 inches in diameter at the mouth, it produced a sugar loaf weighing some 3 pounds. Then came the *grand deux* (13 inches by 6 inches, weighing 5 pounds), the *trois* (9 inches by 7.5 inches, 7–8 pounds), the *quatre* (19 inches by 8 inches, 12 pounds), and the *sept* (22 inches by 10 inches, 18 pounds).[14] Finally, there were much larger molds for poorer-quality sugar-known as *mélis, fondue, bâtarde,* and *vergeois;* these held loaves of up to 60 pounds and more. The liquid sugar was poured into the molds in two to four steps, depending on the size. It was stirred occasionally to prevent a thick crust from forming, and the following day the mold was placed into the draining room (*grenier*).

The sugar lost about half its weight while draining, but its volume remained constant. Since the mold had a hole in the narrow end, much of the syrup simply flowed out once the mold was placed upside

---

12. Duhamel, *Art de rafiner le sucre,* 24.
13. See, for example, the rule forcing Bordeaux merchants to sell clay to La Rochelle refiners. ACCLR, carton 14, no. 4648, June 21, 1732.
14. ADL, 2J354, "Usages des raffineries d'Orléans," n.d.

down in a pot; residue collected in this fashion could be reprocessed and sold. But since not all the undesired liquid left so easily, it was necessary to draw out the rest by means of a clay covering. A layer of exceptionally white, wet clay, usually from Rouen or Saumur, was placed over the mold; the water from this clay passed through the sugar, cleansing it of any remaining impurities and draining them into the pot.[15] It took from eight to ten days to dry out the first layer of clay, and then a second was added, which took another week to dry. The pure, white sugar was removed from the mold; being solid, it retained the shape of the mold and was a loaf of sugar. The loaves were placed into the drying house, a large room with thick walls designed to keep the heat inside. With the loaves arranged carefully on shelves according to size, a fire was lighted and the temperature raised considerably. It remained so for a week, at the end of which the loaves were completely dry.

The finished loaves were then taken to the wrapping room to be packaged for sale to retailers. The finest-quality sugar was wrapped in blue or violet paper. To avoid discoloration, the paper had to be of excellent quality, and French refiners insisted on using Dutch paper. Even small refiners trusted only imported wrapping paper, and some then put a sheet of white paper between the sugar and the wrapper. Poorer-quality loaves were wrapped in a cheap, gray paper that weighed less and kept down the price. The weight of the paper could be significant, as Marseilles refiners learned in 1749, when purchasers in Constantinople complained that the wrappers were too heavy.[16] Buyers threatened to resort to Venetian sources if the fraud was not discontinued.

The best type of sugar produced by French refiners was *sucre royal*, made in small quantities in only a few refineries: in Orléans, for example, it constituted only 3 percent of the total sugar production. Using the highest-quality raw materials and requiring a special refining process, sucre royal was prohibitively expensive, costing 50 percent more than Orléans' second-best sugar. For some it was worth it, and French refiners boasted that it was the best sugar in the world. It

---

15. ADIL, C142, "Opération d'une raffinerie de sucre," 1755. According to "Mémoire sur les différentes espèces de sucre," the sugar might remain in the grenier for one or two months. ADLA, C731, May, 1715.

16. ADG, 7B1408, purchases of paper by Antoine Fontanilhe, January 8, 1775; ACCM, H110, "Extrait d'une lettre de Constantinople sur les abus que se commettent à Marseille pour l'envelope des graines de sucres," 1749.

was "very pure and marvelously transparent . . . even, fine, dry, brilliant, and easy to break."[17] The French claimed that even the Dutch were incapable of producing such a perfect sugar and had to rely on an inferior imitation. Sucre royal was made from the best clayed sugar or even from good refined sugar.[18] It was treated with egg whites instead of lime, drained with the best white clay, and aired out of doors before being put into the drying room. An imperfect sucre royal was produced in a few refineries and sold as *demi-royal*.

Other sugars were either *ordinaire* or *commun*. They were refined in the standard fashion and designed to satisfy a wider market. "Ordinary" sugar included the deux, trois, and quatre, and "common" the sept, mélis, bâtarde, and the like, but the divisions were scarcely hard and fast. In general, ordinaire was made from clayed sugar, whereas the better commun varieties were produced from muscovado; the worst varieties came from refining the drained residue accumulated during the various stages of the refining process. Sophisticated refiners, such as Jean Othod Dédé of Hamburg, claimed to produce many more types of sugar. He believed it possible to create eleven distinct refined sugars and six different *candis*, or large-crystaled sugars formed by a shorter boil, but there are no records of a practicing French refiner manufacturing such a range of goods. Indeed, the refiners of Bordeaux claimed that Dédé's techniques could not possibly work in France, because of the "dearth of manpower, coal, and all things necessary for production."[19]

If the French lacked some of the secondary items, they were certainly well stocked in the prime ingredient, raw sugar. This, of course, was vital given the large quantities required to produce refined sugar. Traditionally, it was accepted that 225 pounds of muscovado yielded 100 pounds of refined sugar, and the government used this ratio for duty purposes. In reality, it probably took less raw sugar, although it is difficult to find reliable statistics on this subject. Public estimates given by individual refiners have little value, since they usually exaggerated the loss to increase the rebates. Thus, in 1777, when the government investigated, refiners in Rouen claimed that it

17. AN, F12 562, "Etat des manufactures orléanaises" (1790), 86–87; Bondois, "L'industrie sucrière," 327.
18. AN, F12 1501, mémoire by the refiners of Bordeaux, 1732–33. See also ADLA, C731, "Mémoire sur les différentes espèces de sucre," May, 1715.
19. ADLA, C731, "Mémoire sur les différentes espèces de sucre," May, 1715; ADLA, C730, "Théorie du raffinage," September 20, 1780; ADG, C4265, April 3, 1781.

took 300 pounds of muscovado to produce 100 of refined; those in Nantes said 225 pounds ("according to the Letters Patent of April, 1717"); and those in Orléans, from 335 to 400 pounds.[20] Figures from other sources were probably more accurate: in 1790, for example, it was estimated that 16,000,000 pounds of muscovado and 5,000,000 pounds of clayed had yielded 13,000,000 pounds of refined sugar at Orléans, for a ratio of between 160 and 175 to 100.[21] In the same year, Bordeaux refiners supposedly produced 7,000,000 pounds of refined from 10,000,000 pounds of muscovado, for a 140 to 100 ratio.[22]

The lower rates may well have reflected certain improvements in refining techniques late in the Old Regime. In 1777 the new minister of the marine, Sartine, offered a prize of 120,000 livres to any refiner who could improve the standard yield by 40 percent. The Boucherie brothers of Bordeaux promptly claimed to have achieved such a breakthrough, and from April, 1778, to March, 1779, the new method was tested in a refinery at Bercy, just outside of Paris.[23] By cleansing the muscovado before refining it, by using a low flame to boil the sugar, and by substituting eggs for ox blood, the Boucheries achieved impressive results: they obtained 81 pounds of refined sugar from 100 pounds of muscovado (instead of the more typical 41 pounds from that amount), and 88 pounds of refined from 100 pounds of clayed. Jealous refiners in other ports, particularly Orléans, immediately contested the results, and the Boucheries never received the advertised prize. They did, however, get an exclusive privilege for twelve years to use the process in a refinery they were constructing on Martinique, and to export their sugar to the United States. Although this project was a financial failure, the Boucheries were a technical success, and soon other refiners were claiming similar results.[24] It now seemed possible to refine sugar with a minimum of waste.

This, of course, was much to the delight of the refiners, ever appre-

---

20. See the various documents in AN, F12 1502.
21. AN, F12 562, "Etat des manufactures orléanaises," 86–87. The figure would be 160 if 1 pound of muscovado equals 1 pound of clayed; 175 if 1 pound of clayed requires 1.4 pounds of muscovado.
22. Malvezin, *Histoire du commerce de Bordeaux,* III, 112.
23. All material on the Boucheries is from AN, F12 1502; and Tarrade, *Le commerce colonial,* 510–15. Tarrade says that the offers were old and that the Boucheries were in touch with Sartine as early as 1776.
24. For example, Lafite du Port (1779) and Gerard de Fonmartin (1784) claimed to get equal or better results. AN, F12 1502. Also, Marseilles refiners responding to a 1780 questionnaire claimed good results. ACCM H109.

ciative of any advances likely to increase profits. As with every other phase of the sugar business, refining was considered to be enormously lucrative. Citing an investigation from Year II (1793–1794), Georges Lefebvre believed that annual profits from refining in Orléans alone amounted to 2,000,000 livres at the end of the Old Regime.[25] The reality was somewhat less impressive, and like the slave trade or speculation in colonial commodities in the ports, the refining businesses usually offered only modest dividends and frequently led to financial ruin. Even in the last two decades of the Old Regime, when the number of refineries in France reached its peak, complaints over the poor state of business were common. Marseilles refiners wrote that "this business has languished for twenty years," a La Rochelle refiner claimed that all local refiners were suffering from a "sharp decline in sales," and Orléans refiners cried out against unreasonably low profit margins.[26] These complaints had some basis in fact, and a careful analysis of the available material shows that refining could be a most difficult enterprise.

Refiners had to cope with high costs, both in terms of initial capital investment and subsequent operating expense. Depending on the time, place, and size of the establishment, the buildings and utensils needed for refining could cost anywhere from 20,000 to 250,000 livres. The biggest variations came with the value of the buildings, which in turn were in proportion to the size of the refinery, and in Old Regime France, refineries came in many sizes. The earliest refining in France occurred on such a small scale that individual apothecaries or grocers produced sugar in their own homes or shops; even homemakers could clarify their own sugar. By the eighteenth century, refining had become more sophisticated, and although artisanal refining still persisted, especially in smaller towns, there were now large, factorylike establishments where refining was undertaken. The early stages in this transition could be exemplified by the life of one merchant, such as Guillaume Lefebvre of Tours. A *marchand confiseur*, Lefebvre had long wanted to refine his own sugar, just as other *confiseurs* did. In 1755 he finally began to do so in a small house but was so successful that he soon needed to move operations to a much larger

---

25. Georges Lefebvre, *Etudes orléanaises* (Paris, 1962–63), I, 113. See also AN, F12 562, "Etat des manufactures orléanaises," 86–87.
26. ACCM, H109, mémoire, 1786; ADCM, C210, no. 115 (1789); ADL, 11J239, "L'art et le commerce du raffineur," cahier 9.

one; he complained that the old house was simply too small, having no space for the molds, lacking proper ventilation, and suffering from condensation. Further, instead of merely producing a limited quantity of sugar for his own modest trade, he wanted to sell to the *grosses maisons* and the public at large. Unfortunately for Lefebvre, his refinery failed in 1766, in spite of the move and further expansion.[27]

If Lefebvre's refinery grew from small to medium, the one at La Rochelle purchased by Jean Perry in 1783 was large, processing nearly 1,000,000 pounds of raw sugar per year.[28] Known as the Ville d'Anvers, the refinery and accompanying house had belonged to the late Théophile de la Croix, one of the most important merchants in the city and a slave trader of note. The original refinery was nearly a century old and had been much embellished by the addition of other properties and buildings, all of which were carefully described in the 1783 act of sale to Perry.[29] The refining part of the estate included three buildings, one for storing the sugar and the other two for processing it. These latter were quite large, having several rooms devoted to the various operations of the refining process, as the description of the refining buildings reveals.

> On the right, upon entering: a stairway to the counter, a cupboard underneath, two offices where the goods are unloaded, a storeroom, a drying room, the stairway of the refinery, a cellar for the sugar with a drying room, the filling room, a cellar without a filling room but with a drying room; above the cellar, a filling room, another a little above, four mounted boilers, two sunken coolers, a small garden, a courtyard next to the boilers where the coal is put, two storerooms . . . a cellar (96 feet by 30 feet) with three drying rooms with fires, a draining room (96 feet by 30 feet), the room for the sugar loaves and drying rooms (64 feet by 19 feet), a draining room for pieces (49 feet by 19 feet), a draining room, and two rooms of 19 feet by 10 feet.
>
> The refinery on the left, upon entering: a large storeroom, two wine cellars, the dining hall, four vats for clay and one for molds, two vats for lime, one with iron for the scum, four for sugar, a storeroom, a long courtyard, two cellars—one for sugar and one for wood—a room above the cellar for pieces of sugar, two draining rooms (26 feet by 17 feet) above

27. ADIL, C142, "Etablissement d'une raffinerie à Tours"; ADIL, C366, "Tableau de la généralité de Tours" (1766), 617–19.
28. ADCM, sale and description in notary Crassous fils (étude Bonniot), October 21, 1783. For production figures for the refinery see ADCM, C210, no. 115.
29. ADCM, notary Crassous fils, October 21, 1783. For the original sale, see ADCM, notary Hirvoix, December 27, 1704.

the lime and scum vats, two draining rooms (89 feet by 21 feet) behind the boiler, a large garden.

Perry purchased the Ville d'Anvers for only 31,000 livres, an extraordinary bargain for the time.[30] In 1740 the Campions of Valenciennes estimated that it would cost 70,000 to 80,000 livres to establish a large refinery there, and in 1753 the refinery of the bankrupt Henry Denis was purported to be worth better than 100,000 livres. Annual inventories of the Orléans company of Veuve Ravôt and Demadières placed the value of the refinery buildings alone at 165,000 livres (1778), 177,000 livres (1780), and 180,000 livres (1783). There is no simple explanation for the low price paid by Perry, although it should be noted that the Ville d'Anvers had always been a cheap investment. In 1704 it sold for 10,000 livres, and after major improvements it was let go in 1705–1706 for 22,000 livres.[31]

Costs for utensils were much more stable, for, whether small or large, all refineries had a similar selection of special equipment.[32] Essential to the operation were vats for boiling and cooling the sugar as well as for holding the limewater and receiving the scum that formed in the process. Various basins and filters were also necessary, as was a wide range of especially designed or adapted implements. The sale of the Ville d'Anvers included various tools for skimming off the foamy scum, for stirring the liquid sugar, for pouring it into molds, for testing its consistency, and even for breaking up poor-quality loaves. The refining industry gave birth to a whole line of hardware, just as it produced its own vocabulary. These implements cost from 6,000 livres to 40,000 livres, but it was generally accepted that 20,000 livres was a reasonable amount for a respectable refinery.[33]

After making an initial investment of 50,000 to 100,000 livres, a

30. Actually he paid 37,200 livres, of which 6,000 was for the utensils. ADCM, notary Crassous fils, October 21, 1783.
31. ADML, 6E229, failure of Henry Denis, July 19, 1758; ADL, 11J201; ADCM, 2C2865, January 29, 1706; ADCM, notary Hirvoix, December 27, 1704.
32. For descriptions of the contents of refineries, see ADCM, 2C2865, January 29, 1706. See also ADIL, C142, "Etablissement d'une raffinerie à Tours"; ADML, 6E229, March 24, 1753; ADML, 5E259, November 18, 1715; ADG, 7B1408, brouillard, July 23, 1774; Butel, *La croissance commerciale bordelaise*, pièces annexes, 52; ADL, 11J220, November 26, 1760. Molds, of which some refineries had several thousand worth from 2,000 to 20,000 livres, were also included in fixed assets.
33. ADCM, notary Crassous fils, October 21, 1783; ADL, 11JJ201, inventory of Société Veuve Ravôt et Demadières, April, 1778; ADLA, C730, March 4, 1786.

refiner had to face huge operating costs, particularly for raw sugar. At any given moment a large refinery might have 100,000 livres' worth, or even more, of raw sugar awaiting processing. On March 15, 1780, for example, the exceptionally large refinery belonging to Veuve Ravôt and Demadières had no less than 282,000 livres' worth of muscovado and clayed sugar "currently in the river"; this same refinery received shipments of sugar costing up to 75,000 livres at a time. Smaller refineries had the same relative amounts invested in raw sugar. Antoine Fontanilhe of Bordeaux, for example, purchased shipments of muscovado worth 10,000 livres each at a time when the fixed assets of his refinery also amounted to approximately 10,000 livres.[34] Only very high sale prices on refined sugar could have overcome such high costs to yield exorbitant profits, but in spite of feeble attempts to fix prices, government supervision and active competition kept prices moderate. At the end of the Old Regime most refined sugar sold to retailers for about 90 livres per hundredweight, while muscovado cost refiners about 40 livres per hundredweight.[35] Obviously, the refiner had little room to maneuver if he actually used 225 pounds of muscovado to produce 100 pounds of refined. Only by getting the most out of his raw sugar and by selling the by-products (syrups and molasses) could he turn even a reasonable profit. This is exactly what Orléans refiners did in 1790: they used the equivalent of 23,000,000 pounds of muscovado to produce 13,000,000 pounds of refined, and then sold 6,000,000 pounds of molasses. In this case, proceeds from sales of sugar products exceeded costs for raw sugar by 30 percent.

Labor and other costs put further restrictions on profits. The size of the work force varied with the size of the refinery. In Bordeaux some twenty-six refineries provided work for 300 men in 1790; this was about 12 men per refinery.[36] The same year, twenty-four refineries in Orléans employed 650 men, or 27 men each. The difference was due to the size of the operation: Bordeaux handled 10,000,000 pounds of raw sugar, Orléans 21,000,000. Output per worker was almost the same, averaging some 32,000 pounds in Orléans and 33,000 in Bordeaux. This was quite typical for late eighteenth-century refineries,

34. ADL, 11J214 and 11J201; ADG, 7B1408, brouillard, July 23, 1774, and September 5, 1774.
35. AN, F12 562, "Etat des manufactures orléanaises," 86–87.
36. Malvezin, *Histoire du commerce de Bordeaux*, III, 112.

and similar figures were reported elsewhere. In 1789, for example, four La Rochelle refineries treated an estimated 2,000,000, 1,000,000, 200,000, and 150,000 pounds of raw sugar; 50, 35, 4, and 6 workers, respectively, were employed in each.[37] In all, there were probably 1,500 to 2,000 men working full-time in French sugar refineries at the end of the Old Regime. Their wages were low, although probably somewhat higher than contemporary averages. In 1785 Veuve Ravôt and Demadière's 26 workers received a total of 4,739 livres, or an average of only 182 livres each.[38] Salaries varied from 100 livres for each of the 7 boys to 320 livres for the foreman, with most being between 170 and 240 livres. On top of these low wages, Ravôt and Demadières paid for the workers' food; this was worth almost twice as much as their salaries. Combining food and wages, the total was 13,839 livres, or 532 livres apiece. A particularly skilled worker could occasionally earn even more, as did M. Maignan, the *maître de cuite* in a small Bordeaux refinery; he earned 700 livres yearly plus 3 percent of the refinery's profits.[39] Skilled occasional labor was also expensive, and bills submitted by plumbers, plasterers, carpenters, coopers, and masons could be high.

Other costs included coal, paper, limewater, ox blood, white straining cloths, and the like, but with the exception of coal they were generally modest. The twenty-four Orléans refineries consumed 23,000,000 pounds of coal in 1790 while processing 21,000,000 pounds of raw sugar; at 36 livres per 1,000 pounds, coal cost nearly 800,000 livres, more than twice as much as labor.[40] In most refineries paper was at most a few thousand livres per year, and limewater amounted to less than 500 livres annually. Most other expenses were negligible.

Late in the Old Regime, total refining costs were in the neighborhood of 6 livres per hundredweight of muscovado treated. Once more, the clearest data come from Orléans, where in 1790 some

37. AN, F12 562, "Etat des manufactures orléanaises," 86–87; ADCM, C210, nos. 115, 117–19.
38. ADL, 11JJ22, March 25, 1785. See also the wages paid by Antoine Fontanilhe at Bordeaux. ADG, 7B1408, brouillard.
39. ADG, 7B1409, January 31, 1784. Maignan claimed that he accepted this arrangement because he was worth 1,000 to 1,200 livres per year.
40. AN, F12 562, "Etat des manufactures orléanaises," 86–87; Lefebvre, *Etudes orléanaises*, I, 113 n. 79.

22,000,000 pounds of raw sugar were refined.⁴¹ Coal cost 800,000 livres, labor an estimated 300,000, paper 100,000, and miscellaneous goods at least 100,000, for a total of 1,300,000 livres, or 5.9 livres per hundredweight. This was in line with at least some contemporary estimates. In 1780, as part of the Boucherie tests, the government made inquiries into the refining business, asking among other things about the costs of refining. Refiners in Marseilles responded that such costs were from 3.5 to 4.5 livres per hundredweight of muscovado, but that in the "current difficult times"—*i.e.*, during the American Revolution—they might be 1 livre higher. Such opinions were not universal, and refiners in La Rochelle estimated total costs at 12 to 12.5 livres per hundredweight.⁴² Why was there such a difference? There are two possible answers: perhaps La Rochelle refiners meant 12 livres per hundredweight of refined sugar and not muscovado, or perhaps they included the handling charges on the raw sugar. In any event, if left unqualified, the figures cannot be accepted.

With operating costs of 6 livres per hundredweight added to the price of raw sugar and with the sale price of refined sugar limited by intense competition, the refiners were in a considerable bind. Many went bankrupt. Refiners in smaller centers suffered from a shortage of working capital and frequently could not overcome their dependence upon bankers and merchants from Paris or the larger ports. Thus, when Henry Denis of Saumur failed in 1753, he had debts of 600,000 livres, of which nearly half was due to Parisians and a quarter to Nantais.⁴³ In larger centers, refiners also suffered financial difficulties, and failures were numerous. At one time or another, nine of thirteen Nantes refineries went under, along with seven of fourteen in Marseilles, and seven of twenty-two in Bordeaux.⁴⁴ Some refiners barely remained solvent. From 1775 to 1784 the de Baussay refinery

---

41. AN, F12 562, "Etat des manufactures orléanaises," 86–87.
42. ACCLR, no. 4662, carton 14, March 3, 1780.
43. ADML, 6E229, July 19, 1758.
44. On Nantes see mémoire by Intendant des Gallois de la Tour, 1733, quoted in Henri Sée, "L'industrie et le commerce de la Bretagne dans la première moitié du XVIIIᵉ siècle," *Annales de Bretagne*, XXXV (1922), 204. See ADLA, E XVI/29, May 6, 1766, on the failure of a small Nantes refinery. On Marseilles see Joseph Billioud and Gaston Rambert, "Une industrie marseillaise: Le raffinage de sucre," *Marseille, revue municipale*, 3ᵉ série, no. 9 (1950), 17–18; and ADDM, H109, mémoire (by Marseilles refiners ?), 1786. On Bordeaux see ADG, C1642, mémoire by the Farmers General, 1742 (?). Apparently most of those that failed in Bordeaux were small.

in La Rochelle had receipts of 1,375,688 livres and expenses of 1,420,101 livres (including 1,174,245 livres for raw sugar), for an average annual loss of nearly 5,000 livres on an initial investment of 100,000 livres. Other—and perhaps most—refiners did better. This may have been especially true for the large refiners, such as in Bordeaux, where refiners were also rich armateurs and speculators in colonial commodities, and such as in Orléans, where the largest French refineries were located. Counting all operating expenses, in 1790 the twenty-four Orléans refineries probably paid out 11,300,000 livres but took in 12,900,000 livres, an increase of 14 percent.[45] Unfortunately, depreciation on what may have been a tremendous capital investment cannot be considered, although it may have been small.

45. ADCM, 4J2915, compte générale, April 28, 1784; AN, F12 562, "Etat des manufactures orléanaises."

8

The Local Refining Industries

> Sugar refineries established in this kingdom are useful to the state: they pay high taxes ... and they support a large population.
> —Anonymous mémoire

Like the import and reexport trades in sugar, the French refining business was organized into a series of local businesses frequently conflicting with one another. The problem was a limited market for French refined sugar. Throughout the Old Regime, French refiners sold almost exclusively to rich French purchasers, usually in Paris, with exports being almost unknown. Refiners thought in terms of securing local monopolies, hindering rivals in other towns, and dominating the lucrative Paris market; they rarely tried to produce for export. The result was paradoxical: in spite of possessing the greatest cane-producing colonies in the world, the French had a refining industry of secondary international importance.

The British, Dutch, and Germans produced far more refined sugar than the French, even if they had smaller or even no colonies of their own to supply them with raw sugar. The British refining industry was supported by the structure of British colonial trade. This was based on an explicit compromise between colonial planters and metropolitan merchants. In return for producing only muscovado and for not dealing with foreigners, British West Indian planters were given a monopoly over the domestic British sugar market and a guaranteed price for their product. For their part, the British port merchants received a monopoly over trade with the colonies. Also, the British received strong encouragement to refine sugar: since the British West Indies were prohibited from producing clayed sugar and since muscovado was inappropriate for immediate consumption, almost all the sugar arriving in British ports had to be refined. This created a huge refining industry, and in the late 1780s, for example, there were an estimated 180 refineries in London alone.

Sugar refining in Holland and Germany was encouraged by different considerations. Since neither country had major sugar-producing colonies, both had to rely on foreigners for sugar. But instead of purchasing refined sugar from France, they purchased only raw sugar, whether muscovado or clayed, which they proceeded to refine and sell throughout northern and eastern Europe. Cheaper labor, more reasonable taxes, and generally more efficient operations enabled the Dutch and Germans to sell refined sugar at a lower price than the French. Thus, instead of losing money by purchasing sugar abroad, they made money by creating a large processing industry. One observer claimed that Hamburg alone boasted more than 200 refineries in 1737; Amsterdam had "more than 60" in 1722 and 110 in 1785.[1]

Faced with competition on this scale and satisfied with profiting from the reexport trade, the French never assumed a leading role in European refining. They did, however, construct a respectable industry that included more than a hundred refineries in the 1780s and that produced more than 25,000,000 pounds of refined sugar annually at the end of the Old Regime. This was a far cry from the early days of French sugar refining, when the trades of apothecary, grocer (*épicier*, or spice merchant), and refiner were virtually indistinguishable. In the mid-sixteenth century there were refiners if not refineries working in Rouen, Marseilles, and Bordeaux, although on a small scale. It was not until Colbert's regime that a true refining industry was established in France, and in the middle of the seventeenth century the major refining centers of Orléans, Bordeaux, and Marseilles began production in earnest. In the eighteenth century there was considerable growth, although in a most erratic fashion. Most refineries were still small and short-lived, and only a few major ones seemed to outlive their founders. During the course of the Old Regime, refineries existed in more than thirty towns in France, with at least half a dozen towns boasting a refinery throughout the eighteenth century.

Two major factors influenced the location of refineries: the availability of raw sugar and the proximity of a market for refined sugar. A map of the French refining business displays this clearly (see Map 2). Almost all the refineries—and certainly all the major ones—were either on the coast or on large rivers with direct access to major ports.

1. Hamburg: Butel, *La croissance commerciale bordelaise*, 252 n. 105. This figure should be taken with a grain of salt, as another estimate also cited by Butel said there were 120 refineries in Hamburg in 1742. But in 1788 there were again supposedly 200 refineries, at least according to M. Gournay, *Almanach générale du commerce* (Paris, 1788), 252. Amsterdam: Jean Pierre Ricard, *Le négoce d'Amsterdam* (Amsterdam, 1722), 10; ADLA, C730, letter from Amsterdam, December 26, 1785.

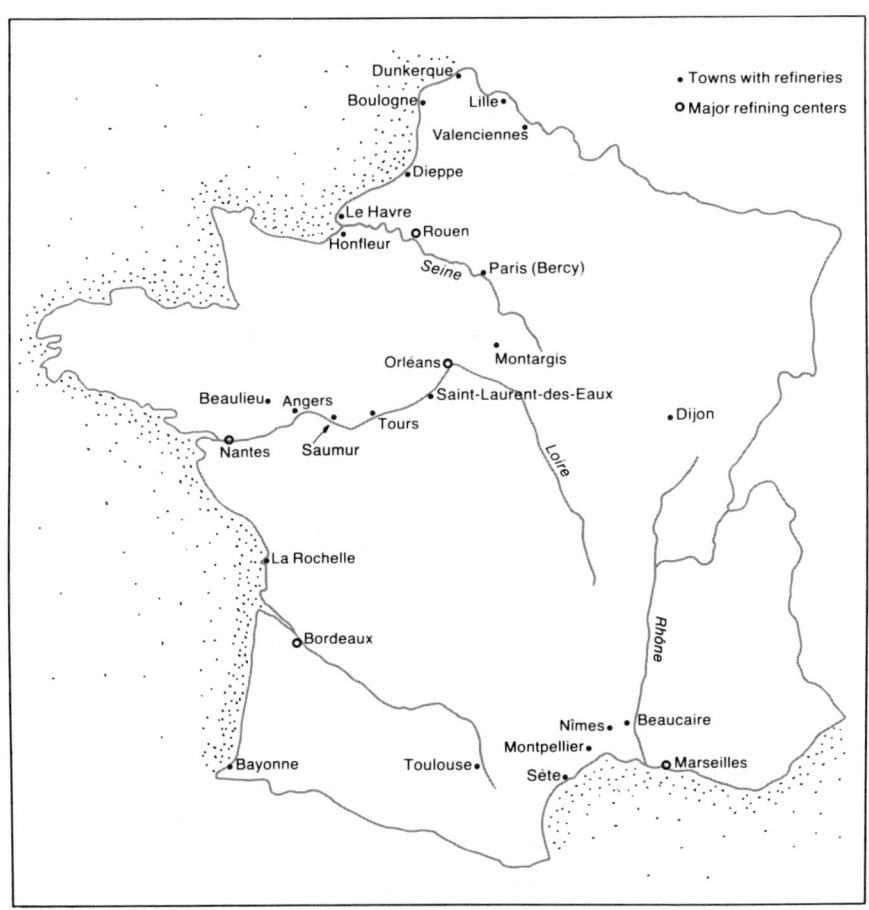

Map 2: The French Refining Industry in the Seventeenth and Eighteenth Centuries

Similarly, most of the refineries were either in large towns or had easy access to Paris or other urban centers. Just as the ports were intermediaries between the Antilles and foreign buyers, so the refineries served to link the ports to inland cities. There were three main groups of refineries: those supplying Paris with sugar, those supplying the north, and those supplying the south. Although the divisions were scarcely hard and fast—Paris was such a large market that it tended to absorb sugar from all available sources—they did exist in a general way, and it makes sense to consider the refining centers according to their chief markets.

There were two major groups of refineries serving Paris, those along the Loire River and those along the Seine. The Loire boasted most of France's sugar refineries in the eighteenth century and was the true center of the industry. From Nantes to Orléans, each major town had one or several refineries. All got their raw sugar from Nantes, and all sold most of the finished product to Paris. Most of the refineries along the Loire Valley were in towns on the river itself, such as Nantes, Angers, Saumur, Tours, and Orléans, but a few were in smaller towns a few miles from the river, such as Beaulieu (Anjou), Saint-Laurent-des-Eaux, and Montargis (Orléanais).[2] In an era when water travel was generally more secure and rapid than overland, the Loire formed a natural highway connecting the major sugar port of Nantes to the capital, since it was relatively easy to go from the Loire basin to Paris. Paris received the majority of its sugar in this way.

In Brittany near the mouth of the Loire was Nantes, for most of the century the leading French port for sugar imports. As we have seen, Nantes reexported a significantly lower percentage of its sugar arrivals than either Bordeaux or Marseilles. Most of the sugar remaining in France was sent up the Loire for further treatment, but a fair amount was refined in Nantes and shipped to Paris. Particularly in the late seventeenth century there was a thriving refining industry at Nantes, which got its start during Colbert's regime. In the 1660s and 1670s five refineries were established in the Nantes suburbs, and another five were built in the 1680s and 1690s.[3] They were helped by the 1681

2. ADLA, C142, October 1, 1776; AN, F12 562, "Etat des manufactures orléanaises" (1790), 76. Beaulieu was near the Breton frontier and was notorious for using smuggled sugar.
3. Most information on Nantes sugar refineries is from Valladier, "Histoire de la raffinerie," I, 1–49. See also AN, Col F3 83, "Mémoire sur le commerce des isles," October 29, 1683, which says there were three refineries operating in Nantes in 1683.

prohibition on reexports of muscovado; this meant that further processing was necessary to sell the sugar. In the eighteenth century, however, high duties placed on Nantes refined sugar entering the Five Great Farms discouraged local refiners and led to a sharp decline in refining activity. On March 2, 1700, a duty of 14 livres per hundredweight was applied to sugar refined in Nantes that entered the main French customs union. Although this was lowered a bit to 13.5 livres in the Letters Patent of April, 1717, it was still too high to allow Nantes refineries to compete with those further up the Loire. Nantes refineries never recovered from these disadvantages or from the last wars of Louis XIV's reign, and between 1717 and 1726, for example, an average of only 2,600 pounds of refined sugar was shipped each year from Nantes to the rest of France, as opposed to more than 3,000,000 pounds of raw sugar. By the 1730s the industry was moribund, and the intendant of Brittany wrote that only four of thirteen refineries remained in business.[4]

For the rest of the eighteenth century, Nantes refiners and would-be refiners never ceased in their efforts to gain some privileges that would enable their industry to revive. Concessions were few, however, in part because of the stiff opposition put up by the refiners at Orléans. As the Nantais saw it, "The Orléans refiners, powerfully protected, have always come to oppose us and have stopped Nantes refiners from getting the least decrease in taxes."[5] Ideally, the Nantais wanted free access to the French market, but barring that, they wanted the right to ship refined sugar duty free across France for sale in Alsace, Lorraine, and other border provinces. The only real concession Nantes got was inclusion in the arrêt of May 25, 1786, subsidizing the exportation of sugar refined in French ports; this came in spite of the excluded Orléanais.[6] How much this arrêt helped the Nantes industry is not clear, because of inadequate documentation, but it may have had a positive influence. In any event some eleven refineries were operating in Nantes at the end of the Old Regime, although most were undoubtedly small.

Some two hundred miles up the Loire River and safely within the

---

4. ADLA, C855, Bureau d'Ingrandes, comptes; BN, msfr 8153, mémoire by Intendant Gallois de la Tour, 1733.
5. ADLA, C733, "Observations des raffineurs de Nantes," 1786.
6. ADSM, C177, May 25, 1786. For the reaction, see ADLA, C733, "Mémoire des raffineurs d'Orléans," September, 1786.

boundaries of the Five Great Farms was the refining capital of eighteenth-century France, Orléans. In 1653 Georges Vandeberque, a recently arrived Dutch immigrant, established the town's first refinery, which would last until the French Revolution.[7] Although two more refineries were established during Colbert's regime, the real boom did not occur until the eighteenth century, when Orléans' geographic and fiscal position proved incomparable. Using readily available supplies of raw sugar from Nantes—most of it muscovado, which was imported into France proper upon payment of only 2.5 livres per hundredweight—Orléans refineries multiplied rapidly, and by 1758 there were at least ten of them. Growth continued until the very end of the Old Regime: There were twenty-two in 1785, twenty-five in 1788, and twenty-seven in 1789.[8] Although some were modest, most were of respectable size, and at least seven handled more than 1,000,000 pounds of raw sugar in a year. Together, the refineries of Orléans were producing an estimated 13,000,000 pounds of refined sugar annually in the 1780s; this was the result of processing some 16,000,000 pounds of muscovado and 5,000,000 pounds of clayed per year.

The Orléans refining industry was the largest, best organized, and most powerful in France. It claimed to produce half of all the sugar refined in the kingdom, a figure probably not grossly exaggerated. Refiners in the town formed a tightly knit group that was clearly on the top of the local merchant community; according to Georges Lefebvre, every merchant's goal was to be a refiner. The influence of the refiners extended beyond the city gates; many established subsidiaries at Nantes and even maintained ships there to procure raw sugar directly from Saint Domingue.[9] The industry was also blessed with important protectors at court, and one refiner claimed in 1734

---

7. Monique Prudhomme, "Une famille de marchands orléanais au début du XVIIIe siècle: Les Sarrebourse" (Mémoire de maîtrise, Université de Tours, 1970), 94. Valladier, "Histoire de le raffinerie," I, 11, incorrectly says Michel Vandeberque. See also Lefebvre, Etudes orléanaises, I, 111.
8. AN, F12 1501, Mémoire from Orléans refiners, 1758; Lefebvre, Etudes orléanaises, I, 111; Calendrier historique de l'Orléanais (Orleans, 1789), 96–97. As time passed, these figures became inflated in popular memory. See, for example, M. Sévin-Mareau, Mémoire sur les causes de la décadence de l'industrie manufacturière et commerciale à Orléans (Orleans, 1828), 5–12, which speaks of thirty-two refineries at Orléans before the Revolution. For production figures, see AN, F12 562, "Etat des manufactures orléanaises," 76; and AN, F12 1502, "Etat général des rafineries de la ville d'Orléans."
9. AN, F12 1639A, mémoire by Orléans refiners, 1786; Lefebvre, Etudes orléanaises, I, 113. See also Chapter 9 below.

that the Duc D'Orléans and the Comte d'Argenson were defending the cause of the Orléanais.[10] Such patrons helped protect the industry from competition from Nantes refineries. But even the Orléanais were not without their complaints, and they particularly disliked their reliance on only one market, Paris. As early as 1711, Orléans refiners requested permission to ship their finished goods across France duty free for sale in Alsace, Franche-Comté, and Lyon. This request was denied by the Conseil de Commerce "because, being in the center of the kingdom, they not only have the city of Paris, which consumes great quantities of their sugar, but also all the neighboring provinces, where they easily sell their sugar by means of rivers."[11] Similarly, when the government decided in 1786 to subsidize exports of refined sugar, the Orleanais were upset that only refiners in the ports were eligible to receive the premiums.[12] In spite of their protests, they could not convince the government to grant them a similar privilege.

Besides Orléans, there were other towns along the Loire with refineries. Angers, Saumur, and Tours each had a refining industry at some time in the eighteenth century. Downstream from Orléans, these towns were still in the Five Great Farms, but their greater distance from Paris and an apparent lack of capital seemed to doom them to secondary status. Angers, the first major town on the Loire inside the borders of the Five Great Farms, had the most success with sugar refining. The industry began there in 1658, when the Dutch immigrant Gaspard van Bredenbec arrived to found the town's first refinery; when he died in 1682, his widow and two sons kept the refinery operating.[13] In the course of the eighteenth century, three other refineries were established, one in 1705, one shortly after, and the third in 1755, but none of these remained in business until the Revolution. One belonged to the Beguyer family, a member of which moved to Nantes later in the century and participated in the slave trade. The

10. ADLA, C733, letter from M. Boillève to M. Noyau, April 2, 1734.
11. AN, F12 55, September 14, 1711. See also ADL, 11J239, "L'art et le commerce du raffineur," cahier 9, which says that Paris took three-quarters of Orléans' refined sugar, with the rest going to neighboring provinces.
12. ADLA, C733, mémoire by refiners of Orléans, September, 1786. See also AN, F12 1639A, mémoire by Orléans refiners (1786?).
13. François Lebrun (ed.), *Histoire d'Angers* (Paris, 1975), 97; Lebrun, *Les hommes et la mort en Anjou aux XVII*e *et XVIII*e *siècles* (Paris, 1971), 74. Michel, *Histoire du commerce et de la navigation à Bordeaux*, II, 304, says the refinery was founded in 1673.

Saumur refining business was more modest. It, too, began in the seventeenth century, when yet another Dutch immigrant, René Tinnebacq, established a refinery. Although Tinnebacq left in 1685, when the Edict of Nantes was revoked, someone else must have taken his place, because the intendant of the Orléanais reported in 1698 that there was a refinery functioning in Saumur.[14] Refining definitely came to an end in the town in 1753, however, when Henry Denis, *marchand rafineur et commissaire des vins*, went bankrupt.[15] Tours' refining industry was even more modest, consisting of one refinery that opened in 1755 and closed in 1766. According to Paul Bondois, this was a small refinery that specialized in producing bonbons.[16]

The second group of refineries serving Paris was located on or near the Seine and included Rouen, Dieppe, Le Havre, and Paris itself. The French refining industry may well have begun in Rouen in 1548, when "Pierre Dubosc, apothecary, signed a contract with Barthazar Sanchez, a Spanish subject, to learn from the latter in two years how to refine sugar and make jams." It is not known whether Dubosc actually built a refinery, but one was definitely constructed in Rouen in 1613 by Jérémie Valens, after another Spaniard, Juan de Palma-Castillo, had tried without success to do so in 1572.[17] The new industry did fairly well in the early seventeenth century, but then special taxes on sugar entering Rouen combined with competition from Loire Valley refiners to throw it into a dismal state from which it never fully recovered.[18] There were but four refineries in the city in 1732 and 1771, and five or six in 1788. This failure of the Rouen refiners to capitalize on their excellent geographic location was a

14. Michel, *Histoire du commerce et de la navigation à Bordeaux*, II, 304; ADLA, C733, "Quand a-t-on commencé à raffiner le sucre en France?" (n.d.); BN, msfr 21773, fol. 75. Two were operating in 1714. ADLA, C730, "Consommation des sucres bruts par an," 1714.
15. ADML, 6E229, July 19, 1758 (referring to the bankruptcy of March 24, 1753). ADIL, C336, "Tableau de la Généralité de Tours," 1766, pp. 617–19, says that the sole Saumur refinery failed "eight to ten" years before.
16. Paul M. Bondois, "Les centres sucriers français au XVIIIe siècle," *Revue d'histoire économique et sociale*, XIX (1931), 76. On Tours see ADIL, C142, "Etablissement d'une raffinerie à Tours," September 10, 1755; and AN, Col F3 83, "Mémoire sur le commerce des isles," October 29, 1683.
17. Laruelle, *Les apothicaires rouennais*, 5; Valladier, "Histoire de la raffinerie," I, 11; AMR, A19, June 30, 1572.
18. Paul Bondois, "Les raffineries de sucre à Rouen sous l'ancien regime" (Typescript in Bibliothèque Municipale de Rouen, 1922), 1–5. For the debate on the special tax at Rouen, see ADLA, C733; and Pierre Dardel, *Commerce et industrie à Rouen et au Havre au XVIIIe siècle* (Paris, 1946), 126–27.

source of considerable distress in the town, and numerous efforts were made to encourage the industry. Most notable were the attempts to abolish the special tax on raw sugar entering Rouen, but these were generally unsuccessful.

Besides Rouen, two other towns in Normandy had refineries producing sugar for the Paris market—Dieppe and Le Havre. Both treated raw sugar arriving directly from the French West Indies, and both shipped the finished product up the Seine to the capital. Dieppe was a refining center of modest size in the late seventeenth century, but the industry declined and ultimately disappeared in the face of competition from the Loire Valley.[19] In 1683 an estimated 500,000 pounds of raw sugar were treated in Dieppe, making it the tenth-largest refining operation in France.[20] The Le Havre refining industry began quite late, apparently after the demise of Dieppe's. In the 1770s two projects for establishing refineries in Le Havre were submitted to the government; both were in search of special privileges, such as tax exemptions on the land, duty-free export rights, and monopoly concessions. The first project was by a group of businessmen who wanted to build in the suburb of Ingouville; the second was by Sieur Duval, who planned to build in Harfleur.[21] The government rejected both requests for special privileges, and the Ingouville group abandoned its idea. Duval persisted and was soon producing a "nice, white" sugar. Finally, two more small refineries were established in Le Havre in the 1780s, one by Becquerel, Isabelle and Company, the other by William Gustave Eichoff, a German Jew. Eichoff was reputed to make "a very nice, white" sugar of "excellent quality."[22]

Shipping the sugar from the lower Seine refineries to Paris was a relatively simple affair made complex only by the number of tolls levied. Pierre Dardel counted a dozen tolls between Rouen and Paris, but he apparently included only major ones. Between Paris and the border of Normandy alone, Gustave Guilmoto found tolls at Sèvres, Neuilly, Saint Denis, Epinay, Argenteuil, Bezons, Le Pecq, Maisons-

19. Savary des Bruslons, *Dictionnaire universel de commerce*, IV, 828; Michel, *Histoire du commerce et de la navigation à Bordeaux*, II, 305; Bondois, "Les centres sucriers français," 39–40. The latest reference I have found for Dieppe refineries is 1733: BN, msfr 21773, arrêt of November 17, 1733, fol. 273–74.
20. AN, Col F3 83, "Mémoire sur le commerce des isles," October 29, 1683.
21. AN, F12 1501, mémoire, June 27, 1775; AN, F12 1502, (1777); Dardel, *Commerce et industrie à Rouen*, 164. Honfleur may also have had refineries. See ADG, C4269, mémoire, August 22, 1730.
22. Gournay, *Almanach générale*, 261.

sur-Seine, Sartrouville, Conflans-Sainte Honorine, Andrézy, Poissy, Triel, Meulan, Lislebelle, Mézy, Mantes, and La Roche-Guyon, with some places having as many as five tolls.[23] Although some were quite venerable institutions—the Abbey of Saint Denis had rights from Carolingian or even Merovingian times—others were of fairly recent origin. Together, these tolls were expensive and represented a considerable hindrance to trade; they may have put the Seine River sugar trade at a disadvantage compared with that of the Loire River. There were far fewer tolls along the Loire, and even merchants at Nantes— who tended to be chronic complainers—admitted that Orléans and Rouen refined sugar cost about the same in Paris.[24]

Paris itself had few refineries of any significance in the Old Regime. It appears that there were no refineries at all until the eighteenth century; the usual sources do not list any in the seventeenth century. In 1719 Sieur Delbeuf and Company asked for permission to establish a refinery in the suburb of Bezons. Although permission was granted, Delbeuf's request for a twenty-year exclusive privilege to refine sugar in the Paris area was denied, and it is not clear if he proceeded to build.[25] In 1758 a refinery was finally established in Bercy, just upstream from the Bastille, and this refinery was apparently the only large one operating in the capital until the Revolution.[26] It was there that the new refining process of the Boucherie brothers was tested late in the Old Regime.[27] If Bercy was the only major refinery in Paris, there may have been some smaller ones. Several *raffineurs de sucre* were active in Paris in the 1770s and 1780s, but whether they merely worked at Bercy or produced small quantities of *candi* on their own or actually owned real refineries is unknown.[28]

There was one other refining center serving the Paris market: La Rochelle. Although not conveniently located to supply Paris, La Rochelle refiners sold fair amounts there and managed to create a

23. Dardel, *Navires et marchandises*, 472; Gustave Guilmoto, *Etude sur les droits de navigation de la Seine de Paris à la Roche-Guyon du XIe au XVIIIe siècles* (Paris, 1889).
24. On tolls and taxes on the Loire, see dossier of calculations, in ADLA, C733. If the Nantais admitted parity, it is more than likely that Loire River sugar was much cheaper.
25. AN, F12 1501.
26. AN, F12 1501, mémoires and letters from refiners of Orléans, 1758; Gournay, *Almanach générale*, 79.
27. See the massive procès-verbal in AN, F12 1502. See also chapter 7.
28. ADS, catalog of names. ADS, C161, June 22, 1738, mentions Sieurs Cottart and Deschamps as "entrepreneurs d'une rafinerie de sucre à Paris."

thriving industry. As early as 1683, La Rochelle had the second-largest refining industry in France, with four refineries using 2,400,000 pounds of raw sugar per year.[29] In spite of various setbacks, the industry grew until there were sixteen refineries in operation in 1789; these processed some 8,000,000 pounds of raw sugar to produce 3,600,000 pounds of refined.[30] This was a remarkable achievement given the ever-declining volume of La Rochelle's colonial trade, competition in local markets from sugar introduced fraudulently from Nantes, and competition in the Paris market from Orléans. Duty-free transit rights certainly helped: after 1706, La Rochelle sugar refined from French West Indian raw sugar could cross France without paying taxes and be sold in the eastern border provinces.[31] This eastern market, along with modest but respectable markets in Poitiers, Niort, and other nearby towns, provided La Rochelle refiners with ample scope for their wares.

Refineries in the rest of France felt the pull of Paris far less than those in La Rochelle and along the Seine or Loire. Those in the north of France had substantial local markets to supply with refined sugar and were in any event all but prohibited by high tariff walls from selling to the capital. The northern provinces were not in the Five Great Farms, and their sugar was far too expensive in Paris to compete with Loire or Seine river sugar. The oldest refinery in the north was built in 1661 in Dunkerque, and throughout the Old Regime there were always one or two refineries operating there. Although they were fairly large in the late seventeenth century, they processed only small amounts of sugar in the eighteenth. One reason for this was the peculiar duty structure of Dunkerque. A free port, Dunkerque could not trade with the rest of France without paying high duties. Although the refiners were prepared to sacrifice Dunkerque's free-port status in order to gain access to the French market, the merchant community in general preferred a small refining industry to the loss of the privilege.[32] The refiners were therefore restricted to the market in French Flanders and bordering areas.

29. AN, Col F3 83, "Mémoire sur le commerce des isles," October 29, 1683.
30. ACCLR, no. 4672, carton 14, "Etat des raffineries," 1789. In the same year, one refiner complained that there were only four refineries operating in La Rochelle. ADCM, C210, no. 115.
31. AN, F12 55, September 14, 1711; Valladier, "Histoire de la raffinerie," I, 26.
32. For example, see ACCDk, deliberations of January 21, February 24, March 28, May 25, and December 29, 1718.

Competition from Lille also hurt Dunkerque. In the eighteenth century, Lille was the major refining center in the north of France, with no fewer than nine refineries operating in 1789.[33] As in Dunkerque, refiners in Lille were virtually prohibited from selling beyond the local area, and they had to compete with cheaper foreign sugar, which seemed to enter without too much difficulty. Other refineries in the north were in Valenciennes and Boulogne, but they were quite small.[34] From 1743 to 1759 a maximum of only 66,000 pounds of sugar entered Valenciennes in one year. The town was simply too poor to support a refining industry: according to one eighteenth-century observer, two-thirds of its seven thousand residents were poverty-stricken, while three-quarters of the remainder were "very mediocre." When a proposal to open a second refinery in Valenciennes was made in 1778, it was hotly debated, with opponents sharply contesting the need for it.

Major refiners in the south of France were less limited to fragile local markets. Bordeaux and Marseilles, in particular, shipped their sugar over large distances. The Bordeaux refining industry was second only to Orléans in the second half of the eighteenth century. Refining had begun in earnest there in Colbert's time, although some grocers or apothecaries may well have refined limited quantities in the sixteenth century. By 1683 there were three active refineries in Bordeaux, handling some 2,000,000 pounds of raw sugar per year.[35] The number of refineries grew rapidly in the eighteenth century: by 1777 there were twenty-six, and there were twenty-three in 1780 and twenty-six again in 1790. In 1790 the refineries produced some 7,000,000 pounds of refined sugar from 10,000,000 pounds of muscovado. Bordeaux refiners had several markets for their sugar, the most significant of which were in the south of France. Here they had

33. Maurice Braure, *Lille et la Flandre Wallonne au XVIIIe siècle* (Lille, 1932), 427. This was probably the source for the figure used by Louis Trénard, "L'alimentation en Flandre français au XVIIIe siècle," *93e congrès des sociétés savantes, Tours, 1968: Section histoire moderne et contemporaine* (Paris, 1971), I, 106. See also Gournay, *Almanach générale*, 304, which says there were eight refineries in 1788.

34. The only reference to refineries in Boulogne is in Gournay, *Almanach générale*, 104, which says there were two in 1788. On Valenciennes, see ADN, C8296, and ADN, C9244, December 5, 1779.

35. Paul Bondois, "Anciennes raffineries bordelaises," *Revue historique de Bordeaux*, XXXI (1938), 81–82. On the growth of Bordeaux's refining industry, see AN, Col F3 83, "Mémoire sur le commerce des isles," October 29, 1683; Butel, *La croissance commerciale bordelaise*, 961; ADG, C4258, March 4, 1780; and Malvezin, *Histoire du commerce de Bordeaux*, III, 113.

virtually no competition: the only other port in the south of France having a large trade with the Antilles was Marseilles, but high duties prevented local refiners from selling much sugar in France. Bordeaux took advantage of Marseilles' handicap and dominated the sugar market in the Midi. Most domestic sales were at the Beaucaire Fair, where cheaper Bordeaux sugar outsold Marseilles sugar in spite of numerous complaints by producers from the latter.[36] According to Paul Butel, Bordeaux refiners sold 4,000 quintaux of sugar at Beaucaire in 1739, compared with 3,000 quintaux in Bordeaux itself, 2,000 in Toulouse, 1,000 in towns near Bordeaux, and 1,000 in Languedoc.[37]

Besides selling their product domestically, Bordeaux refiners also shipped it outside France, particularly to the east and southeast. Such sales were made feasible by the arrêt of August 11, 1699, which exempted Bordeaux refined sugar from most taxes when it was crossing the kingdom for sale abroad.[38] In particular, the Bordelais could sell their sugar in Alsace and Franche-Comté and ship it across France duty free to Italy. Needless to say, the Farmers General attached many conditions to this right: shipments had to follow a prescribed route; they were subject to inspection at any time; and large deposits had to be paid.[39] In spite of such hindrances, the export trade was important to Bordeaux refiners, and they apparently made significant shipments not only to Alsace and Franche-Comté but also to Savoy, Piedmont, and Geneva.[40]

If Bordeaux generally had little competition in the south of France, it had virtually none in the southwest. The only other towns with refineries at any time in the Old Regime were Toulouse and Bayonne, but they had only small establishments. Toulouse had one refinery in the late seventeenth century, and it apparently ceased operations early. Bayonne had at least one refinery; it was founded in 1763 by Sieur LaSalle, who claimed in 1784 that it was a success. "Every month," he wrote, "taxes levied on sugar produced in the refinery amount to 5,000 livres for His Majesty. Besides this considerable

36. For example, see AN, F12 1501, dossier from 1732–33; ADG, C1642, January 18, 1740.
37. Butel, *La croissance commerciale bordelaise*, 422–23.
38. Malvezin, *Histoire du commerce de Bordeaux*, III, 109; Valladier, "Histoire de la raffinerie," I, 33; AN, F12 55, September 14, 1711.
39. For more on the conditions, see ADG, C4269, mémoire (1732?).
40. Further problems were posed by Bordeaux merchants who fraudulently introduced cheap foreign refined sugar into France. See ADG, C1642, June 10 and October 4, 1742.

interest ... [the refinery] is an important utility for the state, for commerce, and for the public."[41] In spite of LaSalle's enthusiasm, the operation was small. Virtually all of its refined sugar went to Spain and did not directly compete with Bordeaux.

The rest of the refineries in the south were in Provence or Languedoc, with Marseilles having the lion's share. Although a sugar trade had been present in Marseilles since the late Middle Ages, a refinery was not established there until 1574; it lasted only six months, with its total production consisting of 952 loaves.[42] Nearly a century passed before a large refinery was built in Marseilles; this was done with the encouragement of Colbert and was, after some early changes, the property of Gaspard Maurelet.[43] Maurelet refined sugar without much competition in Marseilles, because of a special privilege his refinery had, namely the right to introduce 100,000 pounds of refined sugar per year into France at a duty rate of 7 livres per hundredweight instead of the normal 15 livres or even 22.5 livres. When Maurelet sold his refinery in 1713, the new owners received the privilege, but they soon had to face local competition. In the 1720s five or six new refineries were established in Marseilles, and although they were small, they managed in 1740 to persuade the government into granting them the same duty rates as the original refinery. Still, the 7 livres per hundredweight was about double what refiners in other ports were paying. Bordeaux refined sugar, for example, paid nothing on entering France, but raw sugar had to pay 2.5 livres per hundredweight upon entering the port. Although there was no such tax on raw sugar in Marseilles, the tax was still much less than the Marseillais ended up paying to export their sugar to France. At 225 pounds of muscovado to 100 pounds of refined, they paid 5.6 livres per hundredweight; at 150 pounds to 100 pounds they paid 3.75 livres per hundredweight. Marseilles refiners never enjoyed a major share of the French market.

---

41. AN, Col F3 83, "Mémoire sur le commerce des isles," October 29, 1683; Bondois, "Les centres sucriers français," 76; AN, F12 1502, mémoire, 1784–85.

42. Billioud and Rambert, "Une industrie marseillaise," 17–18. Joseph Mathieu, *Marseille: Statistique et historique* (Marseilles, 1879), 284, says that Pope John XXII bought sugar in Marseilles.

43. Billioud and Rambert, "Une industrie marseillaise," 20. Carrière, *Négociants marseillais*, 314, says 1675. See also Paul M. Bondois, "Le raffinage du sucre à Marseille aux XVIIe et XVIIIe siècles," *Annales de Provence*, XIX (1922), 131–32.

The equalization of local duty rates gave Marseilles refining a temporary boost, and some fourteen refineries were in operation by 1754. These were small, treating a total of less than 4,000,000 pounds of raw sugar in their busiest year: Marseilles sugar was simply too expensive to compete effectively on the French market, and only 700,000 pounds of it was sold in France in 1754. Complaining that sugar from Bordeaux or even Montpellier was cheaper, local refiners looked to the export market for help, but this provided little relief. Exports of refined sugar to Italy and the Levant were never large enough to support a major refining industry in Marseilles, and by the end of the Old Regime, refining was significantly down. Only seven refineries were left in 1786, selling a total of 300,000 pounds of sugar.[44] In that year the government finally conceded duty-free transit rights to Marseilles refined sugar, but before this could help revive the industry, the Revolution ended this chapter in the history of Marseilles sugar refining.

The restrictions placed on Marseilles' trade with France enabled towns near Marseilles to develop small refining industries. In particular, Sète and Montpellier managed to create refineries of note, which caused some concern at Marseilles. In 1717 Simon Gilly established the first refinery at Sète; this was a success, in part because on January 15, 1718, the government extended to Sète the concessions offered other ports by the Letters Patent of April, 1717. Sugar from Sète was sold in the south; at the Beaucaire fair, for example, it was considered in 1732 to be "firm and of good quality."[45] It was also sold abroad, especially after it received duty-free transit rights in 1732. Prosperity was short-lived, however, and while Marseilles' refining business grew in the 1740s, Sète's disappeared, a victim of the overwhelming advantages in supply and capital possessed by Marseilles. In the second half of the eighteenth century, Montpellier offered a more serious challenge to Marseilles, which led to the complaints by Marseilles refiners in 1786 that refined sugar from Montpellier was hurting sales of Marseilles sugar. Not much is known of the refineries of Montpellier, except that the largest—and perhaps the only—one was owned

---

44. ACCM, H109, mémoire (by Marseilles refiners ?), 1786.
45. Paul M. Bondois, "La raffinerie de Cette au XVIIIe siècle," *Annales du Midi*, XXXIV (1922), 394–96; AN, F12 1501, July 27, 1732.

by the Sabatier family, formerly or also of Marseilles and Sète.[46] This refinery was in operation at least from 1764 to 1786. Finally, there were at one time or another refineries operating in Beaucaire (at least in 1732 and 1787) and Nîmes (in 1716). They were insignificant, as was the refinery of Dijon (1764–1777).[47]

There was a fourth group of refineries operating in Old Regime France for a brief while, those in the French West Indies. They were active in the latter part of the seventeenth century, having received strong encouragement from Colbert. "You know," wrote Colbert in 1670, "how important it is to the commerce of the French islands in America to have the residents refine their own sugar, thereby making it easier to sell." In 1683 the colonies had at least five refineries, which were treating some 3,000,000 pounds of raw sugar annually.[48] But as noted, these met with stiff opposition from metropolitan merchants and refiners. Finally, the government began to discourage colonial refining, but this merely served to encourage the claying of sugar. A standoff was reached, and throughout the eighteenth century, the French West Indies alone of all the European colonies in the Caribbean produced significant amounts of clayed sugar.

The attempt to establish a strong French West Indian refining industry went counter to traditional economic policy in the Old Regime. Local privilege was fundamental to that policy, and West Indian refineries threatened to subvert it. Too many people stood to lose from a successful West Indian refining industry: shippers, whose cargoes would shrink by more than half; French refiners, who could not withstand the competition; and the thousands of sailors and workers whose livelihood depended upon the metropolitan sugar business. Colbert's vision was too broad—he hoped to eliminate the trade in raw sugar and force the Dutch and Germans to buy only refined sugar from France—and it ran into too many vested interests. Similarly,

---

46. Rambert, *Histoire du commerce de Marseille,* VI, 384; ACCM, H110, mémoire, July 3, 1741; AN, F12 1229, Beaucaire Fair, 1765–77; BN, nafr 2721, requests by Sabatier, June 20 and October 13, 1769; AN, F12 1502, petition by Sieur Bernavon, 1787. Bondois, "La raffinerie de Cette," 399, says that Sabatier had a refinery in Montpellier in 1744, but this may be an error. In 1741 there was definitely a Sabatier refining sugar in Marseilles. ACCM, H110, mémoire, July 3, 1741.

47. AN, F12 1501, July 27, 1732; AN, F12 1502, petition by Sieur Bernavon, 1787; ADLA, C730, April 6, 1716; J. Giroux, "La raffinerie de sucre de Dijon dans la deuxième moitié du XVIIIe siècle," *Annales de Bourgogne,* LIII (1981), 80–90.

48. Michel, *Histoire du commerce et de la navigation à Bordeaux,* II, 303; AN, Col F3 83, "Mémoire sur le commerce des isles," October 29, 1683.

Colbert's successors would not or could not allow any group of refineries from one town to dominate the internal refining industry. Local privileges were established and respected throughout the country, and each refining center had to sell to a local and not a national market.

9

To the Consumer

> It seems that Paris entry duties are infinitely less on luxury items than on necessities.
> —Commerce de Paris

Whether muscovado, clayed, or refined, sugar had to follow a long, complex, and generally costly path before it finally arrived in the hands of a consumer. The barriers to commerce were numerous in eighteenth-century France, and although the sugar trade may have been considerably less hindered than trade in grain or wine, it certainly suffered from a multitude of petty fiscal and physical obstacles. To overcome these problems, merchants involved in the sugar trade attempted to rationalize their businesses in many ways. The biggest established complex networks that enabled them to control virtually all aspects of the trade, from growing the cane in the colonies to selling refined sugar to retailers in France. Relying above all on family ties, merchants managed to create a more efficient operation in the midst of a still largely medieval economic system.

The physical geography of the sugar trade within France was, as noted above, relatively small. There was one huge market, Paris, and it tended to dominate internal trade. To supply Paris with adequate quantities of sugar was indeed the organizing principle behind much of the eighteenth-century sugar trade, and elaborate networks were established for that purpose. The most important of these was along the Loire River, which for the sugar trade was a one-way road from Nantes to Paris. For most of the eighteenth century, more sugar was imported into France proper by way of Nantes than via any other French port, and most of it ended up in Paris after having been refined either in Orléans or one of the smaller towns along the river. The Loire also furnished sugar to the provinces in the center of France, such as Berry or the Nivernais. Also supplying Paris with sugar was the Seine River network, extending from Le Havre to the capital. Although not nearly as significant as the Loire network, it was nonetheless an important supplier to Paris as well as to the rest of the Ile de France and Normandy. Other networks existed in the north and south, with the former using Dunkerque as its main port and the latter Bordeaux. From Dunkerque, sugar—which had frequently arrived first in Nantes—was distributed throughout French Flanders, Artois, and Hainault, whereas Bordeaux supplied the Midi from Aquitaine to Provence, occasionally with some help from Marseilles.

The human geography of the sugar networks was more complex, although it usually was organized around the family unit. From the smallest refiner to the largest wholesale merchant, most businessmen involved with sugar relied heavily on family ties for financing and organizing the business. Almost all commercial companies in the Old Regime were partnerships established for only a few years' duration, although they were renewable. This was certainly true when it came to colonial trade. Only royally chartered companies, usually enjoying certain monopoly privileges, went beyond the simple partnership, and few of these had the capital and the disinterested management to survive long enough to develop into something akin to modern joint-stock companies. The vast majority of merchants engaging in colonial trade were involved in family partnerships. Besides forming partnerships with relatives, most merchants used the services of relatives in the course of conducting business, particularly if sales or purchases beyond the local area were required. The capitalism of eighteenth-century France relied heavily on personal ties. Since modern institutions were largely lacking or could not inspire confidence, individuals had to be trusted; but most could place their faith only in family members. The ideal was to have a family member at every key place in the operation, and many of the larger firms came close to realizing this ideal.

The Loire River—with its overland extension to Paris—was a particularly fertile place for developing family networks to handle the sugar trade. A natural highway linking the Atlantic and the capital, the Loire was the internal sugar route par excellence, boasting abundant quantities of raw materials, processing plants, and the largest market in France. To control and profit from the flow of sugar from the West Indies to Paris, merchants expanded their operations along the Loire, using family members whenever possible. A simple example is provided by the Beguyers. In 1705 René Beguyer established a refinery in Angers that remained in operation until the 1770s.[1] In the middle of the century, members of the family moved to Nantes, where they participated in overseas trade, fitting out ships for the West Indies and even for Africa. It can only be assumed that the Nantes Beguyers sent their West Indian sugar to the family refinery in Angers for further processing. Ultimately, the operation in Nantes eclipsed that at Angers, and the refinery was closed in 1776 or 1777. Following the American Revolution, the business based in Nantes was large enough to allow Jean Beguyer to purchase two small plantations with slaves in Saint Domingue. When the company failed in 1787, it had credits—and debts—of over 2,000,000 livres.

If the Beguyers showed how one family could rely almost exclusively on its own resources to move from refining to shipping, slave trading, and planting on a modest scale, the Colas, Jogues, Sarrebourses, and Vandeberques showed what a group of closely related families could do when acting together. All four families were from Orléans: the Colas arrived there from Paris in the fourteenth century; the Jogues and Sarrebourses were there at least from the beginning of the seventeenth century, and the Vandeberques arrived around 1650.[2] Even in the seventeenth century, they were generally successful. For example, Pierre Jogues was a rich merchant who was named mayor of Orléans in 1663, and Georges Vandeberque established the town's first refinery, which functioned until the Revolution. By the end of the seventeenth century, many links were formed between the families. In 1690 Michel Vandeberque married Marie Sarrebourse, and their siblings Pierre Sarrebourse d'Audeville and Marie Vandeberque also wed nine years later. Business ties accompanied the marriages, and by 1700 the two families were as close financially as they were socially. Meanwhile, the Colas were becoming related to both families. In the 1660s or 1670s Anne Colas married François Sarrebourse, uncle of Marie and Pierre Sarrebourse, and in 1695 Jacques Colas, Anne's cousin, married Elisabeth Vandeberque, sister of Michel and Marie. Finally, the Jogues joined the others early in the eighteenth

---

1. On the Beguyers see Lebrun, *Les hommes et la mort,* 74; ADLA, notary Girard, August 4, 1785; ADLA, notary Lambert, September 10, 1785; and ADLA, 2C3084, January 31, 1791.
2. On the Colas see M. Legaingneulx, *Généologie de la famille de MM. Colas* (Orléans, 1768), 1. On the Jogues see M. Colas de la Noue, "Notes sur la famille Jogues," *Bulletin de la Société Archéologique et Historique de l'Orléanais,* XIV (1907), 639. On the Sarrebourses see Prudhomme, "Un famille de marchands orléanais," 23.

century with marriages to the Colas in 1702 and to the Sarrebourses in 1714. By this time, further marriages had taken place between the Vandeberques and the Colas and between the Vandeberques and the Sarrebourses.

In 1712–1713, the group began to expand geographically, sending members to key places for the sugar trade. By 1726 there were Sarrebourses in Orléans, Nantes, Cadiz, Lyon, Marseilles, and possibly Amsterdam and Saint Domingue. Similarly, members of the Jogues family also moved to Nantes and Cadiz, and Pierre Colas moved to Nantes in the second half of the eighteenth century.[3] Only the Vandeberque men never left Orléans, where they stayed to run the family refinery, which was at the heart of the operation. There they contracted marriages with other refining families, the Mirons, the Seurats, and the Tassins. Although the Sarrebourses apparently died out quickly in Orléans, the Colas and the Jogues survived there throughout the eighteenth century and established refineries of their own. In 1794 no fewer than eight of Orléans' twenty-four refineries belonged to members of the allied families: Colas Malmusse; Seurat Guilleville; Seirat, Miron, and Tassin; Jogues, Guedeville Brothers; Colas Desfrancs; Colas Brouville; Vandeberque Brothers; and Colas Malmusse Brothers.[4] These refineries produced over 40 percent of Orléans' refined sugar.

To supply these refineries with sugar, the families' operations in Nantes grew considerably in the eighteenth century and ultimately came to equal or even surpass those in Orléans. The Nantes business centered on the Sarrebourse family, and especially on Pierre Sarrebourse d'Audeville, the first of the family to move to Nantes. Soon after arriving, Pierre became an active armateur, sending out ships to the Antilles and to Africa.[5] He must have been quite successful at his new profession because in 1725 his fortune was evaluated at 400,000 livres, making it the second-largest commercial fortune in the town. The fortune made, the family apparently withdrew from an active commercial life. It sent out its last ship in 1754, and although Pierre

---

3. René Kerviler, *Répertoire général de bio-bibliographie bretonne* (Rennes, 1886–1908), X, 67–68. The état-civil in ACN lists no Colas before 1780–90.
4. AN, F12 1502, "Etat général des raffineurs de la ville d'Orléans."
5. On Pierre Sarrebourse d'Audeville and family see Jean Meyer, *La noblesse bretonne* (Paris, 1966), 218, 226, 832; Meyer, *L'armement nantais*, 172, 257; and ACN, état-civil, marriage of Marie-Thérèse Portier and Philippe Sébastien Sarrebourse, June 23, 1778.

Grégoire remained a *négociant,* or wholesale merchant, his brother Philippe Sebastien opted for a military career. By the end of the century the family seemed intent upon regaining its earlier noble status. It did not, however, turn its back on its relatives in Orléans, and when Pierre Grégoire's wife died in 1783, he was able to confide in his rather distant cousin there: "I feel that a trip to your city will provide me with many distractions. I have good relatives and friends who would truly like to share my grief."[6]

If the Sarrebourses became less active, the Colas and Jogues picked up the slack. Working as armateurs and commissioned agents, they were deeply involved in the sugar trade at Nantes in the second half of the eighteenth century. They kept in close contact with Orléans and supplied the family refineries with raw sugar. The families also remained close to each other, both in Nantes and in Orléans, establishing a company in the former (Jogues Brothers and Colas) and intermarrying yet again in the latter. Indeed, the 1786 marriage of Robert Colas to Anne Jogues was the last involving a Jogues, for the family had no male heirs. The family was very wealthy, and in Nantes its members paid over 1,000 livres in capitation taxes in 1789, one of the largest assessments in the city.[7]

The dense network created by these transplanted families served to make the sugar trade more efficient and profitable. By the end of the century, members of the four families owned plantations in the colonies, ships to transport sugar to Nantes, and refineries in Orléans. They participated in the slave trade and in virtually every other commerce related to the production of sugar in the Antilles and France. Such a network was an ideal solution to the problems of doing business in eighteenth-century France.

Family networks also existed in the south of France, although the lack of a major market made them more diffuse. Whereas the Loire Valley merchants merely expanded along the one great route taken by the majority of sugar in the north, those in the south could expand in several directions. One of the most popular trade routes in the south was between Toulouse and Bordeaux, and this was the one which the Fontanilhe family tried to exploit in the 1770s and 1780s. Jean Baptiste Fontanilhe was a négociant in Toulouse when he died in the

6. ADL, 11J247, September 12, 1783.
7. ADLA, B3530.

1750s or 1760s, leaving his wife, Anne, in charge of the business.[8] Although one son apparently replaced the father in the Toulouse business, Anne remained firmly in charge of the company, and the other son, Antoine, moved to Bordeaux, where he was well received and named a *bourgeois* in 1768. Antoine was fairly well-off at this time: when he married in 1771, he brought some 60,000 livres into the marriage community. Antoine's choice for a wife was Marie-Rose l'Hermenier Dumont, an orphaned daughter of an artillery officer in Martinique, a choice his mother clearly welcomed. With his own money and his wife's dowry, Antoine purchased a small refinery in 1774 for 92,613 livres, but he still remained close to his family in Toulouse. Not only did he sell sugar to his mother, he relied on her for his own financial stability, and when she died in 1786, he quickly went bankrupt. Obviously, Antoine had failed to establish himself firmly as an independent merchant, and in his case close family ties proved disastrous; as the bankruptcy papers put it, "His failure was caused by his great confidence in his late mother's commercial house."

A much more spectacular family operation was established by the Sabatiers of Montpellier, for whom the sugar trade was but one of several lucrative enterprises. According to Guy Chaussinand-Nogaret, the Sabatiers were a Protestant merchant family resident in Montpellier before the revocation of the Edict of Nantes in 1685. In the early eighteenth century they made a fortune from supplying the French army with uniforms. "From 1719," wrote Chaussinand-Nogaret, "their network was enormous. They clothed almost all the old regiments of France: Lorraine Cavalry, Languedoc Dragoons, Blais, Brittany, Bresse Infantry, Bassigny Infantry, German Infantry of Alsace, Quercy Infantry, Latour Cavalry. Besides complete dress—uniforms, hats, socks, belts, bandoliers—they also furnished arms—rifles, bayonets, sabers, and swords. The zone of their activity was not limited to France; it spread to Spain, Italy, and Sardinia."[9] The operation was so big that it went far beyond the confines of one family and forced the Sabatiers to rely on the next best thing: the Protestant

---

8. On the Fontanilhes, see ADG, 2E1242, December 17, 1768, December 23, 1770, January 4, 1771 (marriage contract), and June 1, 1778; ADG, 7B1408, brouillard (1774–76); and ADG, 7B1416, August 2, 1786.
9. Guy Chaussinand-Nogaret, *Les financiers de Languedoc au XVIIIe siècle* (Paris, 1970), 223–33.

community, either in exile or in France. Around 1740 the Sabatiers became suppliers to the Ministry of the Marine and were drawn into the colonial trade. They became armateurs, sending out textiles to the colonies and bringing back sugar that they processed in their new refinery at Sète.[10] After a short time, they closed the refinery and opened a new one at Montpellier itself because of the latter's good waters. This refinery remained in operation until the end of the Old Regime, by which time the main branch of the Sabatiers' enterprises had been transferred to Paris. Guillaume Sabatier became an influential banker who participated in the administration of the new Compagnie des Indes and ultimately the Bank of France. But all the while the family remained involved in supplying the army and in the sugar trade.

By providing a sound basis for trust, networks of relatives and even coreligionists helped sugar merchants overcome the problems posed by poor communications and by a dearth of reliable institutions. They also helped give the sugar trade a more coherent organization in the face of obstacles raised by antiquated administrative and fiscal structures. In spite of Colbert and in spite of a general trend toward a single customs union in the eighteenth century, internal French trade was still plagued by numerous duties, taxes, and tolls often designed to protect a particular interest as well as to provide—however indirectly—money to the crown. The fact that virtually all of these impositions were collected by private individuals or agencies further hindered trade. The government, in which the power to tax nominally resided, often had little control over what its so-called agents were doing in the field. Complaints against tax collectors were common, but the government frequently had limited power to eliminate abuses.

Import and export duties were set by the crown, but since France was not unified for duty purposes, much of the country was considered "foreign." Only the central part of France formed a duty-free area, which was known as the Five Great Farms. Duties were levied when the sugar entered the Farms—that is, either at the port of arrival or at an internal barrier, the most important of which was at Ingrandes, about twenty-five miles up the Loire from Nantes. The basic duty rates were fixed by Colbert in 1664 and 1665, and they remained

---

10. On the Sète refinery see also Bondois, "La raffinerie de Cette," 399.

relatively constant throughout the Old Regime. As modified by the Letters Patent of April, 1717, the rates were designed to encourage production of muscovado and clayed sugar in the French West Indies, encourage the reexportation of raw sugar from France, protect the metropolitan refining industry, and discourage the import of all foreign sugar. As we have seen, the duties fulfilled all their assigned tasks, and the only changes in the duty structure occurred in 1786, when the government decided to encourage the export of refined sugar by offering subsidies to refiners.

In spite of the overall success of the duty program, the manner of collection greatly disturbed the merchant community and led to seemingly endless disputes; it also made the internal trade in sugar more difficult. Until 1780, customs duties on colonial products were collected by the Domaine d'Occident, a branch of the General Farm since 1732.[11] The Farm was a private organization that leased from the crown the right to collect various impositions. This meant that collectors of duties and taxes were collecting for their own purses, a fact that tended to encourage a vigorous approach. From the merchants' point of view, zealous tax collectors were the cause of all the disputes; the agents for the Farm, on the contrary, blamed merchant greed and fraud.

The great power of the Farm, reinforced by its relative autonomy, made it the sworn enemy of merchants in all the ports. As far as the sugar trade was concerned, the Farm was responsible primarily for collecting duties on imports, but since France did not form a single customs union, this meant that the Farm had a degree of influence over the internal traffic in sugar. To begin with, the Farm regulated the duty-free transit of sugar from the ports to foreign destinations. The Farm determined the routes that had to be followed; sugar that deviated from the prescribed itinerary was considered to be imported and therefore liable to duties. The official routes were not always the most convenient, at least in the eyes of the merchants, but this was a minor problem compared with the Farm's other pretensions.[12] Agents of the Farm had the right to open sealed barrels of sugar in transit at any time, meaning that a shipment that had successfully

11. George T. Matthews, *The Royal General Farms in Eighteenth Century France* (New York, 1958), 131.
12. For dossiers on quarrels between merchants and the General Farm, especially at Ingrandes, see ADLA, C731–32.

crossed most of the country might arbitrarily be halted in a distant province. Furthermore, the Farm insisted that merchants pay deposits to guarantee the ultimate export of the sugar in question. These deposits were as expensive as they were annoying, and they discouraged many merchants from shipping their sugar overland.

More significant than the control over the transit trade was the Farm's regulation of the movement of sugar between different parts of France, and particularly between the provinces outside and inside the Five Great Farms. It was at Ingrandes that the internal trade in sugar was most affected by the Farm. Virtually all sugar traveling from Nantes to Orléans passed by the Bureau d'Ingrandes, and there the full weight of the private tax-collecting bureaucracy was felt. Merchants with sugar had to pay both duties for importing it from Brittany and taxes for the journey farther up the Loire. The real problem came in determining the quality of sugar being imported: the Farm insisted that merchants were trying to import Nantes refined sugar under the guise of West Indian clayed. As early as 1670, Nantes merchants were complaining that their shipments to the interior were being troubled by such accusations, but it was another sixty-one years before the Conseil de Commerce finally directed the tax collectors at Ingrandes to stop seizing disputed sugar. With the sugar's quality determined, the Farmers calculated the amounts owing and issued a detailed receipt upon payment. The printed form (see page 161) listed the various taxes due.[13] The list of taxes was long, and it was one of the few benefits of the Farm that merchants could occasionally pay so many of them at one time. On other routes, many individual tolls and taxes were paid, and sugar was also liable to a tax upon entering Paris itself.[14]

How costly were these impositions? In a word, very: the various duties, taxes, and tolls could come to more than 50 percent of the value of the sugar. A calculation made in 1772 by Nantes merchants provides a good example. On a 1,063-pound barrel of clayed sugar that cost 318.90 livres in Saint Domingue, merchants paid 171.89 livres in various taxes by the time it reached Orléans, including 132 livres in duties. This, however, was only part of the story, since the same barrel also incurred expenses of 158.78 livres, including 62 livres in trans-

---

13. ADLA, C732.
14. Saint-Julien and Bienaymé, *Histoire des droits d'entrée*, 84–85.

Bureau d'Ingrandes
Certificate

We, the receiver and controller of the duties at the Bureau d'Ingrandes, certify that _____, shipper by water living at _____, for _____, merchant living at _____, has presented in this office the quantity of _____ [pounds of sugar] to bring by water to _____, upon which he has paid in accord with the receipt delivered to him today, which is valid with the present for one and the same shipment, the sum of _____ livres.

To wit:

Entrée	Officiers et signatures
Abord	Parisis
Consommation	Acquit, formule et
Jauge et courtage	certificat
Subvention	Double cloison
Domaine d'Occident	Prévôté d'Angers
Concédez	Prévôté de Saumur
Trépas de la Loire	

Done at the said Bureau d'Ingrandes the _____ day of _____, seventeen hundred _____.

[signed] _____

atlantic freight charges and 25 livres in commissions. All told, the price of the sugar had nearly doubled, but not because of exorbitant profit taking. And after leaving the refinery, further charges would raise the price even higher. Transportation to Paris cost some 2 livres per hundredweight, and entry taxes at Paris ranged from 4 livres per ton in 1705 to nearly 40 toward the end of the century.[15]

The different expenses acted to push up the price of sugar to the retailer, and only intense competition among wholesalers kept prices moderate. As a general rule, clayed sugar cost retailers about twice as much as it cost in the ports, while refined was about two and one-half to three times the port price of muscovado. But short- and even medium-term prices could vary dramatically according to availability in the ports. War had the greatest effect on prices. At the 1777 Beaucaire Fair, for example, the price of refined sugar was about 10 percent more than in 1776, going from an average of 74.5 livres per

---

15. ADLA, C730; E. Levasseur, *Histoire du commerce de la France* (Paris, 1911), I, 449; Saint-Julien and Bienaymé, *Histoire des droits d'entrée*, 84–85.

hundredweight to 81.5; this increase was due to the outbreak of the American Revolution and the attendant difficulties in transatlantic commerce. By the end of the Old Regime, retailers were paying nearly 100 livres per hundredweight for Orléans refined sugar and probably about 20 percent less for clayed.[16] This was a considerable amount of money, and retailers consequently tended to purchase relatively small amounts at a time.[17]

Wholesalers and refiners either sold their sugar directly to retailers, or they used the services of a middleman, who could be either an independent distributor or a commissioned salesman. Antoine Fontanilhe, a small Bordeaux refiner, employed M. Lanié as his traveling salesman in the Montauban area and perhaps beyond.[18] Lanié had great success in selling his wares, as a letter to Fontanilhe from a satisfied customer testified: "Sir, your traveling salesman sold us a small lot of first-quality sugar in loaves, which he assured us to be of superior beauty, and so effectively does it turn out to be so that we beg you to ship [more] to us by the first boat." Other customers dealt directly with Fontanilhe without ever using an intermediary; as one wrote, "Sirs, the present is to ask you to tell me by return post how much the following would cost: sugar, clayed sugar or all qualities, indigo." Bigger refiners apparently used slightly different methods, preferring to sell larger lots to distributors who then handled sales to retailers. The Ravôts of Orléans, for example, delivered more than 2,000 pounds of sugar to Famin fils aîné, who had arranged sales to three buyers in Paris.[19] It is not clear whether Famin worked exclusively for the Ravôts.

In most of France, only apothecaries and grocers (*épiciers*) had the right to sell sugar to the public. As early as 1311, grocers in Paris could retail sugar, and in 1336, Philippe VI gave the same permission to apothecaries. In 1484, Charles VIII created the unified guild of grocers and apothecaries and granted them the privilege of dealing in "works and merchandise of grocery, apothecary, works of wax, and jams of

16. AN, F12 1229; AN, F12 562, "Etat des manufactures orléanaises" (1790), 86–87. On additional relationships between prices of clayed and refined, see AN, F12 1229.
17. On purchases by retailers, see ADL, 11J219, February 21, 1769; ADS, D5B6 4659, April 1, October 28, November 16, 1779, January 10, February 10, April 10, 1780, among others; and ADG, 7B1368, December 25, 1785.
18. ADG, 7B1368, December 25, 1785. Of the hundreds of letters extant to Fontanilhe, only three or four are from Lanié, and all of these are from Montauban.
19. ADG, 7B1368, April 14, 1782; ADL, 11J219, February 21, 1769.

sugar." This was reiterated in the seventeenth century by both Louis XIII and Louis XIV, and by the eighteenth century the exclusive right was already an established tradition. If apothecaries used their sugar in preparing medicines, grocers sold it in pure form, although frequently in small lots. The registre de conscience of M. Augustin, grocer at Coulommiers, for example, listed about fifty sales of sugar from 1786 to 1788, with the average sale amounting to only 5 livres for about five pounds of sugar; the largest sale was for twelve pounds, the smallest three. Even this was quite large when compared with the sale of only four ounces made in 1783 by M. Angrand of Paris to M. Lemaître.[20] Amounts that small had to be broken off the larger loaves by means of a special chopper.

It is impossible to know exactly who bought the sugar or how much the average Frenchman consumed. Only a few isolated cases are known, and these are probably far from being typical. Purchasers of sugar who were rich nobles or members of the royal family can occasionally be traced, but there are few precise data about purchasers from the lower orders. Frank Spooner could calculate that one rich Italian family in the seventeenth century spent 3 percent of its food budget on sugar, but Anne-Marie Puiz was unable to discover the amount of sugar consumed by eighteenth-century Genevans. Similarly, Guy Thuillier admitted ignorance about sugar usage in nineteenth-century Nivernais, and most of the major regional studies on eighteenth-century France simply ignore the question.[21] From the silence, it can only be concluded—however tentatively—that the vast majority of rural Frenchmen never tasted sugar.

What can be known with a higher degree of certainty is the per capita consumption rates for France and some French towns in the eighteenth century. As we have seen, total national consumption of sugar grew in the eighteenth century from an average of about 25,000,000 pounds per year in the 1730s to about 57,000,000 pounds in the 1780s (though it peaked in 1770 at over 80,000,000 pounds). Given the steady rise in the population of France after 1730, this

20. Lespinasse, *Les métiers et corporations*, I, 500–505; Jèze, *Etat ou tableau de la ville de Paris*, 317; ADS, D5B6 1196 and 1704.
21. Frank Spooner, "Régimes alimentaires d'autrefois: Proportions et calculs en calories," in J. J. Hémardinguer (ed.), *Pour une histoire de l'alimentation* (Paris, 1970), 370. See also, in the same volume, Anne-Marie Puiz, "L'alimentation populaire et sous-alimentation au XVIIe siècle: Le cas de Genève et de sa région," 37, and Guy Thuillier, "L'alimentation en nivernais au XIXe siècle," 162.

translates into a per capita figure of some 1.5 to 2 pounds for most years, with a maximum of between 3 and 4 pounds. This is well in line with estimates of French sugar consumption early in the nineteenth century: Joseph Mathieu calculated per capita consumption at 1.1 pounds during the bleak days from 1812 to 1816. Urban and particularly Parisian rates were significantly higher than the national average. Official statistics put annual sugar consumption in Paris at 6,500,000 pounds in the 1780s; if most of this is assumed to be refined sugar, this meant a per capita intake of 15 to 25 pounds of the equivalent in raw sugar. And even this may be too modest. Orléans refiners alone claimed to sell some 9,000,000 pounds to Paris; if one converts this to raw sugar and allows for sales from other sources, it suggests that per capita Parisian consumption would be 30, 40, or even 50 pounds. Figures from Marseilles also show higher than average rates. Officials estimated that 750,000 pounds of raw sugar were used locally in 1755, for a per capita rate of nearly 10 pounds.[22] Thus, sugar was consumed in relatively large quantities in rich towns, but it is doubtful if much found its way into poorer rural areas. The contrast between urban and rural life was apparent even in eating habits.

22. Mathieu, *Marseille*, 289; Robert Philippe, "Une opération pilote: L'étude du ravitaillement de Paris au temps de Lavoisier," in Hémardinguer (ed.), *Pour une histoire de l'alimentation*, 61; Julliany, *Essai sur le commerce de Marseille*, III, 214.

10

Conclusion

In 1789 most observers could foresee little but growth for the French sugar industry. Demand was ever increasing, and supply seemed likely to grow to meet it. If Saint Domingue reached its maximum output, they believed that French Guiana would finally be cultivated seriously: three times the size of Saint Domingue, French Guiana supposedly could produce enough sugar to guarantee continued French domination over the European market.[1] And yet within five years the French sugar industry was in ruins, never to rise again in the same form. A combination of political, economic, and agricultural factors destroyed the eighteenth-century trade and helped give rise to a radically different nineteenth-century one. By the time the dust settled in 1815, irrevocable changes had occurred in the structure of the sugar business in France, Britain, Europe as a whole, and the Caribbean.

In many ways the French Revolution was responsible for the collapse of the old system. This was ironic. Few of the leaders of the various revolutionary movements had great interest in the colonies or colonial trade, and fewer still wished to innovate in those areas. Indeed, for the first two years of the Revolution, little was done with regard to the sugar business, which continued to operate at near record levels until the summer of 1791. Then, during the night of August 22–23, 1791, there occurred an event that ended the era of tranquil prosperity and led directly to the end of the eighteenth-century French sugar trade: the slaves in the North province of Saint Domingue revolted. Thousands of slaves living primarily on the sugar-rich Plaine du Nord launched a bloody civil war that would not end until after the colony achieved independence and ceased to be a major producer of sugar. The Saint Domingue, or Haitian, Revolution was a long, deadly affair characterized by bitter fighting between the three racial groups on the island: whites, blacks, and mulattoes. Even

---

1. Projects for the development of Guiana were never lacking in the Old Regime or the new one either. See, for example, AN, F12 549; and Weuves, *Réflexions historiques*, 293–95.

after independence was proclaimed on January 1, 1804, sporadic fighting continued, coming to an end only in the 1820s. By this time, Haiti had long ceased to be a factor in the world sugar trade. The war for independence was fought against the plantation system as much as against France, and political independence was accompanied by a destruction of the institutions of servitude. What had once been the most productive and sought-after tropical colony in the world became overnight a poverty-stricken backwater. Sugar production fell from nearly 200,000,000 pounds per year in the 1780s to virtually nil by the time France recognized Haitian sovereignty in 1825. Never again would the French Empire be the world's leading producer of raw sugar, especially as French Guiana remained unsettled and unproductive.

The loss of Saint Domingue was not the only blow to strike the French sugar industry, although it was by far the most severe. Even before the slave rebellion had spread through the entire colony to disrupt sugar production totally, Saint Domingue—indeed, the entire French West Indian empire—was effectively cut off from France. On February 1, 1793, the National Convention declared war on Great Britain. French overseas shipping had already slowed markedly in anticipation of such a war, and within weeks of the declaration it ceased altogether. With the exception of a brief period following the Peace of Amiens (1802), France was unable to import sugar in any significant quantities from its remaining colonies until 1815. This twenty-two-year hiatus forced most sugar merchants to withdraw from the business and invest their money elsewhere.

The war, and most particularly the British blockade of Napoleonic France, not only cut off the supply of West Indian sugar, it also encouraged the French to seek alternate sources of sugar. They found one in the sugar beet. In the 1740s Andraeas Marggraf had published a paper in Berlin showing the possibility of extracting sugar from beets.[2] Some fifty years later, his pupil Franz Carl Achard turned his attention to the problem, and in 1802 he established the first factory for producing beet sugar. Although Achard had little financial success, word of his endeavors reached France, where they were soon copied. In 1811 Napoleon decided to encourage the creation of an indigenous

---

2. On beet sugar see Deerr, *History of Sugar*, II, 471ff.; and Aykroyd, *Sweet Malefactor*, 96–101.

sugar industry and thereby relieve France from a costly dependence on British West Indian sugar. Within two years a large sugar beet industry was operating in France. Although it foundered after the wars, it quickly returned to prosperity, and by 1835 some four hundred factories were producing nearly 80,000,000 pounds of beet sugar, or a third of total French consumption.

The rest of the sugar came from the colonies of Guadeloupe, Martinique, and Reunion, but changes had taken place there, too. In 1794, reacting to the threat of the complete loss of Saint Domingue and anxious finally to give full application to the Declaration of the Rights of Man and Citizen, the National Convention abolished slavery and the slave trade in the French Empire. Although Napoleon reimposed slavery and legalized the slave trade, the writing was on the wall. In 1807 Great Britain abolished its slave trade and began a crusade to have other nations follow suit. At the Congress of Vienna, a victorious Britain forced Louis XVIII to accept the French trade's abolition (which Bonaparte had decreed in 1815), and it was clear that the days of West Indian slavery were also numbered. In 1833 Britain abolished slavery in its colonies, and France did the same in 1848. The old plantation system based on slave labor was dead.

Contemporary with the demise of slavery were technological changes, particularly in the refining of sugar. Most significant was the development of centrifugal refining in the 1840s: spinning replaced boiling, as a machine now spun the impurities out of the sugar. Other technological advances affected the processing of cane in the colonies; new mills were developed to extract a far higher percentage of the juice from the cane. These advances were accompanied by changes in the organization of the sugar business, both in the Antilles and in France. In the nineteenth century the "central factory system" was developed in the Caribbean; the cane of several plantations could now be processed in one large factory. There was also a move toward centralization in France, as large refineries sold to a national market and not just local ones.

These changes underline the multifaceted nature of the sugar trade in eighteenth-century France. There were actually several sugar businesses in the Old Regime, and although they were linked by their common reliance upon one commodity, they usually operated semi-autonomously: the businesses of planting, importing and reexporting, and refining often had little to do with one another. Being distinct, these branches of the sugar trade developed at different speeds and in different directions, which is one reason why, when viewed as a whole, the eighteenth-century French sugar business presents a varied and even contradictory image. This is particularly true when the "modernity" of the sugar trade is considered. Although originally cast in Old Regime molds, parts of the sugar trade developed in some ways into modern forms. This was certainly the case in economic matters: several features of the sugar business were strikingly atypical of the classic Old Regime and, together with innovations in a few other industries, presaged nineteenth-century developments. Particularly novel were, first, the organization of sugar plantations and large refineries, and, second, the attempts by some merchants to amalgamate the various branches of the trade and to overcome if not eliminate the barriers to trade within the kingdom.

Both the plantation and the refinery exemplified the new forms of industrial organization being developed on the eve of the industrial revolution.[3] Both accentuated the difference between capital and labor, and both demanded that labor be specialized and disciplined to a degree otherwise almost unknown before the eighteenth century. Even in the eighteenth century, few industrial workplaces were as tightly controlled as the plantation and the large refinery, where, on one estate or under one roof, up to several hundred workers might be ruled by one foreman or manager. Textile manufacturing, for example, required specialization, but it lacked discipline in that it was usually "organized" by short-term arrangements between a merchant and local cottagers.[4] As Pierre Goubert noted, "Most of the producers in this sector [i.e., the industrial sector] were country-dwellers, in fact peasants whose main employment was agricultural."[5] Only in certain exceptional fields usually related to mining or, perhaps, shipbuilding was there a large, concentrated, and perma-

---

3. David Landes, *The Unbound Prometheus: Technological Change and Industrial Development in Western Europe from 1750 to the Present* (Cambridge, England, 1970), 2.

4. Tihomir J. Markovitch, *Les industries lainières de Colbert à la Révolution* (Geneva, 1976), 476–77; William M. Reddy, *The Rise of Market Culture: The Textile Trade and French Society, 1750–1900* (Cambridge, England, 1984), 13. There are numerous regional studies with examples of such arrangements between merchants and peasants.

5. Pierre Goubert, *The Ancien Régime: French Society, 1600–1750* (New York, 1974), 55. Much the same sentiments were expressed earlier by E. Tarlé, *L'industrie dans les campagnes en France à la fin de l'Ancien Régime* (Paris, 1910), 79.

nent work force such as was found on the plantations and largest refineries.⁶ Similarly, few industries required such large capital outlays as planting and, to a much lesser degree, refining. Again, mining stands out as a rare example of frequently huge investments; in most other industries little cash was usually needed.⁷

In one other major way the sugar industry looked forward to the nineteenth century, although here it was not so unique: the largest sugar interests tried to unite the various branches of the business and tried to establish networks that would overcome the obstacles to trade created by tradition and by a government and society that respected tradition. In effect, the largest sugar merchants were attempting both to rationalize the trade and to make it national rather than local. Parallel developments can be seen in several other late eighteenth-century French businesses, from grain to textiles.⁸

In spite of these significant modernities, the sugar business was still firmly rooted in the Old Regime. Even in its overall economic organization, it was as traditional as it was novel. Above all, there was the role played by merchants. As was usual in Old Regime businesses, merchants were of exceptional importance in the sugar trade. Growers and processors of sugar were either rivaled or eclipsed by merchant middlemen who handled the purchase of sugar in the colonies and its sale in the French ports for distribution throughout Europe. This was in sharp contrast to the later situation. In the nineteenth and twentieth centuries, refining for the national market was the dominant feature of the business, and merchant middlemen in

6. See, for example, Gabriel Pelletier, *Les forges de Fraisans, la métallurgie comtoise à travers les siècles* (Dole, 1980), 90. In 1788 a total of 197 workers were employed at Fraisans, "one of the largest operations in the province" (95). On shipbuilding, see T. J. A. LeGoff and Jean Meyer, "Les constructions navales en France pendant la second moitié du XVIIIᵉ siècle," *Annales: Economies, Sociétés, Civilisations*, XXVI (1971), 173–85, which, although not dealing directly with economic issues, implies a large, well-organized industry at Nantes and Bordeaux.

7. Pelletier, *Les forges de Fraisans*, 87, says that the forges of Fraisans were worth 114,000 livres in 1724, "une fortune!" More typical of the Old Regime was the printing industry, which remained largely artisanal. See, for example, Jean Pierre Klein, *Histoire d'une imprimeur: Berger-Levrault, 1676–1976* (Paris, 1976), 50–51, which discusses the largest printer in Strasbourg; this business had sixteen workers in 1788 in a factory worth some 26,000 livres in 1787.

8. On rationalizing the grain trade, see Steven Kaplan, *Provisioning Paris: Merchants and Millers in the Grain and Flour Trade During the Eighteenth Century* (Ithaca, 1984), and Rudé, *The Crowd in the French Revolution*, 23–25. On textiles, see L. M. Lemuller, *Guillaume Ternaux, 1763–1833: Créateur de la première intégration industrielle française* (Paris, 1978), and Serge Chassagne, *Oberkampf: Un entrepreneur capitaliste au siècle des lumières* (Paris, 1980).

the ports were largely eliminated. In the eighteenth century, however, refiners dealt with only a small percentage of the sugar arriving in France and could not begin to rival the importers; indeed, when refiners became large enough, they tended to move to the ports to become merchants themselves. Although merchants and planters were more evenly balanced, particularly later in the Old Regime, when the planters' reluctance to pay off their debts in full weakened the merchants' position, merchants played a key role in the business as a whole. Again, this was typical of the Old Regime. Like the Oberkampf textile business, among many others, the sugar trade was "more commercial than industrial," and the merchants who made it so ran—or at least tried to run—traditional, low-overhead operations, usually out of their homes.[9] The key was a quick turnover of goods and of the small but easily expandable capital, and the successful merchant was one who avoided large capital investments while keeping things moving rapidly. Toward the end of the Old Regime, of course, this was becoming increasingly difficult to achieve, a fact that helped lead to the efforts to bring together the various branches of the sugar business in a more rational whole.

The commercial organization of the sugar trade reflected not only financial interests but also social ones, and in this the sugar trade was more uniformly traditional. Business was not just of a certain economic type; it was conducted in a certain way. Because of a lack of reliable institutions, business was highly personal in the eighteenth century, and the vast majority of firms dealing with sugar—either in the ports or at refineries—were one-man operations or simple partnerships. Although the economy had progressed far enough for distant bankers to provide credit to the sugar merchants, it still scarcely allowed for the creation of joint-stock companies in this domain. In addition, the extension of credit was done in a curious fashion: it was usually provided surreptitiously in the acceptance of bills of exchange.[10] At the same time, extending credit to merchants was one of the last links in a long chain of patronage that frequently began at the highest levels of government and society. When a lowly sugar mer-

---

9. Chassagne, *Oberkampf*, 100. For a discussion of "commercial capitalism" as practiced in the Old Regime, see George V. Taylor, "Types of Capitalism in Eighteenth Century France," *English Historical Review*, LXXIX (1964), 478–97.

10. Raymond Roover, *L'évolution de la lettre de change, XIVe–XVIIIe siècles* (Paris, 1953).

chant like Jean Beguyer of Nantes went bankrupt in 1787, the cause was quite clear: he was ruined by the failure of Claude Baudard de Saint-James, trésorier général de la marine.[11] Credit facilities were thus midway between the traditional and the modern. Organized in a most chaotic fashion, they still managed to allow commerce to grow.

Although necessary for the smooth functioning of "big business," the commercially active wealthy of Paris or other financial centers played only an insignificant role in the day-to-day operations of the sugar business. Here it was strictly a question of personal contact, and given a fundamental lack of confidence encouraged by an inadequate institutional framework—the idea of a limited liability corporation, for example, was still embryonic in France—family ties became of paramount importance. For many merchants, family and business organization were all but identical, and most of the important sugar-trading companies were in fact family companies, usually partnerships between fathers and sons, between brothers, or between in-laws. This last was of the greatest significance, for only through marriage could a family survive both as a family and as a business. Marriage was therefore central to a family's social and economic development, and successful matches guaranteed this future. The relationship between business and marriage was explicitly recognized, with many marriage contracts providing for the creation of new partnerships between the in-laws. When Pierre Sarrebourse of Orléans married Marie Vandeberque in 1699, the contract said, "He will enter into a company with Sarrebourse de Mondonville, his uncle; Michel Vandeberque, his brother-in-law; and Jacques Sarrebourse, his brother, on August 1, 1700, with a one-quarter interest."[12] Even when it was not a question of establishing a new partnership, marriages were arranged—or at least consented to—with an eye sharply focused on the financial side of the match. Thus, when Antoine Fontanilhe heard that his sister had received an offer of marriage, he wrote to his brother: "Our sister is at an age to be established. Her intention is such. One does not often find opportunities like the present one. . . . I say therefore that if the deal proposed for my sister is really as described, it must be accepted according to the proposed conditions. The request for a thousand *écus* is very mod-

11. ADLA, notary Varsavaux, March 5, 1789 (deposited, February 20, 1791).
12. ADL, 3E10464, November 7, 1699, quoted in Prudhomme, "Une famille de marchands orléanais," 28.

est. . . . We must establish this girl. Listen only to the voice of friendship and to the goodness of your heart to do the best for the family."[13]

Economic and social aspirations were intertwined in other ways. It was of course the goal of the company to make money, and in this many were singularly successful. The major sugar merchants in the ports were quite wealthy. Owning plantations in the colonies and ships to transport the commodities back to France and dealing in vast quantities of sugar, coffee, indigo, and cotton, the large merchants were among the richest people in France who did not rely on the court for their fortunes. The cities where they lived were also wealthy and, indeed, internationally famed. For example, Arthur Young, although unimpressed by Paris in relation to London, declared Bordeaux to be far richer than even Liverpool.[14]

Money, however, was only one goal of the merchants, and for many it was merely a means to an end. The end was status, or, in more concrete terms, entry into the nobility. Throughout the eighteenth century it was common practice for the most successful sugar merchants to gain noble standing either by purchasing an ennobling office or by receiving it from the government in recognition for services rendered the state. The crown honored merchants in this way in order to encourage French commerce. Traditionally, participation in commerce was considered a demeaning act, and most truly noble families avoided it. Louis XIV and XV went out of their way to combat this attitude by declaring explicitly that nobles were free to participate in maritime trade and by offering noble status to the most successful common merchants. This policy, however, seemed at first to be self-defeating, and until the middle of the eighteenth century, merchants tended to abandon their profession upon entering the nobility. As one anonymous author complained in the late 1720s: "In France, commerce is not perpetuated in the family. The merchant only thinks of getting rich as a means to place his son in an office. Thus, little by little, clever merchants are lost to the state and to commerce." Like Jean Pellet, a colonial commodities merchant in Bordeaux, ennobled merchants in the first half of the eighteenth century tried to quit commerce and live like true nobles. In the second half of the century, there was a marked shift in attitude. Attaining noble status was just

13. ADG, 2E1242, June 1, 1778.
14. Young, *Travels in France*, 55–56.

as common a goal, but its realization no longer entailed retiring from trade. Many of the major sugar merchants were ennobled in the 1750s; yet most remained active in commerce.[15] And in 1789 many *cahiers de doléances* asked for an end to the entire system of venal ennoblement.[16]

In spite of institutional and social handicaps, the French sugar industry grew rapidly in the eighteenth century. Simple economic factors were behind this growth. Sugar succeeded in creating an ever-growing market for itself in Europe, a demand that the French alone seemed capable of meeting. As demand and supply increased, real prices fell, thereby creating yet further demand. The increased volume of the sugar being traded more than offset the fall in real prices to make it an attractive commodity to trade.

If the sugar business was attractive, it was also competitive; if high volume allowed for more money to be made overall, the fierce competition restricted profit margins in each of the various phases of the operation. From the planters in the French West Indies to the grocers in Paris, businessmen dealing in sugar were compelled by competition to limit their markups. Thus, the 100 pounds of sugar that cost 20 to 25 livres in the Antilles might yield 50 pounds of refined and retail for 40 to 50 livres. This was not a great difference, especially considering freight charges, losses in transit, taxes, and the number of merchants involved. Clearly, each of the middlemen limited his markup to a small percentage. Wild speculation did not exist in the normal conduct of the business, and only under special circumstances could a merchant hope to get away with doubling or tripling the price. During difficult wars, such as the Seven Years' War or the French Revolution, large fortunes could be made overnight by merchants daring to challenge the Royal Navy; in other words, only abnormal situations created an absence of competition that allowed profits to reach exceptionally high levels.

Fierce competition not only limited profits at each step, but it also engendered bitter disputes among the different types of businessmen involved. A limited understanding of the economic factors at play

---

15. BN, msfr 7800, "Mémoire concernant le commerce de la France" (post-1727), fol. 56; Jean Cavignac, *Jean Pellet, commerçant en gros (1694–1772)* (Paris, 1967); Stein, *French Slave Trade*, 185–91.

16. For example, in Nantes. See *Archives parlementaires de 1787 à 1860, première série (1787 à 1799)* (Liechtenstein, 1969; Paris, 1966–71), IV, 94–101.

encouraged businessmen to blame one another for any perceived problems. Hence, the planters blamed French shippers for unduly low prices fetched by sugar in the colonies and for selling poor-quality merchandise there. "The cupidity of men" was seen as the cause of these abuses, which included the sale of "rotting beef capable of poisoning the hardiest people."[17] In France similar complaints were heard. Shippers and wholesalers had different interests that could conflict, and both could be opposed to refiners. Even consumers could be enraged if the price of sugar became too high.

In spite of the conflicts and complaints, most people concerned with the selling of sugar did well. Like their counterparts in the British West Indies, French planters as a group made reasonable profits, reaping dividends from their initial capital investments.[18] Shippers and wholesalers always made money from freight charges and commissions, and occasionally made more through speculation. Refiners and retailers, usually catering to upper-class tastes, also made modest amounts from sugar. Even consumers benefited from the business in that the real price of sugar declined in the eighteenth century, thereby allowing it to reach a larger market. Indeed, the only people who did not as a group gain from the trade were the slaves whose labor made the entire operation possible. But the price of a growing and profitable sugar business is best measured in human and not monetary terms. More than one million Africans were forced by the French alone to emigrate and to live and die in bondage.

The sugar business was part of the Old Regime. In many ways it exemplified the Old Regime, particularly in its curious amalgam of traditional and modern features. It was one of many luxury trades serving the needs of the upper strata of French society; yet it was so large that it could scarcely be conducted within the confines of normal eighteenth-century business practice. That the conflicting and irrational elements in it were accommodated in the traditional structures reflects the flexibility and appropriateness of those structures for eighteenth-century France; it also attests to the ingenuity of the individual merchants involved.

17. Weuves, *Réflexions historiques*, 34.
18. Ward, "Profitability of Sugar Planting," 208–209.

Selected Bibliography

SECONDARY SOURCES

Alpers, Edward A. *The East African Slave Trade.* Nairobi, 1967.

———. "The French Slave Trade in East Africa." *Cahier d'études africaines,* X (1970), 80–124.

Anstey, Roger. "The Volume and Profitability of the British Slave Trade, 1761–1807." In *Race and Slavery in the Western Hemisphere: Quantitative Studies.* Edited by Stanley L. Engerman and Eugene D. Genovese. Princeton, 1975.

Arcy, F. d'. "Aperçu de l'histoire du sucre sous l'ancien régime." *Revue historique des Antilles,* IV (1929), 11–32.

———. "L'industrie sucrière aux isles au XVIIe siècle." *Revue historique des Antilles,* II (1929), 3–16.

Armytage, Frances. *The Free Port System in the British West Indies, 1766–1822.* London, 1953.

Augier, F. R. *The Making of the West Indies.* London, 1960.

Aykroyd, W. R. *Sweet Malefactor.* London, 1967.

Banbuck, C. A. *Histoire politique, économique et sociale de la Martinique sous l'ancien régime (1635–1789).* Paris, 1935.

Batie, Robert Carlyle. "Why Sugar? Economic Cycles and the Changing of Staples on the English and French Antilles, 1624–54." *Journal of Caribbean History,* VIII–IX (1976), 1–41.

Berbain, Simone. *Le comptoir français de Juda (Ouidah) au XVIIIe siècle.* Paris, 1942.

Billioud, Joseph, and Gaston Rambert. "Une industrie marseillaise: Le raffinage de sucre." *Marseille, revue municipale,* 3e série, no. 9 (1950), 14–26.

Bois, Paul, et al. *Histoire de Nantes.* Toulouse, 1977.

Boizard, E., and H. Tardieu. *Histoire de la législation des sucres (1664–1891).* Paris, 1891.

Bondois, Paul. "Anciennes raffineries bordelaises." *Revue historique de Bordeaux,* XXXI (1938), 81–83.

———. "Les centres sucriers français au XVIIIe siècle." *Revue d'histoire économique et sociale,* XIX (1931), 23–76.

———. "L'exportation du sucre au XVIIIe siècle: La question de la Flandre française." *Annales du Nord,* IX (1923), 123–28.

———. "L'industrie sucrière française au XVIIIe siècle." *Revue d'histoire économique et sociale,* XIX (1931), 316–46.

———. "Le raffinage du sucre à Marseille aux XVIIe et XVIIIe siècles." *Annales de Provence*, XIX (1922), 131–44.
———. "La raffinerie de Cette au XVIIIe siècle." *Annales du Midi*, XXXIV (1922), 392–400.
———. "Les raffineries de sucre à Rouen sous l'ancien régime." Typescript in Bibliothèque Municipale de Rouen, 1922.
Bosher, John F. *The Single Duty Project*. London, 1964.
Braure, Maurice. *Lille et la Flandre Wallonne au XVIIIe siècle*. Lille, 1932.
Butel, Paul. *La croissance commerciale bordelaise dans la seconde moitié du XVIIIe siècle*. Paris, 1973.
———. *Les négociants bordelais, l'Europe, et les Iles au XVIIIe siècles*. Paris, 1974.
Carrière, Charles. *Négociants marseillais au XVIIIe siècle*. Paris, 1973.
Cavignac, Jean. *Jean Pellet, commerçant en gros (1694–1772)*. Paris, 1967.
Chaussinand-Nogaret, Guy. *Les financiers de Languedoc au XVIIIe siècle*. Paris, 1970.
Chiche, Marie-Claire. *Hygiène et santé à bord les navires négriers au XVIIIe siècle*. Paris, 1957.
Colas, M. de la Noue. "Notes sur la famille Jogues." *Bulletin de la Société Archéologique et Historique de l'Orléanais*, XIV (1907), 639–40.
Curtin, Philip D. *The Atlantic Slave Trade: A Census*. Madison, 1969.
———. *Economic Change in Pre-Colonial Africa*. Madison, 1975.
Daaku, Kwame Yeboa. *Trade and Politics on the Gold Coast, 1600–1720*. Oxford, 1970.
Daget, Serge. *La France et l'abolition de la traite des noirs de 1814 à 1831*. Paris, 1969.
Dardel, Pierre. *Commerce et industrie à Rouen et au Havre au XVIIIe siècle*. Paris, 1946.
———. *Navires et marchandises dans les ports de Rouen et du Havre au XVIIIe siècle*. Paris, 1963.
Debien, Gabriel. *Les colons de Saint Domingue et la Révolution*. Paris, 1953.
———. *Les engagés pour les Antilles*. Paris, 1952.
———. *Les esclaves aux Antilles françaises*. Basse-Terre, 1974.
———. *Etudes antillaises*. Paris, 1956.
———. "Les grand'cases des plantations à Saint Domingue aux XVIIe et XVIIIe siècles." *Annales des Antilles*, XV (1970), 1–39.
Deerr, Noel. *The History of Sugar*. 2 vols. London, 1949–50.
Dorveaux, Paul. *Le sucre au moyen age*. Paris, 1911.
Drescher, Seymour. *Econocide*. Pittsburgh, 1977.
Drummond, J. C., and Anne Wilbraham. *The Englishman's Food*. London, 1957.
Elzinga, S. "Le tarif de Colbert de 1664 et celui de 1667 et leur signification." *Economische-Historisch Jaarboek*, XVI (1929), 221–73.
Filiot, J. M. *La traite des esclaves vers les mascareignes au XVIIIe siècle*. Paris, 1970.

Franklin, Alfred. *La vie privée d'autrefois*. Vol. III of 27 vols. Paris, 1888.
Frostin, Charles. *Histoire de l'autonomisme colon de la partie française de Saint Domingue aux XVIIe et XVIIIe siècles*. Paris, 1972.
_____. *Les révoltes blanches à Saint Domingue aux XVIIe et XVIIIe siècles*. Paris, 1975.
Galenson, David W. "The Rise and Fall of Indentured Servitude in the Americas: An Economic Analysis." *Journal of Economic History* XLIV (1984), 1–26.
_____. *White Servitude in Colonial America*. Cambridge, England, 1981.
Geggus, David. "Les esclaves de la Plaine du Nord à la veille de la Révolution." *Revue de la Société Haitienne d'Histoire et de Géographie*, XLIII (1985), 16–51.
Giroux, J. "La raffinerie de sucre de Dijon dans la deuxième moitié du XVIIIe siècle." *Annales de Bourgogne*, LIII (1981), 80–90.
Goubert, Pierre. *The Ancien Régime: French Society, 1600–1750*. New York, 1974.
Grant, William L. "Canada Versus Guadeloupe: An Episode of the Seven Years' War." *American Historical Review*, XVII (1912), 735–43.
Guilmoto, Gustave. *Etude sur les droits de navigation de la Seine de Paris à la Roche-Guyon du XIe au XVIIIe siècles*. Paris, 1889.
Hémardinguer, J. J., ed. *Pour une histoire de l'alimentation*. Paris, 1970.
Inikori, J. E. "Market Structure and the Profits of the British Slave Trade in the Late Eighteenth Century." *Journal of Economic History*, XLI (1981), 745–76.
_____. "Measuring the Atlantic Slave Trade." *Journal of African History*, XVII (1976), 197–223.
_____, ed. *Forced Migration: The Impact of the Export Slave Trade on African Societies*. New York, 1982.
Jeulin, Paul. *L'évolution du port de Nantes*. Paris, 1929.
Joinville, Pierre de. *Le commerce de Bordeaux au XVIIIe siècle*. Paris, 1908.
Josa, Guy. *Les industries du sucre et du rhum à la Martinique (1639–1931)*. Paris, 1931.
Julliany, Jules. *Essai sur le commerce de Marseille*. 3 vols. Marseilles, 1842.
Kerviler, René. *Répertoire générale de bio-bibliographie bretonne*. 17 vols. Rennes, 1886–1908.
Labrousse, Ernest. *La crise de l'économie française à la fin de l'ancien régime et au début de la Révolution*. Paris, 1944.
Lacombe, Robert. *Histoire monétaire de Saint Domingue et de la République d'Haiti jusqu'en 1874*. Paris, 1958.
Landes, David. *The Unbound Prometheus: Technological Change and Industrial Development in Western Europe from 1750 to the Present*. Cambridge, England, 1970.
Laruelle, E. *Les apothicaires rouennais*. Rouen, 1920.
Lasserre, Guy. *La Guadeloupe, étude géographique*. 2 vols. Bordeaux, 1961.
Lebeau, Auguste. *De la condition des gens de couleur libres sous l'ancien régime*. Poitiers, 1903.

Lebrun, François. *Les hommes et la mort en Anjou aux XVIIᵉ et XVIIIᵉ siècles.* Paris, 1971.
_____, ed. *Histoire d'Angers.* Paris, 1975.
Lefebvre, George. *Etudes orléanaises.* 2 vols. Paris, 1962–63.
Legaingneulx, M. *Généologie de la famille de MM. Colas.* Orléans, 1768.
Léon, Pierre. *Marchands et speculateurs dauphinois dans le monde antillais au XVIIIᵉ siècle.* Paris, 1963.
Lespinasse, René de. *Les métiers et corporations de la ville de Paris.* Vol. I of 3 vols. Paris, 1886.
Levasseur, E. *Histoire du commerce de la France.* Vol. I of 2 vols. Paris, 1911.
Lippman, E. O. von. *Abrégé de l'histoire du sucre.* Paris, 1894.
Lovejoy, Paul E. "The Volume of the Atlantic Slave Trade: A Synthesis." *Journal of African History,* XXIII (1982), 483–96.
Ly, Aboulaye. *La Compagnie du Sénégal.* Paris, 1958.
Malvezin, Théophile. *Histoire du commerce de Bordeaux.* 4 vols. Bordeaux, 1892.
Martin, Gaston, *Nantes au XVIIIᵉ siècle: L'ère de nègriers.* Paris, 1931.
Mathieu, Joseph. *Marseille: Statistique et historique.* Marseilles, 1879.
Mathiez, Albert. *La vie chère et le mouvement social sous la terreur.* Paris, 1927.
Matthews, George T. *The Royal General Farms in Eighteenth Century France.* New York, 1958.
Mettas, Jean. "Honfleur et la traite des noirs au XVIIIᵉ siècle." *Revue française d'histoire d'outre-mer,* LX (1973), 14–19.
Meyer, Jean. *L'armement nantais dans la deuxième moitié du XVIIIᵉ siècle.* Paris, 1969.
_____. *La noblesse bretonne.* Paris, 1966.
Michel, Francisque. *Histoire du commerce et de la navigation à Bordeaux.* 2 vols. Bordeaux, 1866–71.
Mintz, Sidney. *Sweetness and Power: The Place of Sugar in Modern History.* New York, 1985.
Newton, Arthur Percival. *The European Nations in the West Indies, 1493–1688.* London, 1933.
Pariset, François, ed. *Histoire de Bordeaux.* Vol. V of 8 vols. Bordeaux, 1968.
Parry, J. H. *The Establishment of the European Hegemony, 1415–1715.* New York, 1961.
Peytraud, Lucien. *L'esclavage aux Antilles françaises avant 1789.* Paris, 1897.
Prudhomme, Monique. "Une famille de marchands orléanais au début du XVIIIᵉ siècle: Les Sarrebourse." Mémoire de maîtrise, Université de Tours, 1970.
Rambert, Gaston. *Histoire du commerce de Marseille.* 7 vols. Marseilles, 1951–66.
Rawley, James A. *The Transatlantic Slave Trade: A History.* New York, 1981.
Rinchon, Dieudonné. *Pierre Ignace Liévin van Alstein, capitaine négrier.* Dakar, 1964.

Robert, Henri. *Trafics coloniaux du port de la Rochelle au XVIIIe siècle.* Paris, 1960.
Roover, Raymond de. *L'évolution de la lettre de change, XIVe–XVIIIe siècles.* Paris, 1953.
Rubin, Vera, and Arthur Tuden, eds. *Comparative Perspectives on Slavery in New World Plantation Societies.* Annals of the New York Academy of Sciences, CCXCII. New York, 1977.
Rudé, George. *The Crowd in the French Revolution.* Oxford, 1959.
Saint-Julien, A. de, and G. Bienaymé. *Histoire des droits d'entrée et d'octroi à Paris.* Paris, 1887.
Schnakenbourg, Christian. "Notes sur les origines de l'industrie sucrière en Guadeloupe au XVIIe siècle (1640–1720)." *Revue française d'histoire d'outre-mer,* LV (1968), 267–92.
_____. *Les sucreries de la Guadeloupe dans la seconde moitié du XVIIIe siècle.* Paris, 1972.
Schumpeter, Elizabeth. *English Overseas Trade Statistics, 1697–1808.* Oxford, 1960.
Sée, Henri. "L'industrie et le commerce de la Bretagne dans la première moitié du XVIIIe siècle." *Annales de Bretagne,* XXXV (1922), 187–208, 433–55.
Sheridan, Richard B. *The Development of the Plantations.* Barbados, 1970.
Stein, Robert. *The French Slave Trade in the Eighteenth Century: An Old Regime Business.* Madison, 1979.
_____. "The French Sugar Business in the Eighteenth Century: A Quantitative Study." *Business History,* XXII (1980), 3–17.
_____. "Measuring the French Slave Trade." *Journal of African History,* XIX (1978), 515–21.
_____. "The Profitability of the Nantes Slave Trade, 1783–1792." *Journal of Economic History,* XXXV (1975), 779–93.
_____. "The Revolution of 1789 and the Abolition of Slavery." *Canadian Journal of History,* XVII (1982), 447–67.
_____. "The State of French Colonial Commerce on the Eve of the Revolution." *Journal of European Economic History.* XII (1983), 105–17.
Tarrade, Jean. *Le commerce colonial de la France à la fin de l'ancien régime.* Paris, 1972.
Taylor, George V. "Types of Capitalism in Eighteenth Century France." *English Historical Review,* LXXIX (1964), 478–97.
Thésée, Françoise. *Les négociants bordelais et les colons de Saint Domingue.* Paris, 1972.
Thésée, Françoise, and Gabriel Debien. *Un colon niortais à Saint Domingue, Jean Barrée de Saint Venant.* Niort, 1975.
Thomas, Robert Paul, and Richard Nelson Bean. "The Fishers of Men: The Profits of the Slave Trade." *Journal of Economic History,* XXXIV (1974), 885–914.
Valladier, Hector. "Histoire de la raffinerie de Nantes." 3 vols. Typescript in Archives Départmentales, Loire Atlantigue.

Vignols, Léon. "Le travail manuel des blancs et des esclaves aux Antilles." *Revue historique*, CLXXV (1935), 308–15.
Ward, J. R. "The Profitability of Sugar Planting in the British West Indies, 1650–1835." *Economic History Review*, XXXI (1978), 208.
Watson, Andrew M. *Agricultural Innovation in the Early Islamic World: The Diffusion of Crops and Farming Techniques, 700–1100*. Cambridge, England, 1983.
Young, Arthur. *Travels in France*. Edited by Jeffrey Kaplow. New York, 1965.

PUBLISHED PRIMARY SOURCES

Avalle, M. *Tableau comparatif des productions des colonies françaises aux Antilles avec celles des colonies anglaises, espagnoles, et hollandaises de l'année 1787 à 1788*. Paris, 1799(?).
Bonnefons, Nicolas de. *Le jardinier français*. Paris, 1651.
Calendrier historique d'Orléanais. Orléans, 1789.
Campbell, John. *Candid and Impartial Observations on the Nature of the Sugar Trade*. London, 1763.
Camus, Michel. "Correspondance de Bertrand Ogéron." *Revue de la Société Haitienne d'Histoire et de Géographie*, XLIII (1985), 3–188.
Cazaud, M. *Account of a New Method of Cultivating the Sugar Cane*. London, 1779.
Concise Observations on the Nature of Our Common Food so Far as It Tends to Promote or Injure Health. London, 1787.
Depping, G. B., ed. *Correspondance administrative sous le règne de Louis XIV*. 4 vols. Paris, 1850–55.
Discours historique sur la cause des désastres de la partie française de Saint Domingue. Paris, 1792(?).
Duhamel du Monceau. *Art de rafiner le sucre*. Paris, 1764.
Dutrône la Couture, Jacques François. *Précis sur la canne*. Paris, 1790.
Edwards, Bryan. *The History, Civil and Commercial, of the British West Indies*. 5 vols. 1819; rpr. New York, 1966.
Forbonnais, M. *Recherches et considérations sur les finances de France*. Basel, 1758.
Gazette de Santé, 1786.
Gillispie, Charles Coulston, ed. *A Diderot Pictorial Encyclopedia of Trades and Industry*. Vol. I of 2 vols. New York, 1959.
Girod-Chantrans, Justin. *Voyage d'un suisse dans différentes colonies de l'Amérique*. Neuchatel, 1785.
Gournay, M. *Almanach générale du commerce*. Paris, 1788.
Guybert, Philibert. *Toutes les oeuvres du médecin charitable*. Paris, 1637.
Hilliard d'Auberteuil, Michel René. *Considérations sur l'état présent de la colonie française de Saint Domingue*. 2 vols. Paris, 1776.
Jèze, M. *Etat ou tableau de la ville de Paris*. Paris, 1760.
Lacombe de Prezel, Honoré. *Les progrès du commerce*. Paris, 1760.
Lavarenne, M. *Le vray cuisinier françois*. Paris, 1628.
Lemery, Louis. *Traité des alimens*. 3rd ed. Paris, 1755.

Lemery, Nicolas. *Traité universel des drogues simples.* Paris, 1698.
Menon, M. *La cuisinière bourgeoise.* Paris, 1746.
Moreau de Saint Méry, Médéric Louis Elie. *Description topographique, physique, civile, politique, et historique de la partie française de l'isle de Saint Domingue.* 1797; rpr. Paris, 1958.
Nostredamus, Michel de. *Excellent et moult utile opuscule à tous necessaire qui désirent avoir connaissance de plusieurs exquises receptes.* Lyon, 1552.
Paris, Louis, ed. *Négociations, lettres, et pièces diverses relatives au règne de François II.* Paris, 1841.
Poncelet, P. *Chimie du goût et de l'odorat.* Paris, 1755.
Ponet, Pierre. *Histoire générale des drogues.* Paris, 1694.
Raynal, G. T. *Histoire philosophique et politique des établissements et du commerce des Européens dans les deux indes.* 6 vols. Geneva, 1775.
Rebecque, J. Constant de. *L'apothicaire français charitable.* Lyon, 1786.
Ricard, Jean Pierre. *Le négoce d'Amsterdam.* Amsterdam, 1722.
Sainte-Marie, Poyen. *De l'exploitation des sucreries.* Pointe-à-Pitre, 1803.
Savary des Bruslons, Jacques. *Dictionnaire universel de commerce.* 4 vols. Copenhagen, 1762.
Sévin-Mareau, M. *Mémoire sur les causes de la décadence de l'industrie manufacturière et commerciale à Orléans.* Orléans, 1828.
Tertre, R. P. du. *Histoire générale des Antilles.* 3 vols. 1667–71; rprs. Fort-de-France, 1973.
Weuves, M. *Réflexions historiques et politiques sur le commerce de France avec ses colonies de l'Amérique.* Geneva, 1780.

Index

Angers: and Nantes, 108, 153; refineries in, 141
Anstey, Roger, 37
Arcy, F. d', 8
Armytage, Frances, 79
Avalle, M., 73

Bayonne, 116–17
Beaucaire Fair: and sales of sugar from Bordeaux and Marseilles, 113, 147; and sales of sugar from Sète, 149; sugar prices at, 161–62
Beet sugar, 166–67
Beguyer family, 141, 153–54, 170–71
Belgium, 109, 116
Belin (plantation), 45, 47
Bondois, Paul, 66, 142
Bongars (plantation): slaves, 46; planting rotation, 61; profits, 85
Bordeaux: sugar imports and reexports, 3, 109–13, 153; refining, 10, 146–47; slave trade, 20, 24; trade route in south, 156–57
Boucherie brothers, 127, 133, 144
Boulogne, 146
Bouzols (plantation), 61, 62
Brazil, 4, 6, 8, 41
Bredebec, Gaspard van, 141
Brittany, 109. *See also* Nantes
Butel, Paul, 111–12, 147

Campbell, John, 100–101
Canada, x
Canary Islands, 3
Chaussinand-Nogaret, Guy, 157
Code noir, 51–53
Colas family, 154–56
Colbert, Jean Baptiste: and French colonization, 4–5; and sugar trade, 5–8, 9, 98, 158–59; and the slave trade, 19, 38; and refining, 136, 140, 150
Colonial system, 6–7
Columbus, Christopher, 3
Commercial capitalism, 169–74
Compagnie des Indes Occidentales: and sugar, 5, 107; and slaves, 21, 30
Crouzet, François, 86
Curtin, Philip D., 45–46

Debien, Gabriel, 57, 58
Denis, Henry, 130, 133, 142
Denmark, 20, 109, 112
Dieppe, 142, 143
Dijon, 150
Dohrmann (refiner), 123
Drescher, Seymour, 74
Dunkerque: sugar imports and reexports, 116, 153; refineries, 145–46
Dutrône la Couture, Jacques François, 66

Egypt, 1, 114
Engagés, 17–18
Ennoblement, 172–73

Family networks, 153–58, 170–72
Foache, Stanislas, 43–44, 45, 64, 81, 83
Fontanilhe, Antoine, 131, 156–57, 162, 172–73
Francis I, 2–3
French Revolution: role of sugar in, ix; and slave trade, 22–23; and sugar trade, 88, 97–98, 165–66
Frostin, Charles, 57

Gabriel le Sucrier, 2–3
Galifet (plantations): size, 45; slaves, 47; workdays, 56; sugar production, 75; profits, 85
General Farms, 95, 159–61
Germany: sugar purchases, 10, 100; and Nantes, 109; and Bordeaux, 111–12; refineries in, 135–36; mentioned, 2
Government policy: and national interest, ix–x, 93–94, 98–99, 117; before 1717, pp. 6–9, 67–69, 98; and reexports, 104. *See also* Letters Patent (April, 1717)
Great Britain: and slave trade, 20, 29–30; and sugar trade, 97, 99–101; consumption of sugar, 100; exports of coal, 122; refineries in, 135
Guadeloupe: settlement and growth, 5, 40–42, 44; and slave trade, 32, 38; plantations on, 74–75; smuggling, 76; economic conditions, 86; British occupation, 97; and Marseilles, 113–14; mentioned, x, 167

183

Guiana (French Guiana): sugar production, x; and slave trade, 32; potential growth, 165
Guilmoto, Gustave, 143–44
Guybert, Philibert, 11, 12

Hilliard d'Auberteuil, Michel René, 75
Holland: refineries in, 8, 126, 135–36; sugar purchases, 10, 99, 100; slave trade, 20, 29; and Nantes, 109; and Bordeaux, 111–12; and Dunkerque, 116; mentioned, 125
Hyeres, 3

Inikori, J. E., 37
Italy: purchases of sugar, 10, 100; and Nantes, 109; and Marseilles, 114; and Bordeaux, 147

Jogues family, 154–56

Labat, Père, 43
Langheté, Sieur, 116
La Rochelle: and slave trade, 20, 24; sugar imports and reexports, 115–16; refining, 123, 144–45
Lavarenne, 13
Lefebvre, Georges, 128, 140
Lefebvre, Guillaume, 122–23, 128–29
Le Havre: and slave trade, 24; sugar imports and reexports, 115; refineries, 143
Lemery, Louis, 12
Lemery, Nicolas, 12
Letters Patent (April, 1717): duty rates set by, 68, 139; effects of, 98, 108–109, 115, 159; summarized, 98–99; mentioned, 10, 127
Levant, 10, 100, 106, 114
Lille, 119, 146
Louisiana, 32
Lovejoy, Paul, 20–21
Lune, Pierre de, 13

Madeira, 3
Maillard plantation, 56
Malvezin, Théophile, 112
Marseilles: sugar imports and reexports, 1, 113–15, 153; and slave trade, 24; refining, 146, 147, 148–50; sugar consumption, 164
Martin, Gaston, 36
Martinique: settlement and growth, 5, 40–42, 63; and slave trade, 32, 38; plantations on, 44, 75; British occupation, 97; and Bordeaux, 111; and Marseilles, 113–14; mentioned, x, 167
Mathieu, Joseph, 164
Maurelet, Gaspard, 148
Mesmerism, 50
Meyer, Jean, 86
Montpellier, 149–50, 157–58
Moreau de Saint-Mery, Médéric: on colonial population, 42–43; on slaves, 47–49; on planters, 57, 59

Nantes: and slave trade, 20, 23–24; wealth, 23–24, 103; sugar imports and reexports, 107–109, 160–61; refining, 122, 138–39; merchant families, 154–56; mentioned, 94
Napoleon, 23, 166–67
Narbonne, 1
Nîmes, 150
Nostredamus, Michel de, 121

Ogéron, Bertrand d', 4–5
Olive and Duplessis, Sieurs, 40
Orléans: and Nantes, 108; refining, 120–34 *passim*, 140–41; merchant families, 154–56; prices, 160–61; mentioned, 10, 118

Paris: consumption of sugar, ix, 10, 164; and ports, 107, 152–53; and refining towns, 138–45; refining in, 144
Parry, J. H., 4
Pellet, Jean, 172
Perry, Jean, 129–30
Plantations: origins and growth, 17, 40–42; described, 43–44; organization, 54–58, 168–69; profits, 84–86. *See also* Slaves
Polverel, Etienne, 23
Poncelet, P., 11
Portugal: sugar production, 3–4; slave trade, 20, 29, 30; and Nantes, 109. *See also* Brazil
Profits: of the slave trade, 36–39, 87–88; of plantations, 82, 84–89; of colonial merchants, 82–83; of port merchants, 101–104; of refiners, 133–34; global, 173–74
Puiz, Anne-Marie, 163

Ravôt et Demardières, 130–32, 162
Rawley, James A., 19
Raynal, G. T., 42
Rebecque, J. Constant de, 11
Reunion, 167

Richardson, David, 37
Rochefoucault plantation, 46–47, 75–76
Romberg, Bapst and Co., 80
Rouen: slave trade, 20; tariffs, 118; refining, 142–42
Rum. *See* Sugar, by-products of
Ryswick, Treaty of, 5

Sabatier family, 150, 157–58
Saint Christophe, 5
Saint Domingue: revolution in, x, 50, 88, 165, 166, 167; settlement and growth of, 4–5, 42–43; and slave trade, 32–33; plantations, 42, 43–44, 81–82; natural problems, 63; types of sugar produced, 98; and Nantes, 108; and Bordeaux, 111; and Marseilles, 114
Saint Lucia, x
Saint Malo, 20
Sarrebourse family, 154–54, 171
Saumur: and Nantes, 108; refining, 141–42
Schnakenbourg, Christian, 44, 61, 74–76, 86, 96
Sète, 149, 150, 158
Slavery. *See* Slave trade; Slaves
Slaves: origins, 26–27, 47–49; demographics, 42–47 *passim*, 56–57, 87–88; prices of, 45, 87–88; legal status, 51–53; plantation work, 54–56, 60–67. *See also* Slave trade
Slave trade: origins, 18–19; growth and abolition, 19–23, 87, 167; organization, 23–36; profitability, 36–39, 87–88. *See also* Slaves
Smuggling, 76–79
Société des Amis des Noirs, 22
Sonthonax, Léger Félicité, 23
Spain: sugar production, 2, 3; and Saint Domingue, 4–5; slave trade, 20; sugar purchases, 100; and Nantes, 109; and Marseilles, 114; and Bayonne, 116–17; mentioned, x–xi
Spooner, Frank, 163
Sugar: arrivals, 94–98, 104, 107–17 *passim*; barrels, 70–71; by-products of, 70, 71–73, 78; consumption, ix, xi, 2, 9–13, 100–101, 163–64; duties and tariffs, 7–9, 68–69, 95, 98–99, 158–162; introduction into Europe, 1–2; introduction into New World, 3–4; losses in transit, 71, 94–95; prices, ix, 2, 88–89, 102–104, 160–62; reexports, ix, 8–10, 98–100, 106–17 *passim*; retailing of, ix, 12, 152, 162–63; sales by planters, 76–80; uses of, 10–13; value, ix, 10, 102–104
—cane: growing in France, 2–3; processing, 6, 64–67, 167; growth and harvesting, 60–64; types, 61
—clayed: defined, 8, 9; processing of, 66–67; popularity of, 67–68, 98; and refined sugar, 101, 160; quantities produced, 103
—muscovado: defined, 8; amounts needed for refined sugar, 9, 126–27; processing of, 66–67; quantities, 67–68, 103
—refined: popularity of, 10, 101; defined, 120; types, 125–26. *See also* Sugar—refining
—refining: in French West Indies, 8–9, 67–69, 150; origins, 8, 120–21; processes, 120–26; costs, 126–34; profits from, 133–34; location in France, 136–51; industrial organization, 168–69

Tarrade, Jean, 85, 94
Tascher de la Pagerie, G., 74–75
Thésée, Françoise, 81
Thuillier, Guy, 163
Tobago, x
Tolls, 143–44, 152, 158–62
Toulouse: refining, 147; merchant families, 156–57
Tours: and Nantes, 108; refining, 141, 142
Trézel, Daniel, 41

Valenciennes, 146
Vandeberque family, 140, 154–55, 171
Venice, 1, 2, 114

Warfare: effects on sugar trade, 9–10, 96–98, 166; effects on slave trade, 21

Young, Arthur, 23–24, 103, 172

DATE DUE			
DEC 18 1995			
DEC 10 1995			
	261-2500		Printed in USA